Review of Scottish Culture 14

In memory of Sir Kenneth John William
Alexander, 14 March 1922–27 March 2001,
economist, educationist and enthusiast for all
aspects of the culture of Scotland.

Review of Scottish Culture 14

Edited by
Alexander Fenton
with
Hugh Cheape and **Rosalind K. Marshall**

Tuckwell Press Ltd
The European Ethnological Research Centre
and
The National Museums of Scotland
Edinburgh

Address for Reviews, Correspondence, Subscriptions:
Editors, ROSC, European Ethnological Research Centre, c/o National Museums of Scotland,
Chambers Street, Edinburgh EH1 1JF

ROSC is published annually, at a price of £14 per issue
Published with the financial aid of the Trustees of
The National Museums of Scotland

ISBN 1 86232 230 9

Typesetting and origination by Brinnoven, Livingston
Printed and bound by Bookcraft, Midsomer Norton, Bath

Editorial Notes and Comments

In pursuance of our policy of dedicating each issue of *The Review of Scottish Culture* to a notable Scot, we are here publishing two appreciations of Sir Kenneth Alexander, by Ian Olson, who knew him when he was Chancellor of the University of Aberdeen, and by Iseabail MacLeod, for the time when he chaired the Scottish National Dictionary Association. These are largely personal memories, so we give here the main points of Sir Kenneth's career. He was born in Edinburgh in 1922, went to school there, and received his higher education at the School of Economics, Dundee. After 13 years of university teaching at Leeds, Sheffield and Aberdeen, he was Dean of the Scottish Business School for two years. From 1963–80, he held the Chair in Economics at the University of Strathclyde, though he had leave of absence during the last four years whilst he carried out the prestigious and exacting task of chairing the Highlands and Islands Development Board. There followed a five year spell as Principal and Vice-Chancellor of Stirling University.

Not being one to spare himself, he was involved as Chairman, Director or Advisory Committee Member with a variety of businesses (shipbuilding, publishing, media, etc.), adult education, government departments and agencies and cultural bodies. He championed the Gaelic College in Skye, Sabhal Mór Ostaig, from its earliest beginnings and was active in promoting the teaching of Gaelic. He chaired the Scottish National Dictionary Association in support for Scots. In furtherance of his care for matters cultural, he acted as President of the Saltire Society from 1975–82, and he was also Chairman of the Edinburgh Book Festival. In recent years he was Chancellor of the University of Aberdeen, and in that respect there is a personal reminiscence to relate. He was one of the delegates to a conference called Europa Gente, organised in Venice in 1986. The organisers were not familiar with all the delegates, nor had they all a good command of the English language. As we were seated listening to a lecture one day, a girl came with a telegram and held it out to me, Alexander Fenton, saying 'this is for Mr Alexander'. But it was for Sir Kenneth Alexander, and it was his invitation to become Chancellor of Aberdeen University. We celebrated that night in a good Italian restaurant.

One of the best things about editing *ROSC* is that there never seems to be any shortage of good quality material. In this issue there is a chronological spread from the fifteenth to the twentieth centuries. Priscilla Bawcutt throws much light on the reading of English books by Scots in the fifteenth and sixteenth centuries, showing that many more were in circulation than has been assumed, and that there were in any case no inhibitions or difficulties in reading and making further use of such sources. Their influence on Scottish literature and thought is assessed. Sport is catered for by a discussion of horse-racing in the sixteenth and early seventeenth centuries, and its gradual development from value largely as entertainment to a new kind of professional status which still remains with us. Another contribution that is concerned with public participation is the one on Grangemouth Children's Day, Bo'ness Fair and Lanimer Day in Lanark, by John Burnett and Malcolm MacCallum. These were local holidays, as distinct from days for fairs and markets, and the remarkable aspect of them is the variety of the sources of inspiration that led to their adoption as current phenomena. Vanessa Habib adds to the story of textiles in Scotland (see her article on The Dutch Weavers in Scotland, 1731–52, in *ROSC 11* (1998–9), 55–66) by a discussion of the printed tapestry carpet and the pioneering work of the Edinburgh firm of Richard Whytock. This is equally a contribution to design history, and ties in also with the article on the import of textile dyes to Scotland in the eighteenth century, discussed in the last issue (13 (2000–1), 18–29). Morrice McCrae is concerned with the lack of adequate medical support facilities and doctors in the mid-nineteenth century in the Highlands and Islands. He looks at the historical background of the Jacobite disturbances, the Poor Law and its various modifications, the potato blight and the geographical isolation of many parts of the area as a whole, and then analyses the results of a questionnaire on medical support sent out in 1850 to ministers in all parishes in the Highlands and Islands by the Royal College of Physicians of Edinburgh. The sorry state of affairs made it clear that relying solely on support from philanthropic sources was not satisfactory and that state support was the only option. In 1850 this was radical thinking – but it may be seen as laying a groundwork for, eventually, the National Health Service. Elaine Thomson continues the medical theme, as well as looking at the roles of women between the 1880s and the 1920s, in her analysis of the lady members of the Executive Committee of the Edinburgh Hospital for Women and Children. In doing so, she deepens her study of the Hospital and its patients that appeared in the last issue (13 (2000–1), 66–77). The economics of farming in the first half of the nineteenth century in the Rhynie district of Aberdeenshire are examined by Susan Storrier, on the basis of diaries from the farm of New Noth. Another diary, kept by a schoolmaster, Donald Sinclair, in Islay in the 1830s–70s, is used to tell the story of his life, and of his existence as a schoolmaster. Since it touches on illness and on medical matters, it forms a useful complement to the material discussed by Morrice McCrae. It can also be compared with the article by R T Glaister on rural school buildings, though these were in a very different part of the country. Another aspect of education, this time at university level, is revealed in Professor A D Boney's article on the misdemeanours of servants at the Old College, University of Glasgow. The servants, many of whom had years of service, were obviously men with minds of their own. Finally, there is material provided some years ago by our old friend the late Jane Durham, of Scotstoun, Kildary, Ross-shire, regarding the acquisition and installation of a threshing mill during World War II. This gives a good picture of wartime conditions, and of the effects of shortages and bureaucratic delays.

The Editors

Contributors

Professor Priscilla Bawcutt, Department of English Language and Literature, Modern Languages Building, The University of Liverpool, Chatham Street, Liverpool, L69 7ZR.

A D Boney, formerly Professor of Botany, University of Glasgow.

John Burnett, Department of Social and Technological History, National Museums of Scotland, Edinburgh.

Professor Emeritus Alexander Fenton, European Ethnological Research Centre, c/o National Museums of Scotland, Edinburgh.

Jane Durham, late of Scotstoun, Kildary, Ross-shire.

James B S Gibson, Ontario, Canada.

Robert T Glaister, The Open University.

Vanessa Habib, Textile Hstorian, Edinburgh.

Helen Kemp, European Ethnological Research Centre, Edinburgh.

Malcolm MacCallum, Curator of the History of Sport, National Museums of Scotland, Edinburgh.

Iseabail MacLeod, Scottish National Dictionary Association, 27 George Square, Edinburgh EH8 9LD

Dr Morrice McCrae, Aberdour, Fife.

Ian Olson, MD, University of Aberdeen.

Brian Smith, Shetland Archivist, Lerwick, Shetland.

Kristina Söderpalm, Gothenburg Historical Museum, Sweden.

Susan Storrier, European Ethnological Research Centre, Edinburgh.

Susan Sinclair, St Andrews, Fife.

Dr Elaine Thomson, Lecturer in Marketing, Napier University, Edinburgh.

Dr Eila Williamson, AHRB Research Assistant, RED:S Project, English Department, University of Southampton.

Sir Kenneth Alexander

It is doubtful if any one person's experience could encompass the extraordinary life of such a multifaceted man as Ken Alexander. On the other hand I feel certain that anyone who knew him, in whatever role, at whatever stage of his career, would have had a similar experience. For although, to be honest, it is often difficult to comprehend why those who ride what the Civil Service ironically term the Magic Roundabout – the Great and the Good who flit from quango to high office to commission and round again – should qualify for such heady careers, in Ken's case this was always clear indeed. For over and above his innate intelligence and his high professional competence, he had at least two features that made him universally liked, appreciated and admired. The first was his modest, kindly and friendly nature, his complete approachability – you were never made conscious of his 'status' regardless of the post he held – so that even those who met him but briefly gained the feeling thereafter that he was an old friend – and always 'Ken'. The second feature was his total commitment; if Ken took something on, he did so wholeheartedly and without reservation.

My direct experience of him started quite late in his career, when in 1987 the Business Committee of the General Council – the graduate body – on which I served, proposed him as Chancellor of the University of Aberdeen. The 1980s were difficult times for universities emerging from a series of harsh UGC cutbacks, and we felt it important to have more than a figurehead, to have someone with both wide experience and visionary enthusiasm. That Ken was both admired and respected by Right and Left, by high and low was indeed important; that he was quietly but deeply committed to Scotland and her cultural life, from fireballs to film, was even more so.

He was elected unanimously, and installed on an unseasonably hot April day (the woolly-semmited assembly fainting quietly under mediaeval robes), taking his oath of office in excruciating Latin (strangely, something he never mastered), and conferring his personal choice of honorary doctorates. He started, characteristically, with Jessie Kesson, the Elgin slum girl who had battled her way to the top of the writing profession. In his inaugural address he made it clear that he wanted to be no figurehead, that he would do all in his power to enable the university to press forward to an ambitious future. It mattered to him that a higher, liberal education – 'the precious pearl of knowledge' – should be open to all, especially to 'raise those of humble origin to the highest rank', as Aberdeen's 500 year old Foundation Bull instructed.

Despite recurrent and serious illness he served the University as friend and guide for the next decade, helping her to prepare for a Quincentenary in 1995, encouraging major projects such as the creation of a chair in Scottish Ethnology. (When its supporting institute was opened in November 1999, Ken, though by this time no longer Chancellor, appeared in the midst of bitter snow flurries, hatless and coatless, gaunt but cheerful, bringing as his gift a Michael Knowles portrait of Jessie). Furthermore, his years as Chancellor (and indeed until his death) coincided with my editorship of the *Aberdeen University Review*, perhaps the oldest postgraduate general literary and scientific journal in existence. Ken proved an valuable contributor, never turning down any request for article or review, always on time or before, his thoughtful contributions reflecting a wide knowledge and understanding of Scottish life and culture.

Since its beginning in 1913, the *Review* has published much significant poetry – from Thomas Hardy to Ian Crichton Smith – and, indeed, it was not long after David Daiches had offered his

Sir Kenneth Alexander

poetry of maturity to the *Review* that in 1992 I received, out of the blue, the following poem from Ken. I later gave it pride of place in a Quincentenary anthology entitled *No Other Place* (Tuckwell, 1995); it speaks for me still of that honest, brave and thoughtful man:

On Climbing Beinn Hiant

Kenneth Alexander

There is something holy about these rocks,
Celestial, transcendent, immanent and serene.
They may serve a purpose,
But it is far from clear.

Fifty-eight million years ago
There were many convulsions,
Omnipotent, supernatural, unmeasurable.
Then two million years later
        God's sense of the appropriate

Moved the earth again
To put the Blessed Mountain up a bit,
And Maclean's Nose out of joint.

Sir Kenneth Alexander with his wife, Angela

Has He waited fifty-six million years
For us to discover His purpose?

Perhaps we have all been too busy
Worrying about the meaning of life?
A fairly obvious thing, surely,
Compared to assessing the virtue
Of all these cryptic stones?

Ian Olson

Sir Kenneth Alexander was President of the Scottish National Dictionary Association from the early 1980s and, although then Principal of the University of Stirling, he found time to help and support us in fund-raising and publicity. For ten years from 1986 he was also Chairman of the Executive Council. (As far as we know he was the only person who occupied both these posts.) In both capacities, he was an enormous help to SNDA as it struggled to find funding for the two thrusts of its plans in word collection and further publications. He used every opportunity to bring the SNDA's work to people's attention and was an enormous support in our struggle to get government funding for the dictionaries. We are glad that he lived to see that aim achieved in a modest annual grant from the Scottish Arts Council.

His skilled chairmanship of meetings saved us from many a boring hour as he deflected the more long-winded contributors with great diplomacy and shafts of humour. He is greatly missed by all of us and we treasure the memories of his kindness, of his great skill as a chairman, and of his infectious laughter.

Iseabail MacLeod

Contents

Editorial Notes and Comments   v

Contributors   vii

Sir Kenneth John Wilson Alexander   viii
Ian Olson
Iseabail MacLeod

English Books and Scottish Readers in the Fifteenth and Sixteenth Centuries   1
Priscilla Bawcutt

The Printed Tapestry Carpet: The Pioneering Work of Richard Whytock
of Edinburgh 1784–1857   13
Vanessa Habib

Horse-Racing in Scotland in the Sixteenth and Earlier Seventeenth Centuries:
Peebles and Beyond   31
Eila Williamson

Grangemouth Children's Day, Bo'ness Fair and Lanimer Day at Lanark   43
John Burnett and Malcolm MacCallum

The Great Highland Famine and the Lack of Medical Aid   58
Morrice McCrae

The Unsung Heroines of Victorian Feminism: The Executive Committee of the
Edinburgh Hospital for Women and Children, c1885–c1920   74
Elaine Thomson

Analysis of Some Aspects of a Farm Diary from New Noth, Aberdeenshire, 1801–1850   81
Susan Storrier

The Journal of Donald Sinclair, Schoolmaster, Islay, 1835–1871   86
Susan Sinclair

Rural School Buildings in the Eighteenth Century   93
Robert T Glaister

Servants of the Old College, University of Glasgow: Misdemeanours and Disciplinary
Methods   105
A D Boney

A Wartime Threshing Machine   119
Jane Durham and Helen Kemp

Shorter Notes

Repairing an Easter Ross Mill in 1787   128
  Alexander Fenton

James Brown Gibson, 5 July 1892–12 July 1914   128
  James B M Gibson

Captain Gustav Ekeberg's Sojourn in Shetland, 1745   130
  Kristina Söderpalm and Brian Smith

Noticeboard

The Launch of Scottish Life and Society: A Compendium of Scottish Ethnology   133

A Complete List of Publications from the European Ethnological Research Centre 135

Dr Alan Gailey   137

Centre for Research on Families and Relationships (CRFR)   137

Strictly Mundial World Music Festival – Zaragoza, Aragon, Spain,
15–18 November, 2000   138

Understanding Tradition: a Multidisciplinary Exploration, University College,
Cork, 22–23 June 2001.   139

The Michaelis Jena Ratcliff Prize for Ethnology, 2000–2001   140

Reviews   141

A Guide to Contributors   174

English Books and Scottish Readers in the Fifteenth and Sixteenth Centuries

Priscilla Bawcutt

Readers of this journal are unlikely to dispute the importance of books. Books do far more than furnish a room, they furnish minds: with facts, ideas, values and entertainment. A book which is forgotten today may once have been a best-seller, and give an unrivalled glimpse into the *mentalité* of a past age. There are excellent studies of Scottish book collectors during the late Middle Ages and Renaissance: Durkan and Ross's classic *Early Scottish Libraries*, and articles on individuals, such as William Elphinstone, Henry Sinclair, bishop of Ross, and Adam Bothwell, bishop of Orkney.[1] Most of these studies, however, are concerned with the learned stratum of society: among the owners bishops and other churchmen predominate; their books tend to be written in Latin or other foreign languages; and they are mostly printed – in Paris, or Basle or Venice. They thus foster the prevalent impression that Scotland's cultural links were chiefly with continental Europe, not England. This indeed is often explicit. Durkan and Ross comment: 'The fewness of English writers is really rather astonishing, T A F Cherry notes 'the absence of English works' from Sinclair's library, and queries: 'Were Anglo-Scottish relations so restricted?' Duncan Shaw makes similar comments on Bothwell's collection, and concludes: 'the role of English books and printers . . . was not very significant' in Scotland.[2] Most recent of all is a categoric statement that 'English-language books seem to have had no market in Scotland'.[3]

These negative pronouncements seem to me misleading, creating a false image of Anglo-Scottish cultural relations in the fifteenth and sixteenth centuries. They seem swayed, in part, by the justifiable desire of some scholars to stress Scotland's humanistic credentials and participation in the Renaissance. Unfortunately this is sometimes coupled with an undervaluation of writings in the vernacular. Such contempt for the vernacular is clear in Shaw's remark that English literature had 'its greatest circulation among those who could read no language but their own'.[4] This is not wholly true; in any case, we should surely be interested in the growing literacy of the laity, and in the sort of books read by lairds, merchants, and even women.

The generalizations quoted earlier were based largely on surviving printed books, which contain indications of Scottish ownership. As evidence, this seems concrete and tangible, but it is highly selective and potentially misleading. Large, learned works tend to survive better than popular ones, which are cheap and flimsy and often read to destruction. If one looks at all the different types of evidence for Scottish reading habits in this period, a more varied picture emerges. English books – in which I include manuscripts, not only prints, and poems and other short pieces of writing – contributed significantly to that picture. Anglo-Scottish literary relations were remarkably close, even during periods of political tension and actual warfare.

What then is the evidence? In the first place there survive more English books with signs of Scottish ownership than is realised.[5] In addition to those actually printed in England, I would include the two Chepman and Myllar prints of

English poems, and the English manuscripts possessed by several Scottish lairds. One is the copy of Trevisa's translation of Higden's *Polychronicon* now in Aberdeen University Library (MS 21), which was owned by John Hay of Yester in 1554; it supplements other signs of Scottish interest in Higden's famous work, such as the extracts in the Asloan Manuscript.[6] Another is a much-travelled manuscript of Lydgate's *Siege of Thebes,* of which more will be said later. Equally significant are the copies of English works made by Scottish scribes. One of the most interesting is the large poetic anthology containing Chaucerian poems and *The Kingis Quair,* now in the Bodleian Library (MS Arch. Selden. B. 24); it was compiled in the reign of James IV for Henry, Lord Sinclair, 'fader of bukis' in Gavin Douglas's admiring phrase.[7]

A practice then remarkably common, yet sometimes ignored by scholars, was the copying of printed books, in part or whole. Some scribes obligingly copied not only the text but also the printer's colophon. One illustration of this custom is the manuscript of John Mirk's *Festial* that belonged to 'Oliuer sinclar off Rosling knycht'. (Oliver was the father of bishop Henry Sinclair.) *The Festial* was a very popular work; designed in the first place for parish priests, but later modified for lay reading, it became 'an early printed best-seller'. Numerous printed editions were published before 1500, but we know that its Scottish scribe used one printed at Rouen in 1499, because he copied its colophon.[8] Almost a century later, in 1586, Robert Denham, or Denholm, of West Scheill, compiled a curious medical-cum-astrological manuscript, which incorporates the words 'Imprented be me Robert Weir dwellyng at the singe of Sant Ihon the Ewangelist in Sanct Myrtyne parrische at Charyng Crosse'. The work in question *(De Cursione lune)* was printed *c*1535 by Robert Wyer.[9]

Testaments often furnish important informa-tion about book ownership, but the Scottish evidence, especially from the early period, is not as abundant as in other countries. Even those that do survive can be disappointing: Gavin Douglas, an exceptionally well read poet, makes no mention in his of the books he undoubtedly possessed. Yet the testament made by the protestant Marjorie Roger in 1584 illustrates their value, revealing 'an impressive English collection', and itemising works by Tyndale, Cranmer, Jewel, Becon and Foxe.[10]

Overlapping with this category are the inventories of booksellers' stock, made after their deaths. Those of Thomas Bassandyne (1577) and Robert Gourlaw (1585) give valuable clues as to what books Scots were buying in the early years of James VI's reign.[11] These are supplemented by other records. One such concerns the seizure by English pirates of a Scottish ship bound from London to Leith in 1586. Its cargo included a 'Packet of Books', whose titles and prices are listed. Among the largely pious works, such as twelve *'Imitations of Christ'* and five *'Seven Sobs'* (William Hunnis's *Seven Sobs of a Sorrowful soule for sinne),* were fifty copies of an English romance, the 'Squire of Low Degree'.[12]

Other important, if usually late, sources of information, are lists of personal libraries. That of the precocious James VI (1573–83) contains some contemporary English classics, such as Elyot's *The Governour,* and also, interestingly, aids to coping with works in foreign languages: *Caesar* and *Vegetius,* both 'in English'; and not only Castiglione's *Il Cortegiano,* but also Hoby's 'The Courtiour in english'.[13] Included in Adam Bothwell's collection is one tantalising title: *Wthopia Mori scotica.* Durkan and Ross say regretfully: 'We have met no Scots-owned copy of *Utopia'.*[14] But the word *scotica* suggests that there possibly once existed a Scots-translated *Utopia.* I would also include in this category the *Compt Buik* of David Wedderburn, a book-loving merchant of Dundee (b1587), which provides haphazard notes about his extensive library. This contained classical poetry, Scottish chronicles, and a large number of English books. Some of these can be identified precisely. Wedderburn's 'buik of walking sprittis', for instance, was also stocked by Bassandyne, and represents the English translation of a Latin work possessed by Bothwell, *Lavaterus, de Spectris.*[15] One cannot, alas, be so certain about which edition of Chaucer Wedderburn lent to 'the gude wyf of Pitlathy' in 1616.[16]

Lastly, there is much information about their reading to be gleaned from Scottish poets and other writers. Its nature varies greatly: with Dunbar it is a matter of echo and brief allusion; Douglas, however, sometimes sounds like a modern scholar, giving precise references to chapter and verse.[17] John Rolland says vaguely that his very popular *Sevin Seages* 'was translatit furth of prois in Scottis Meter'. This prose, however, was not the Latin *Historia Septem Sapientium*, but *The seven Wise masters of Rome*, an English version (printed by Copland, *c*1555).[18] Another valuable source is *The Complaynt of Scotland* (*c*1550). Its anonymous author, possibly Robert Wedderburn, was highly anglophobe, yet revealed his wide acquaintance with English writings in the 'monologue recreatiue', or pastoral interlude: here remarkably learned shepherds list tales and songs, starting with 'The taylis of cantirberrye' and ending with an English love song: 'My hart is leiuit on the land'.[19]

It can be illuminating to juxtapose small and scattered pieces of evidence. Consider the case of William Caxton. As far as I am aware, no surviving book printed by Caxton bears the signature of a Scottish owner. But to conclude that Caxton's publications were unknown in Scotland would be absurd. There are numerous indications to the contrary, of which a few may be cited. In 1483 three English books were stolen from Robert, second Lord Lyle; the first, 'of the philosophouris sawis', was almost certainly *The Dicts or Sayings of the Philosophers*, printed by Caxton in 1477.[20] In the 1490s two other Caxton publications were copied by Scottish scribes: one was *The Cordial, or the Four Last Things* (1479), and the second *The Book of the Order of Chivalry* (1489), a copy of which was included in Adam Loutfut's heraldic manuscript (1494).[21] In 1506 Sir David Sinclair bequeathed to a friend his 'Buk of Gud Maneris'; this is likely to be the work of that name printed by Caxton in 1487, or its reprint of 1500.[22]

An even more interesting illustration of Caxton's impact on Scotland, however, comes from those who were aware of him principally as an author. Whether Henryson's *Fables* were indebted to Caxton's *Aesop* (1484) is a matter

of debate.[23] There can be no doubt, however, that Douglas read Caxton's *Eneydos* (1490) very attentively, and carried out a brilliant demolition job on 'this buke of Inglys gros'. As he famously said, it was no more like Virgil's *Aeneid* than 'the deuill and Sanct Austyne'.[24] John Mair also pursued a running battle with Caxton. Mair, like George Buchanan and James VI, erroneously believed him to be not merely the printer but the author of *The Chronicles of England* (1480; 1482), the first printed history of England. He frequently called attention to Caxton's 'raving', 'incoherencies' and 'silly fabrications'.[25] Nonetheless Mair made much use of Caxton, and this led, ironically, to the later belief that he had translated him into Latin: *Caxtonum Latine reddidit*.[26]

Caxton is still famous, but only a few have probably heard of William Baldwin. He is best known today as the editor of *The Mirror of Magistrates*, yet in his own time he was equally famous for his *Treatise of Morall Philosophye, contayning the Sayinges of the Wise* (1547), reputed to have had 'more editions before 1660 than any other text except the Bible'.[27] This highly didactic work clearly impressed George Bannatyne, who in 1568 included in his renowned poetic anthology twenty-four 'wyis sentences drawin furth of the buik callit Morall philosafie'. Bannatyne was not alone in his taste for Baldwin's 'pythie meeters'. Gourlaw's inventory contained one copy, described with remarkable honesty as 'imperfyte'; the 'Packet of Books' had ten copies, and David Wedderburn possessed a copy, listed next to 'Erasmus in inglis'.[28] Some of the verses that Bannatyne included were still popular in Scotland a generation later, and inscribed on the painted ceilings of country houses, such as Delgatie and Prestongrange.[29]

I wish now to discuss categories of books, but obviously must be selective, and will limit myself to three topics that concerned ordinary people quite as much as intellectuals: health, religion, and entertainment.

Medical Treatises

We do not know the precise nature of the English book 'of medecyn' that was stolen from Lord

Lyle in 1483, nor of the 'potingary bukis in Inglis' purchased in 1507 for James IV.[30] But another English work on health that appealed to Scottish readers may still be read today. This is Lydgate's *Dietary* – written in verse, as was then the norm for much didactic literature, and full of sensible counsel on health, by no means confined to diet in the modern sense. It accompanied the 1487 text of Barbour's *Bruce* (Cambridge, St John's College, MS 191), and at least two other copies were made by Scotsmen in the sixteenth century (in the Makculloch Manuscript and the Bannatyne Manuscript).[31]

Bassandyne stocked various works on health, both in Latin and the vernacular; among them were 'thrie Thressour of ane pure man', ie three copies of *A good booke of medicines called the treasure of pore men*. This was one of the most popular medical works in Tudor England, first published *c*1526, and repeatedly reprinted in the sixteenth century.[32] A small battered manuscript in Edinburgh University Library (Dc 8 130), compiled *c*1595, contains copies of this and Andrew Borde's *Dietary of Health* (1547). The first owner was the Protestant Adam Wallace, reader at Crosbie Kirk in Kyle, and the book seems to have been 'in constant use' by Adam and his son David.[33] Another manuscript of *The Treasure of pore men*, now lost, is said to have been owned by Lilias Ruthven, Lady Drummond (d 1579).[34]

Religious literature.

Two historians have recently argued that students of medieval Scotland have shown more interest in ecclesiastical politics, such as disputes over benefices, than in religion. They call for a 'proper assessment' of two neglected areas: the nature of popular piety, and the degree of connection between medieval Lollardy and early Protestantism. They note the value of 'comparative evidence from outside Scotland, crucially that from Flanders and the Rhineland', yet make no mention of the impact upon Scotland of English religious writings.[35]

There is a wealth of evidence to show that Scottish readers from the early fifteenth century onwards often turned to England for spiritual nourishment. *Piers Plowman*, England's greatest medieval religious poem, was known to Gavin Douglas; and in the later sixteenth century, by which time it was viewed as a precursor of the Reformation, both Bassandyne and Gourlaw stocked copies of the printed editions (1550, 1561).[36] Another fourteenth-century religious poem, *The Pistel of Susan*, was known to Andrew Wyntoun; its distinctive metrical form, the alliterative thirteen line stanza, later became immensely popular with Scottish poets.[37] Sir Oliver Sinclair's copy of the *Festial* has already been mentioned. R J Lyall has shown that Scotticized versions of another English religious work, the *Speculum Vitae*, attributed to William of Nassington, were made in the late fifteenth century.[38] David Boswell of Glasmont and Balmuto (d *c*1493), whose son obtained the estate of Auchinleck in 1504, possessed *Dives and Pauper*, another religious treatise, printed by Wynkyn de Worde in 1496.[39]

Medieval Scotland is curiously lacking in a native tradition of mystical prose. But there is some evidence to suggest that a manuscript now in Paris (Bibliothèque Sainte Geneviève, 3390), containing writings by the northern English mystic Richard Rolle of Hampole, once had Scottish owners, including 'my lord Saltoun and Abernethy', who may be Alexander, fourth Lord of Saltoun (d 1527).[40] Around 1500 a so far unidentified George Bassandyne possessed an edition of *The Chastising of God's Children* (printed *c*1494); this devotional work, intended for nuns, contains a series of translations from Suso's *Horologium Sapientiae* and Van Ruysbroek's *Spiritual Espousals*.[41]

Popular piety in Scotland took many forms, of which only a few can be considered here. Its most famous literary manifestation is a carefully composed anthology of devotional prose and verse, chiefly on the subject of the Passion (British Library, MS Arundel 285).[42] But religious feeling was expressed elsewhere, more casually, but no less intensely: in short prayers or verses copied on the blank pages of protocol books, or the margins of books of hours, or interspersed with the notes on logic made by Magnus Makculloch. Many of these, despite a superficial Scottish colouring, are undoubtedly English in origin. Some short examples are the prayer: 'In my beginning God me speid, / In grace and vertew to proceid'; the 'Earth upon earth' verses misattributed to various Scottish poets, including Dunbar; a quatrain upon the paradoxes of the Incarnation; and eight lines on the 'Arma Christi', beginning 'A sheilde of redd a crose of grein'. The latter was scribbled as late as the seventeenth century in a manuscript belonging to the Earl of Dalhousie.[43]

Many medieval English poems belong to the type known as Appeals from the Cross, in which Christ speaks of his great suffering, and pleads with sinful man to love him in return. These poems are often intensely moving and highly dramatic, and it is not surprising that they attracted Scottish readers, who wished to have copies for themselves. One such which opens 'This is goddis awne complaint', was copied *c*1500 into the Gray Manuscript, and curiously attributed to an otherwise unknown 'Glassinbery'.[44] Another with the admonitory refrain 'Luk on my wondis and think on my passioun', is an extract from a poem by Lydgate. This was copied into a book of hours belonging to the Hays of Yester, presumably by a member of that family.[45] Another self-contained passage from a poem by Lydgate ('The Testament') follows Dunbar's 'Passioun' in Manuscript Arundel 285.[46]

One impressive poem of this type was copied at least twice in the early sixteenth century: 'Now herkynnis wordis wunder gude'. It appears in fragmentary form in the Makculloch Manuscript, and also in Arundel 285, where it is entitled 'The Dollorus Complant of Our Lorde apoune the croce crucifyit'.[47] Comparison with the English texts, all northern in language and provenance, illustrates some of the uses to which such a poem might be put. One (dated *c*1500) occurs in the Resurrection play of the Towneley cycle, associated with Wakefield. Here the poem has been shortened and adapted to its dramatic context. It is voiced by Christ, who stands triumphant but bloodstained before the audience.[48] The earliest known version of the poem, however, occurs in a fifteenth-century manuscript, possibly of Carthusian origin (British Library, Add 37049); here the text is accompanied by a drawing of Christ on the Cross: 'an actual tree bearing branches of love and charity; surrounding it are the instruments of the Passion'. A tiny contrite figure, in clerical dress, looks reverently towards Christ.[49]

Many fine poems in praise of the Virgin Mary were written by Scottish poets, such as Dunbar and Henryson. But when the theologian John Ireland wished to do honour to the Virgin, the vernacular poem he chose for inclusion in *The Meroure of Wyssdome* was English: 'Moder of God, and virgin vndefould'. Ireland believed this poem to be by Chaucer, as did the compiler of the Selden Manuscript, which contains a closely similar text, with exactly the same explicit.[50] Modern scholars, however, attribute the poem to Hoccleve.

Let me turn briefly from religious orthodoxy to dissent, and the likely role of English books in its spread. Lollardy until recently was believed to be essentially an English phenomenon, with 'only a few traces . . . north of the border'.[51] Yet the historian Walter Bower, writing in the 1440s, was clearly aware of the principal writings of Wyclif, such as the *Dialogus* and *Trialogus*. He testified that 'the opinions and writings of this heretic are still retained by some Lollards in Scotland and are carefully preserved at the instigation of the devil'.[52] A generation later John Ireland still took the heretical doctrines of Wyclif 'of ingland' and his 'folowaris in this land' very seriously. He attacked them in the *Meroure of Wyssdome,* and devoted a section of his unpublished Commentary on the Fourth Book of Sentences (Aberdeen University Library, MS 264) to condemning the *errores Weicleif et aliorum*.[53]

In England group-reading of the vernacular Bible, and particularly the New Testament, was a practice strongly associated with Lollards. It is of interest, therefore, that one of the surviving books owned by a member of the Sinclair family, Sir William Sinclair (d 1580), is an English manuscript of a Wyclifite New Testament.[54] Unfortunately, the exact date when it came to Scotland is unknown. Even more significant is a work once termed 'the only literary relic we possess of the Scottish Lollards'. This is Murdoch Nisbet's translation, or Scotticisation, of a Wyclifite New Testament, made *c*1520 for himself and his Ayrshire friends. Interestingly, at a later date he added to this medieval work extra material from Luther's Preface to the New Testament (1522) and Tyndale's Prologue to the Epistle to the Romans (1534, 1536?).[55] The work was preserved in the Nisbet family until the early eighteenth century, and provides a small but telling piece of evidence in support of the vague assertions by later Scottish writers that the Gordons of Earlstoun and Campbells of Cessnock 'entertained the disciples of Wicliff', and read the New Testament in the 'vulgar tongue'.[56]

Imaginative Literature.

Imaginative literature is a vast subject, and it is necessary to be selective. There is no space to discuss the popularity of English love songs, such as those copied by George Bannatyne, or which underlie some of *The Gude and Godlie Ballatis*.[57] I must restrict myself to two poets particularly esteemed at this time, Geoffrey Chaucer and John Lydgate, and to romances, the forerunners of modern novels in their wide, popular appeal.

There can be no doubt that Chaucer excited Scottish readers in the fifteenth century as much as he did English ones. Chaucer altered the course of poetry in both countries, and this was recognised in the glowing tributes paid to him by Scottish poets, from James I to Henryson, Dunbar, Douglas, and Lindsay. Some called him their 'master', not in any slavish sense, but because they learnt so much from him. Five hundred years after his death it is perhaps hard for modern readers to comprehend what was new about Chaucer. I would single out his mastery of story-telling, his metrical variety, and, above all, the brilliance and subtlety of his style. Today it is common to see him as essentially the poet of *The Canterbury Tales*. But late medieval readers regarded Chaucer as a great love poet, and the most admired and influential of his works

was *Troilus and Criseyde*. Most Scottish poets responded to this poem in some way or another: by quotation, allusion, imitation, or adoption of its metrical form – termed 'Troilus verse' by James VI.[58] Probably the greatest but most enigmatic response to Chaucer was Henryson's *Testament of Cresseid*. This, however, is not the place to add to the thousands of words already expended on Henryson and the other great Makars.[59] Here two less familiar 'Chaucerians' will receive some attention.

The first and most unexpected is Hary, a poet who never mentions Chaucer, and who terms the English 'Our ald Ennemyis cummyn of Saxonis blud'.[60] It is difficult to conceive a more anglophobic work than *The Wallace*, yet Hary's idealized portrait of its hero in book X owes much to Chaucer, notably his descriptions of the Knight in the General Prologue, and of Lycurgus and Emetrius in *The Knight's Tale*. Chaucer's influence may also be detected in the seasonal or astrological set-pieces which punctuate the action, and in the conclusion to the whole poem, 'Go nobill buk . . . Go worthi buk' (XII 1449 ff), which recalls the ending of *Troilus and Criseyde*. In one wholly fictional episode Wallace meets the queen of England, and remarks: 'in spech of luff suttell ye Southeron ar' (VIII 1411). Half-critical, half-admiring, this is revealing, alluding to that area of poetry where Chaucer was rightly perceived to be a master. The love scenes in *The Wallace*, though clumsy, owe much to *Troilus and Criseyde*, and to the short love complaints of Chaucer and his followers – precisely the sort of poems that Henry, Lord Sinclair could read in the Selden Manuscript.[61] For Hary, as for his greater contemporaries, Chaucer was a model of the high style. His debt to this literary tradition is worth stressing, since he is sometimes seen, quite mistakenly, as indebted chiefly to oral tradition.

Another unexpected testimony to Chaucer's impact comes from John Ireland. Precisely when and how he encountered Chaucer's writings is unknown, but in *The Meroure of Wyssdome* (completed in 1490) he responds to him thoughtfully and interestingly. Much of what he says is couched in general terms: Chaucer is a good teacher, who induces 'personis to lefe vicis and follow wertuis [virtues]'.[62] But one passage is much more specific:

And thus thi hienes may knaw, and all vthir, that the science and prescience of god causis na necessite in vs nore oure deidis. And for the instruccioun of thi hienes, I haue now tretit part of this mater, for it pertenis mare to my crafft than to Chauceir, that has tretit this mater in the buk of Troylus, and richt excedandly for a temporale man and clerk nocht greit [without a degree] in theologie. And suppos [although] his tovnge and langage be faire and sueit in metire and well componit, yit in gret sentens this maner of speking [by this Ireland means prose] is mare lovit [more esteemed] and acceptabile, as Arestotiles in his Rethoric sais and declaris *quod sermo* [misread as *fermo* in STS edition] *solutus est preferendus illi qui metro clauditur*. Sa dois Cicero, the oratour of Rome and Latyn tovnge, and Demosteyne, the oratour of Grece; thai usit this maner of speking, and als the haly writ and doctrine of Ihesu is put in this maner of speking and nocht in ryme nore metyre. And quhen Chauceir himself cummys to sad [serious] and gret materis, he usis this maner of speking, as in the Persounis taill [Parson's Tale] and vtheris.[63]

Ireland here refers to the 'predestination soliloquy' in book IV of *Troilus and Criseyde* (953–1085). One scholar says that he 'applauds Chaucer's discussion',[64] but Ireland's tone is a little ambivalent. When he says 'for it pertenis mare to my crafft than to Chauceir', it suggests the antagonism of the professional, or theologian, towards the amateur, or layman. Ireland himself has been discussing predestination, and has affirmed that God's fore-knowledge 'causis na necessite in us nore oure deidis'. Contrast this with Troilus's fatalism:

For al that comth, comth by necessitee;
Thus to ben lorn, it is my destinee.
(IV, 958–9).

Ireland's ambivalence is apparent in the word *excedandly* (line 7). Ireland's editor glossed it

as 'excellently' , but the word can mean 'surpassingly' (of something good), or 'excessively' (of something bad). According to *OED*, *exceeding* contains the notion of 'overstepping the limits of propriety or custom'. Ireland admires Chaucer, yet is uneasy about the way he oversteps the usual limits of a 'temporale man'. Elsewhere he praises Chaucer's 'gret eloquens', but he has reservations about his use of verse rather than prose for theology. Ireland's preference for prose is something that he feels strongly about, and a topic to which he returns elsewhere.[65]

Lydgate's poems were also highly valued by Scottish readers at this time. One important reason was that he provided access to the great stories of antiquity concerning Troy and Thebes. Two Scottish copies were made of his huge *Troy Book* in the late fifteenth and early sixteenth centuries, one owned by Sir Thomas Ewen, chaplain of St Giles (1509–29). There is also evidence that the editions of this work printed in England (1513; 1555) were available in Scotland.[66] Lydgate's *Siege of Thebes* certainly had a number of Scottish readers. These included Thomas Boyd, Earl of Arran, who borrowed a copy from Anne Paston in 1472, during his exile in England.[67] Another manuscript of *The Siege of Thebes*, now in the United States, had several Scottish owners; the most interesting of these are Marion Lyle of Houston, daughter of the second Lord Lyle, and Duncan Campbell, seventh laird of Glenorchy, who inscribed his flamboyant signature on this manuscript in 1598.[68] At almost the same time (in 1596) David Wedderburn recorded the loan of his 'Sege of Thebes' to a friend.[69]

The work of Lydgate that Scots seem most to have admired, however, is a mournful poem on love, usually known as 'The Complaint of the Black Knight'. Not only do there survive complete or partial copies of it in three literary miscellanies (Selden, Asloan, and Bannatyne), but it was one of the very first works to be printed in Scotland. The Chepman and Myllar print bears the enthusiastic comment of one early reader: *liber probus atque amabilis atque pro auriculis audiendus* [a worthy and delightful book and pleasing to the ears]. It seems rather hard on Lydgate that in *Early Scottish Libraries* the last word *audiendus* is misread as *arduus*, and elsewhere rendered as 'hard on the ears'.[70]

It is a curious fact that all Scottish copies of this poem associate it with Chaucer: three have the title 'the maying and disport of Chaucer', and the Bannatyne extract ends 'quod Chauser'.[71] Lydgate's poems were in some respects better known than his name. Short passages from his longer works often circulated anonymously. The Book of the Dean of Lismore, among its Gaelic contents, contains a few Scots and English pieces, all anti-feminist. One of these (on the iniquity of Delila) is attributed to 'Bochas', or Boccaccio. In fact it represents two stanzas from Lydgate's *Fall of Princes,* a very free rendering (via a French version) of Boccaccio's *De Casibus Illustrium Virorum.*[72] Lydgate's translation was far better known than the *De Casibus* throughout the sixteenth century.[73]

In Scotland, as in England, romances seem to have been immensely popular with all sections of society, from kings downwards. James I, on the last evening of his life, is said to have entertained himself in 'reading of Romans', along with chess, tables, and 'other honest solaces'. In the 1390s Sir James Douglas of Dalkeith bequeathed to his heir not only legal books but also romances [*romancie*].[74]

It is unfortunate that few Scottish romances survive; but we know the names of more than twenty English romances which seem to have circulated in Scotland, along with other types of narrative, such as tales of Robin Hood and the outlaw ballad of Adam Bell, Clim of the Clough and William of Cloudesley.[75] The chief subject of romance was chivalry: knights engaging in battle, usually in exotic locations; there was often a love interest, and occasionally an admixture of piety. In tone most romances were escapist, and in form somewhat shapeless – 'large, loose baggy monsters' – to steal a phrase from Henry James.

A few titles of those known to Scottish readers will indicate their chivalric flavour: *Sir Eglamour of Artois,* one of the first texts to be printed by Chepman and Myllar; *The Squire of Low Degree; Sir Ywain; Guy of Warwick; Hypomedon;* and *Sir*

Lamwell.[76] *Sir Bevis of Southampton* seems to have been the most famous of all romances, both in England and Scotland, where it is mentioned by Dunbar, Lindsay, and *The Complaynt of Scotland,* and figures in Gourlaw's inventory.[77] *Sir Bevis* illustrates the longevity of romance themes; already over two centuries old, when Dunbar referred to it, chapbook versions were being produced in the eighteenth century. Scottish readers were also aware of more modish and up-to-date romances, such as those in prose, often translated from French: Douglas mentioned *Paris and Vienne* and *The Recolles of Troy,* both of which were translated and published by Caxton, and a later generation of readers knew the prose romances of Lord Berners, *Arthur of Little Britain* and *Huon of Bordeaux.*[78]

Two works are of particular interest, because they indicate that the contemporary taste for what may be loosely termed 'crusading romances' had reached Scotland; this was a time when the threat of Islam was keenly felt throughout Europe. The first is *The Siege of Milan,* mentioned in *The Complaynt of Scotland,* but long unidentified. Regarded by some critics as the best of the English Charlemagne romances, it narrates a fictional episode in which Lombardy has been conquered by the Saracens; the central figure is not Charlemagne himself but his heroic bishop Turpin.[79] It is interesting that in *The Complaynt* this work is mentioned in proximity to a small cluster of other Charlemagne romances: *The Four Sons of Aymon* (translated from the French and published by Caxton *c*1489), *The Brig of Mantribill* (some version of the Ferumbras story), and the Scottish *Rauf Coilyear.* It has been suggested that both *Rauf Coilyear* and Hary's *Wallace* were influenced, stylistically, by *The Siege of Milan.*[80] Mention might also be made of the metrical form employed in this romance and *Sir Eglamour,* 12-line tail-rhyme. This metre was unknown in Scottish poetry until Dunbar put it to brilliant and humorous use.

The second work is *The Three Kings' Sons*: a Burgundian prose romance, dated *c*1463, which tells how the princes Philip of France, David of Scotland, and Humphrey of England assisted the king of Naples to rid his kingdom of the

Turks. The story abounds in jousts and tournaments, and illustrates the late medieval taste for harnessing chivalry to a worthy cause, in this case fighting the Turks. John Mair refers to the work in his *History of Greater Britain*, mentioning not only the French original, but what he calls a similar book *in nostra lingua vernacula*.[81] It should be noted that Mair does not distinguish between the Scots and English languages; for him the crucial difference is between Latin and what he variously calls 'the language used of us Britons', 'English', and 'our vernacular'.[82] No Scots version of *The Three Kings' Sons* is known, but there does exist an English translation, which survives in a single handsome manuscript, written and illuminated *c*1480 (British Library, MS Harley 326).[83] It seems highly likely that Mair's book 'in our vernacular tongue' is the English translation; this does not necessarily mean, of course, that Mair saw what is now the sole surviving manuscript.

Mair mistakenly took the fictional prince David, who is only a secondary figure, not the hero, to be David, earl of Huntingdon (1152–1219). This has excited the interest of historians, but the story of *The Three Kings' Sons* does not concern the third Crusade (1188–94).[84] It is quite unhistorical, an *histoire* only in the French sense. The action take place chiefly in Naples and Sicily, not the Holy Land. Mair was clearly adventurous in his reading, and there may be other references to vernacular romances in his voluminous works. Although of little interest to philosophers or theologians, they would be precious to literary historians.

I will conclude with an obvious yet important point concerning language. Lowland Scots and English were closely related, sharing a basic grammatical structure and a common core of vocabulary. Most Scots, whether anglophiles or anglophobes, recognised this. Dunbar hailed Chaucer as 'of oure Inglisch all the lycht'; even the author of *The Complaynt* conceded that Englishmen and Scots were 'of ane langage'.[85] This undoubtedly facilitated the ready acceptance of English books; and if copies were desired, it was easy to make the small adjustments which would naturalise them into Scots. In a few cases such Scotticization was so successful that the English origins of some poems were soon forgotten, and remained so for centuries.

This linguistic closeness contributed to the success of one particular class of English writings: translation. Well-educated Scots read Latin and other foreign works in the original. But beginners and the less learned needed translations. There were, of course, some outstanding Scottish translations in this period, such as Douglas's *Eneados*; but there existed nothing to compare with the sheer mass and variety of those available in English. Several instances have been mentioned earlier, such as those associated with the names of Lydgate and Caxton, but many more were clearly circulating in Scotland. Continental culture, it should be noted, did not always reach Scottish readers directly; it often came via English intermediaries, through the medium of English translators.

Critics who discuss Anglo-Scottish literary relations at this time pay much attention to Chaucer, and those courtly poets who wrote in a distinctive southern form of English. Yet the northern counties of England are closest to Scotland, linguistically as well as geographically. One might expect that works composed in this area would have travelled to Scotland particularly easily. Indeed many of the English works mentioned in this article are northern in dialect or provenance. This area of cross-border literary contacts and influences is much neglected but full of interest, and would repay further investigation.

Notes and References

1 See Durkan, J and Ross, A. *Early Scottish Libraries*, Glasgow, 1961; Macfarlane, L J. William Elphinstone's Library Revisited. In MacDonald, A A, Lynch, M and Cowan, I B, eds. *The Renaissance in Scotland: Studies in Literature, Religion, History and Culture*, Leiden, 1994, 66–81; Cherry, A F. The Library of Henry Sinclair, Bishop of Ross, 1560–1565, *Bibliotheck*, 4 (1963), 13–24; and Shaw, D. Adam Bothwell, a Conserver of the Renaissance in Scotland. In Cowan, I B and Shaw, D, eds. *The Renaissance and Reformation in Scotland*, Edinburgh, 1983, 141–69.

2 Durkan and Ross, *op. cit.*, 15; Cherry, *op. cit.*, 15; Shaw, *op. cit.*, 168.

3 Ford, M L. Importation of Printed Books into England and Scotland. In Hellinga, L and Trapp, J B, eds. *The Cambridge History of the Book in Britain*, vol III: 1400–1557, Cambridge, 1999, 195.

4 Shaw, *op. cit.*, 168.

5 *Cf.* Durkan and Ross, *op. cit.*, 174; Ford, *op. cit.*, 195.

6 See Craigie, W, ed. *The Asloan Manuscript*, STS, 1923–5, I, 153–71; also the allusions to 'policornica' in *Asloan Manuscript*, I, 194, and Stewart, A, ed. *The Complaynt of Scotland*, STS, 1979, 67.

7 See Boffey, J and Edwards, A S G, eds. *The Works of Geoffrey Chaucer and the Kingis Quair: a Facsimile of Bodleian Library, Oxford, Manuscript Arch. Selden. B. 24*, Cambridge, 1997.

8 St John's College, Cambridge, MS G 19, fol 164 (both colophon and signature). On the *Festial*, see Erbe, T, ed. *Mirk's Festial: a Collection of Homilies*, EETS, 1905; also Doyle, A I. Publication by Members of the Religious Orders. In Griffiths, J and Pearsall, D, eds. *Book Production and Publishing in Britain 1375–1475*, Cambridge, 1989, 115.

9 This manuscript is American National Library of Medicine, MS 49. See Faye, C U and Bond, W H. *Supplement to the Census of Medieval and Renaissance Manuscripts in the United States*, New York, 1962, 138.

10 Lynch, M. *Edinburgh and the Reformation*, Edinburgh, 1981, 84–5.

11 For the inventories, see [Laing, D], ed. *The Bannatyne Miscellany*, II (1836), 191–202; 209–215; Bald, M A. Vernacular Books imported into Scotland: 1500 to 1625, *Scottish Historical Review*, 23 (1926), 254–67; and the more detailed analysis in Ferguson, F S. Relations between London and Edinburgh Printers and Stationers (–1640), *The Library*, 4th series, 8 (1927), 145–98.

12 *Cf.* Robertson, D. A Packet of Books for Scotland, *Bibliotheck*, 6 (1971–3), 52–3.

13 See Warner, G F. The Library of James VI, *Miscellany of the Scottish History Society*, 1 (1893), xi–lxxv [lii and lvii].

14 See the catalogue, printed in Cameron, A I, ed. *The Warrender Papers*, II, SHS, 1932, 396–413 [404]. *Cf.* Durkan and Ross, *op. cit.*, 15.

15 See Millar, A H, ed. *The Compt Buik of David Wedderburne Merchant of Dundee 1587–1630*, SHS, 28 (1898), 87; Ferguson, *op. cit.*, 163; Cameron, *op. cit.*, 403.

16 Millar, *op. cit.*, 105.

17 *Cf.* Bawcutt, P. The Library of Gavin Douglas. In Aitken, A J, *et al.*, *Bards and Makars*, Glasgow, 1977, 107–26.

18 See Black, G F, ed. *The Seuin Seages*, STS, 1932, xiv–xv; 9 and 325.

19 *Complaynt of Scotland*, 50–51.

20 See Thomson, T, ed. *Acts of the Lords Auditors of Causes and Complaints*, Edinburgh, 1839, 112*. For full discussion, see Bawcutt, P (note 68 below).

21 The two manuscripts are NAS, GD 112/71/(1); and British Library, Harley 6149.

22 See Ferguson, *op. cit.*, 145.

23 For a survey of opinion, see Fradenburg, L O Henryson Scholarship: the Recent Decades. In Yeager, R F, ed. *Fifteenth-Century Studies: Recent Essays*, 1984, 74–5.

24 *Eneados*, I Prol, 138–42; Bawcutt, P, *Gavin Douglas: a Critical Study*, Edinburgh, 1976, 80.

25 See John Major [Mair], *A History of Greater Britain*, trans. A Constable, SHS, 1892, 145, 191–4. *Cf.* Buchanan, *History of Scotland*, trans. J Aikman, 4 vols, Edinburgh, 1827–9, 1, 426; and Warner, *op. cit.*, lxxiii.

26 Major, *History*, xxiv.

27 Maslen, R W. William Baldwin and, the Politics of Pseudo-Philosophy in Tudor Prose Fiction, *Studies in Philology*, 97 (2000), 31. See also King, J N. *English Reformation Literature*, Princeton, 1982, 358–406.

28 See Ritchie, W Tod, ed. *Bannatyne Manuscript*, 4 vols, STS, 1928–34, II, 218. *Cf.* Ferguson, *op. cit.*, 170; Robertson, *op. cit.*, 52; Millar, *op. cit.*, 169.

29 Personal communication from Michael Bath.

30 See note 20 above; and Balfour Paul, Sir J, ed. *Accounts of the Lord High Treasurer of Scotland*, Edinburgh, 1902, IV, 92.

31 See MacCracken, H N, ed. *Minor Poems of Lydgate*, 2 vols (EETS, 1911 and 1934), II, 703–7.

32 See Ferguson, *op. cit.*, 166; and Slack, P. Mirrors of Health and Treasures of Poor Men: the Uses of the Vernacular Medical Literature of Tudor England. In Webster, C, ed. *Health, Medicine and Mortality in the Sixteenth Century*, Cambridge, 1979, 237–73.

33 On this manuscript, see Comrie, J D, *History of Scottish Medicine*, 2 vols, Edinburgh, 1932, 1, 188–90. On the Wallaces, see Sanderson, Margaret H B, *Ayrshire and the Reformation: People and Change 1490–1600*, East Linton, 1997, 111 and 162.

34 Cowan, Samuel, *The Ruthven Family Papers,* London, 1912, 160–61.

35 Boardman, S. and Lynch, M. The State of Late Medieval and Early Modern Scottish History. In *Freedom and Authority: Scotland c1050–c1650,* East Linton, 2000, 44–59.

36 See *Palice of Honour,* 1714 (in Bawcutt, P, ed. *Shorter Poems of Gavin Douglas,* STS, 1967); Ferguson, *op. cit.,* 163 and 172.

37 Amours, F J, ed. *The Original Chronicle of Andrew of Wyntoun,* 6 vols, STS, 1903–14, IV, 22 (line 4334).

38 Lyall, R J. The Lost Literature of Medieval Scotland. In McClure, J D and Spiller, M R G, eds. *Bryght Lanternis: Essays on the Language and Literature of Medieval and Renaissance Scotland,* Aberdeen, 1989, 35–6. On the *Speculum Vitae,* see Raymo, R. Works of Religious and Philosophical Instruction. In Hartung, A E, ed. *A Manual of the Writings in Middle English,* vol. 7 (1986), 2261–2.

39 The Pierpont Morgan Library copy of *Dives and Pauper* (no. 734) contains a note to this effect.

40 See Baxter, J H. An Aberdeen Manuscript in Paris, *Scottish Historical Review,* 24 (1927), 326–7; and Cumming, W P. A Middle English MS in the Bibliothèque Ste Geneviève, Paris, *PMLA,* 42 (1927), 862–4.

41 Cambridge, Magdalene College, Pepys Library, no 2051. *Cf.* Bazire, J and Colledge, E, eds. *The Chastising of God's Children,* London, 1957.

42 The manuscript is published in Bennett, J A W, ed. *Devotional Pieces in Verse and Prose,* STS, 1955; see MacDonald, A A. Passion Devotion in Late-Medieval Scotland. In MacDonald, A A *et al,* eds. *The Broken Body: Passion Devotion in Late-Medieval Culture,* Groningen, 1998, 108–31.

43 On these verses, see Brown, C and Robbins, R H. *Index of Middle English Verse [IMEV],* New York, 1943, *Supplement,* 1965, nos 430 and 430.5; 704; 4181 (also Bawcutt, P. Dunbar and an Epigram, *Scottish Literary Journal,* 13.2 (1986), 16–19); and 91. For the latter, see Sullivan, E W, ed. *The First and Second Dalhousie Manuscripts: Poems and Prose by John Donne and others,* facsimile edn, Missouri, 1988, 21.

44 See Stevenson, G, ed. *Pieces from the Makulloch and the Gray MSS,* STS, 1918, 46–50; *IMEV,* no. 3612; and Woolf, R. *The English Religious Lyric in the Middle Ages,* Oxford, 1968, 216–17.

45 Cambridge, Magdalene College, Pepys Library, MS 1576; for the Lydgate poem, see MacCracken, *op. cit.,* I, 216–21.

46 Bennett, *Devotional Pieces,* 270–74; corresponding to MacCracken, *op. cit.,* I, 357–62.

47 *IMEV,* no. 1119. See Stevenson, *Pieces from the Makulloch and the Gray MSS,* 33–6; Bennett, *Devotional Pieces,* 261–5.

48 See Stevens, M and Cawley, A C, eds. *The Towneley Plays,* 2 vols, EETS, 1994, I, 342–6.

49 Woolf, *op. cit.,* 202–7 [with illustration].

50 *The Meroure of Wyssdome,* vol I, ed. C Macpherson, STS, 1926, 166–70; Boffey and Edwards, *op. cit.,* 2 (poem 7).

51 Thomson, John A F, *The Later Lollards: 1414–1520,* Oxford, 1965, 203.

52 Watt, D E R *et al.,* ed. *Scotichronicon in Latin and English,* 9 vols, Aberdeen and Edinburgh, 1987–98, VII, 69.

53 *Meroure of Wyssdome,* vol. III, McDonald, C, ed. STS, 1990, 84–6.

54 Oxford, Bodleian Library, MS Fairfax 11; *Cf.* Lawlor, J H. Notes on the Library of the Sinclairs of Rosslyn, *Proceedings of the Society of Antiquaries of Scotland,* 32 (1897–8), 90–120 [107].

55 British Library, MS Egerton 2880. See *The New Testament in Scots,* Law, T G, ed, 3 vols, STS, 1901–4. *Cf.* Lindsay, T M. A Literary Relic of Scottish Lollardy, *Scottish Historical Review,* 1 (1904), 261; and Sanderson, *op. cit.,* 42–47.

56 *Cf.* Lindsay, citing Wodrow, *op. cit.,* 271.

57 An instance is the poem by an 'inglisman' (in fact William Elderton) in *Bannatyne Manuscript,* III, 254–6; and its religious 'parody' in Mitchell, A F, ed. *Gude and Godlie Ballatis,* STS, 1897, 213–19.

58 Craigie, J, ed. *Poems of James VI,* 2 vols, STS, 1955–8, I, 81.

59 A good starting-point is Kratzmann, G. *Anglo-Scottish Literary Relations 1430–1550,* Cambridge, 1980.

60 McDiarmid, M P, ed. *Hary's Wallace,* 2 vols, STS, 1968–9, book I, line 7. Embedded references are to this edition.

61 Instances are Chaucer's *Complaint of Mars* and *Complaint of Venus.*

62 *Meroure of Wyssdome,* I, 164.

63 *Meroure of Wyssdome,* I, 73–4; slightly modernised.

64 McDonald, C. John Ireland's *Meroure of Wyssdome,* and Chaucer's *Tale of Melibee, Studies in Scottish Literature,* 21 (1986), 23.

65 See *Meroure of Wyssdome,* III, 164; and I, 164.

66 See Bergen, Henry, ed. *Lydgate's Troy Book,* 4 vols, EETS, 1906–35, IV, 46–50; and Van Buuren, C. John Asloan, an Edinburgh Scribe, *English Studies,* 47 (1966), 366–8.

67 See Davis, N, ed. *Paston Letters and Papers.* Oxford, 1971, I, 574–5.

68 See Bawcutt, P. The Boston Public Library Manuscript of John Lydgate's *Siege of Thebes:* its Scottish Owners and Inscriptions, *Medium AEvum,* 70 (2001), 80–94.

69 Millar, ed. *Compt Buik,* 89.

70 See Beattie, W, ed. *The Chepman and Myllar Prints: A Facsimile,* Edinburgh, 1950, 109; Durkan and Ross, *op. cit,* 129 and 136; Durkan, J. The Cultural Background in Sixteenth-Century Scotland. In

McRoberts, D, ed. *Essays on the Scottish Reformation 1513–1625*, Glasgow, 1962, 299.

71 Ritchie, ed. *Bannatyne Manuscript*, IV, 87.

72 NLS, MS Adv. 72.1.37, p. 184. The passage corresponds to Bergen, H, ed, *Fall of Princes*, 4 vols, EETS, 1924–7, I.6371–7, and 6441–7.

73 *Cf.* Edwards, A S G. The Influence of Lydgate's *Fall of Princes c*1440–1559: a Survey, *Medieval Studies*, 39 (1977), 424–39.

74 *Cf.* Brown, M. *James* I, Edinburgh, 1994, 186; and MacQueen, H L. *Common Law and Feudal Society in Medieval Scotland*, Edinburgh, 1993, 94.

75 For Scottish interest in these tales, *cf.* Bawcutt, ed. *Poems of William Dunbar*, Glasgow, 1998, no 39: 'Now lythis off ane gentill knycht', 25–30; Douglas, *Palice of Honour*, 1718; Ferguson, *op. cit.*, 177.

76 The evidence derives chiefly from *Complaynt of Scotland*, 50–51, and Bassandyne and Gourlay. For information about the romances, see Burke Severs, J, ed. *A Manual of the Writings in Middle English 1050–1500*, vol I (1967).

77 See Dunbar, *Poems*, no 39: 34-5; Lyall, R J, ed. Lindsay, *The Thrie Estaitis*, Edinburgh, 1989, 174; *Complaynt*, 50; Ferguson, *op. cit.*, 177.

78 See Douglas, *Palice of Honour*, 576, and *Eneados*, I Prol. 206; *Complaynt*, 50; Ferguson, *op. cit.*, 170; and Bald *op. cit.*, 258.

79 This poem is included in Mills, M, ed. *Six Middle English Romances*, London, 1973.

80 *Cf.* McDiarmid, ed. *Hary's Wallace*, I, cxxv. The name 'Schir Gawteir' in *Rauf Coilyear*, 957, may derive from *The Siege of Milan*, 377–8.

81 Major, *History of Greater Britain*, 165 (see note 25).

82 Major, *op. cit.*, 160, 195, and 204–5.

83 For information about both romances, see Furnivall, F J, ed. *The Three Kings' Sons*, EETS, 1895; Burke Severs, ed. *Manual*, 163–5; Grinberg, H. *The Three Kings' Sons* and *Les Trois Fils de Rois*, *Romance Philology*, 28 (1975), 521–9; and Meale, C. Book Production and Social Status. In Griffiths and Pearsall, *op. cit.*, 212 and plates 19 and 20.

84 *Cf.* Stringer, K J. *Earl David of Huntingdon 1152–1219*, Edinburgh, 1985, 39–40; also MacQuarrie, A. *Scotland and the Crusades*, Edinburgh, 1997, 30–31.

85 Dunbar, *Poems*, no 59.259; and *Complaynt*, 84.

The Printed Tapestry Carpet: The Pioneering Work of Richard Whytock of Edinburgh 1784–1857

Vanessa Habib

Introduction

In the *New Statistical Account* for the parish of Lasswade, Midlothian, compiled in 1843, Richard Whytock's carpet factory at St Ann's was described as an ingenious and innovative venture:

> . . . Besides carpets on the principle of the Tournay and Axminster kind, made to fit all sizes and shapes of rooms without seam, and which are made at only a few other places in this country, Richard Whytock and Co, the proprietors, manufacture a new sort of Brussels carpet, of great beauty, which resembles tapestry in its general effect, and which they call Tapestry Brussels; also a fabric in velvet pile, quite novel in its appearance. These two fabrics are produced by a new process of their own invention, which is applicable also to other fabrics, to which they purpose to apply it. As the principle is patented, it is not kept secret. It consists of a combination of the two hitherto rival methods of producing Figures on cloth, namely, the arts of weaving and printing; and, at the same time, is a simplification of both processes to a wonderful degree . . . The productions of the manufactory are already in much request in London, and have found their way to various parts of the world.[1]

These comments suggest that the company was assured of future success. Yet although celebrated for this patent in his own lifetime, little is now known of the carpets and furnishing fabrics manufactured by Whytock. None of the surviving Tapestry carpets have been positively identified with him. His other varied manufacturing activities have been forgotten. He was the founder of the furnishing company known as Whytock and Reid which, remarkably, still trades in Edinburgh today and which bears the Royal Warrant, an honour first bestowed on Whytock by Queen Victoria in 1838.[2] During his lifetime this company, then known as Whytock and Co, expanded into many branches of upholstery work and cabinet making, carving and gilding, of high quality.

Early Years

Richard Barnet Whytock seems to have started business in Edinburgh with his brother William in 1806, selling drapery and haberdashery goods, which included printed cambrics, shawls, blankets, quilts and trimmings.[3] Later, with a new partner, Robert Grieve, he began to specialise in furnishings and upholstery work. An advertisement in the *Edinburgh Advertiser* in 1810 set out their intentions:

> . . . Coloured Drawings of all the Fashionable Drapery for Beds and Window Curtains will be regularly received, and Upholsterers of the best taste will be recommended to their purchasers,

as they mean to give their attention wholly to the Mercantile part of the Trade.

Pattern Books, containing 100 patterns each, sent to any part of Scotland, if required. Liberal discounts allowed to Upholsterers.

Richard Whytock, one of the Partners, is now in London, selecting from the best Manufacturers the newest and most admired patterns, and the whole will be arranged on or about the 1st of September.

As there is no shop or warehouse in Scotland entirely in the same Trade, Whytock, Grieve and Co solicit, with some degree of confidence, the patronage of the Nobility and Inhabitants of Scotland in general . . .[4]

By 1818 Whytock had moved premises again and begun his manufacturing career in earnest. He employed skilled workmen from London, to make elaborate decorative fringes for furniture drapery, which was becoming increasingly fashionable in Edinburgh.[5] During this period he also formed a new and long lasting partnership with Henry Henderson, to make furnishing fabrics, particularly silk and worsted damasks. Henderson's manufactory was in Queensberry House in the Canongate, once a fine Old Town residence of the Duke of Queensberry. From 1825, Whytock was awarded several large premiums by the Board of Trustees for Manufactures for these fabrics – the Board's judges commenting in one year on the 'great beauty of the silk', and he himself also later became a judge in their annual competitions.[6] An early indication of his interest in carpets came in 1826 when he shared a premium with the Kilmarnock company of Gregory Thomson and Co for carpeting in imitation of Brussels.[7] Whytock was made a Burgess of the Canongate in 1828 and his Burgess Ticket survives, on which he is described as a manufacturer there (Figure 1).[8] He clearly hoped to make and to sell furnishings to the expanding urban community in the New Town and had moved by 1827 into the heart of it, to No 7 George Street and had taken an additional partner, the wallpaper stainer William McCrie.[9] Whytock supplied Lady Helen Hall, at her address in George Street, with Brussels, common and stair

carpet in 1830–31.[10] A vignette on the heading of his account shows the elegant façade of the Georgian showrooms (Figure 2).

In 1830 he was asked to go to Brussels by the Board of Trustees, to report on the Exposition of the Manufactures of the Netherlands, which the Scots were anxious to emulate. He had expected to see a 'grand display' of carpets, but was disappointed:

> There were to be sure several handsome Carpets from Tournay made in one piece like our Axminster Carpets but I considered the patterns inferior, and the colour in no degree superior to our own. Some very handsome Carpets which at first I imagined to be made in one piece I afterwards discovered to be made in breadths of two feet or little more joined together and with borders sewed on. Of the fabrics usually called Brussels or Wilton there were a good many specimens but I did not see a single pattern that I would have been at the trouble to carry home nor were the fabrics so good as those made in this Country.[11]

He also noted some Figured silks from Lyons, made on the Jacquard loom 'now common at home, and even considerably improved since they were introduced'.

The Printed Tapestry Carpet

Although William McCrie's name has never been associated with the Tapestry carpet, his subsequent career as a wallpaper stainer and his partnership with Whytock suggest that they may have experimented with the printing of worsted yarns.[12] The idea was not new, but Whytock was the first to apply it to heavy carpet yarns.[13] By printing bars of colour across a group of warp threads, each colour the length of a loop of warp, the effect could be created of a multi-coloured Brussels carpet without the dead pile lying in the body of the carpet when one of generally five or six colours was not required in the pattern. This would economise on the number of coloured warp threads used in each longitudinal line of patterning in Brussels and cut pile Wilton carpets and at the same time increase the

1. Richard Whytock's Burgess Ticket, granted in 1828. Reproduced by kind permission of Stoddard Carpets, Stoddard International plc.

2. Letterhead showing the now demolished shop of Richard Whytock at 7 George Street, with St Andrew Square and the Melville Monument in the background. National Archives of Scotland.

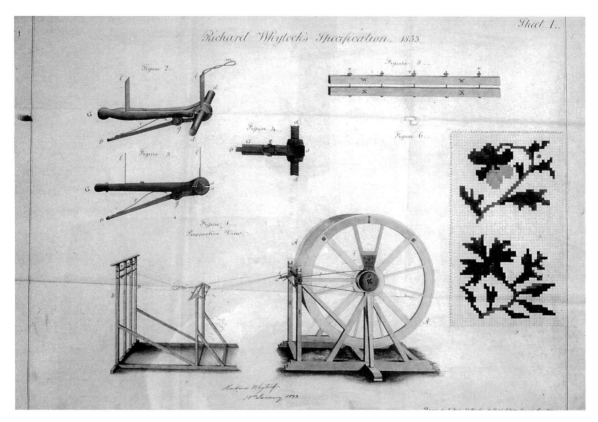

3. Patent specification drawing by John Farey of Whytock's wooden printing drum, six feet in diameter. National Archives of Scotland.

number of colours which could be used in a design. A drawing which accompanies his patent specifications in the National Archives of Scotland, shows a simple design of Viola and Dianthus and the sequence of colours to be printed on a group of pile threads wound round a printing drum (Figure 3). Initially the colour was applied with a series of rulers or sticks pressed against the threads from a horizontal shelf at the side of the cylinder. This was later changed to a colour roller revolving in a colour box underneath the cylinder. Only one thread in the pattern repeat could be printed at a time, but several repeats could be printed simultaneously.[14] Originally Whytock had made an arrangement with two of the leading Kidderminster carpet manufacturers to put his idea into practice, but they were sceptical of its success and did not take

it up.[15] He was thus left to develop the process himself, which he patented in 1833. But there were several technical problems connected with the printing process at first, including the difficulty of accurate registration, printing of pastel shades and the formation of large areas of even background colour. The latter was caused by the unpredictability of the final shade of each pile thread which showed up when laid side by side.[16] Another difficulty was the security of the pile, in comparison with the traditional Brussels structure. Nevertheless, the first carpet made by this method was exhibited in 1832 and called the 'Edinburgh Carpet'.[17] It caused a great deal of interest amongst the Board of Trustees and Whytock advertised his 'new and splendid fabric in Carpet' in the Edinburgh press, confident that it would rival conventional carpets.[18] According

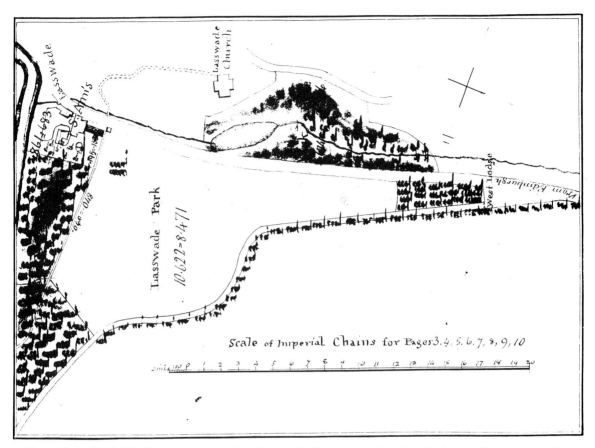

4. Part of the Melville Estate, surveyed by James Hall in 1841, showing St Ann's. National Archives of Scotland.

to James Skene, in evidence given to the Ewart Select Committee, Whytock could print up to fourteen colours by 1835.[19] A later writer claimed that as many as 150 shades had at one time been employed on an intricate pattern, but in general thirty to forty shades came to be used in this process.[20]

In 1833 the carpet manufactory moved to larger premises leased from Lord Melville at St Ann's, Lasswade, a village near Edinburgh on the river Esk (Figure 4). Here the partners also made hand knotted carpets in the Persian and Turkish style.[21] The Board of Trustees had actively encouraged the manufacture of several different types of carpet in Scotland from the mid-eighteenth century and a specimen collection of the best Axminster, French tapestry,

Turkey and Persian carpets could be examined in their offices in Edinburgh. Whytock, frequently a judge in their annual competitions, purchased many of the prize-winning carpets and carpet designs. In 1830 a significant increase was made in the premiums offered for Turkey carpets.[22] Gregory Thomson and Co. of Kilmarnock were awarded the first prize and their entries were bought by both Whytock and William McCrie.[23] The following year they were again winners with a premium of £150, for four Axminster or Turkey carpets, described by the judges as 'an article of the highest merit, greatly surpassing their expectations'.[24] One of these carpets was also purchased by Whytock.

Whether he had entirely surmounted the technical difficulties involved in manufacturing the Tapestry carpet is not known, for he had apparently already leased the patent to an English house by 1835.[25] But early in 1838 he was appointed Patent Carpet Manufacturer to the Queen, and a report in the *Scotsman* after the Coronation in July, describing the festivities at St Ann's, noted a large new room at the factory, eighty feet long.[26] With a colour maker named George Clink he continued to work on the warp printing process, bringing out a second patent in 1839 for an improved method of colouring the worsted warps by the use of small dye baths, through which steam would pass to fix the colour.[27] But according to his joiner and long-term employee, William Lunn, this work proved a very costly experiment and the idea was not taken up.[28]

At the end of 1839, Whytock contributed to the Exhibition of Scottish Manufactures held at the Assembly Rooms in Edinburgh. He showed a Patent Velvet Carpet with a border, examples of Taboret and Damask, a Tapestry stool and several Persian Rugs.[29]

In 1840 Whytock and Co were asked to supply some of the furnishings for the newly-built home of John Kincaid Lennox Esq at Lennox Castle near Campsie.[30] These included several specially made carpets. A bordered Turkey Tapestry carpet and Turkey rug were ordered for the dining room and a super Tapestry carpet with a crimson damask Persian rug for the library. In this room the carpet was to be surrounded by a border of oak flooring.[31] In charge of the overall decorative scheme in the house was the painter and interior decorator, D R Hay, whose theories of the use of colour in interiors were to become influential and may have encouraged William McCrie to design a range of wallpapers to harmonize with Whytock's furnishings in 1843.[32] No rooms decorated by them have so far been identified, but house sales in Edinburgh of the early 1840s reveal several handsome and luxurious examples of Tapestry carpets within newly decorated interiors.[33]

In 1846, Whytock applied for an extension to his patent, claiming that the manufacturing difficulties he had so far encountered had meant that he had not made much money out of it.

He said in evidence that he had made less than 302,000 yards of Tapestry carpet, and had merely 57 looms at work on it.[34] After the extension was granted in August 1846, John Crossley and Sons of Halifax bought the patent rights for the sum of £10,000, allowing Whytock and Henderson to continue to use the process at Lasswade. It appears that Crossley had been making Tapestry carpets under licence since 1844 and already had 130 looms at work on them.[35] This company was to become the centre of Tapestry carpet production in subsequent years, having made several technical improvements to the printing process and having been able to mechanise the whole operation. However a long article in the Art Union in 1847, one of a series called 'Visits to British Manufactories', makes it clear that Whytock was producing Tapestry carpets of high quality at Lasswade, even though he had licensed his patent to other concerns. The writer commented:

> There are no doubt, few of our readers . . . who have not 'stepped' upon the soft and delicate carpet we are describing, which although found chiefly in the mansions of the wealthy, are not beyond the reach of those who, with means comparatively limited, covet home luxuries, and desire in all things beautiful specimens of art.[36]

The article expanded on the economies of printing without having to cut blocks or engrave cylinders and also stated that the number of colours currently in use was 'frequently more than twenty'. With the extension of Whytock's patent for a further five years, the firm of Pardoe and Hoomans in Kidderminster were also to be granted a licence. A further connection with Kidderminster at this period was the arrival at Lasswade of Henry Widnell, who became a partner of Henry Henderson.[37]

Of particular interest are the five illustrations of designs by William Hunter who worked for Whytock (Figure 5). He had intended to become a portrait painter but was persuaded to become a designer (and in the 1841 Census is described as an artist), perhaps influenced by the prospect of a regular and substantial salary.[38] Whytock was

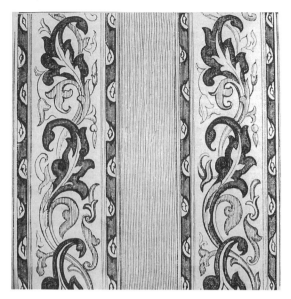

5. Carpet designs by William Hunter.

interested in the training of designers and bought patterns at the Board of Trustees competitions, but the copying of designs was universal and he later wrote that he knew of several extensive manufacturers of Brussels carpet who had boasted that they had never paid for a pattern.[39] In 1836 the Trustees Drawing Academy at Edinburgh instituted pattern drawing classes under the direction of the artist Thomas Barker Holdway, whose designs were also purchased by Whytock.[40] Holdway got the Trustees to pay for a visit to Paris, to study how French designers were trained.[41] French design was acknowledged to be of far higher quality than in Britain. But it was also conceded that carpets were only bought by the wealthiest class of the community, whereas in Britain, 'every apartment is carpeted; the great consumption is, therefore, in the moderately priced article, for which in France there would be no demand'. Though the designs were beautiful, the material was sometimes considered to be 'dry and poor'.[42]

Yester House

A rare survivor of the Tapestry velvet carpet, similar in style to William Hunter's illustrations and dating from the same period, though the maker is unknown, is presently at Yester House in East Lothian.[43] In two large pieces, each about 25ft by 14ft, in adjoining rooms and partially bordered, it has a laid velvety pile (Figure 6). The pattern shows a medallion containing a dark red orchid, with the bulb at the base of the plant on a cream ground and a larger medallion with a garland of greenhouse flowers including orchids.[44] The carpet is made from strips 27 inches wide with a repeat of 48 inches and a mitred border 17½ inches wide. All the pile threads in the design appear to be different from one another and so must have been printed individually, and the effect is one of great richness of colour and depth of shading. The composition of naturalistically drawn groups of flowers is handled with great restraint, bearing in mind the rococo excesses of the next few years, and reflects the contemporary passion for gardens and conservatories. Although the quality of the workmanship and the early date suggest Whytock as the maker, the remarks of Bertram Jacobs that Whytock printed his warps in pairs, making 130 prints across a 27 inch strip whereas Crossley, on the recommendation of his designer McCullum, printed 260 individual threads across the width, must be taken into account.[45] On general inspection the Yester carpet appears to have ten tufts to the inch which are all printed individually. However, the 1851 Census does record an Archibald McCallum as a pattern designer at Lasswade. It is interesting to note that in 1846, the director of the Botanic Garden in Edinburgh began a course of lectures on pictorial botany for students at the Trustees Drawing Academy, and several manufacturers including Whytock were invited to send their designers to attend.[46] A Tapestry carpet of slightly later date made by Crossley and Sons, which is illustrated in the *Journal of Design and Manufactures* for 1850, shows a complicated but much more mechanical design. Awarded a medal by the Society of Arts, part of its attraction was the juxtaposition of different sections of the pattern, shown in three different engravings. Though some examples of Tapestry Brussels strip carpeting have survived, notably in the Coloroll Carpets collection, Tapestry velvet carpet was too delicate to bear much usage and the most renowned surviving examples are the showcase carpets attributed to Crossleys for the Great Exhibition in 1851, made in two halves, each about 18ft by 6ft.[47]

Henderson and Widnell

It is likely that Henry Widnell joined Whytock and Co in Lasswade at the time of the extension of the patent. His arrival seems to have coincided with Richard Whytock's withdrawal from manufacturing carpets although he remained active in the development of other kinds of fabrics and continued to commission and sell fine carpets in his Edinburgh shop.[48] However, by 1851, the Census for Lasswade suggests that there were already two companies at work in the area as Henry Henderson was described as a carpet manufacturer, aged 52, with two

6. The Yester House carpet, showing the border; the overall view; a detail of the central garland. By kind permission of Mr and Mrs Francis Menotti.

firms, employing 185 men and 85 women.[49] The following year Henderson and Widnell acquired ground at Polton in the neighbouring parish of Cockpen for another manufactory.[50] At the Great Exhibition they were awarded a medal for the quality of their carpets and two of their designs, showing all-over patterns of natural groups of flowers and leaves, were illustrated in the *Art Journal Catalogue*.[51] The Journal commented: 'we have seen carpets produced by this firm, equal in texture, richness of colour and beauty of pattern to any foreign fabric of a similar description'. Henderson and Widnell also exhibited a portière in the style of Louis XIV, measuring 10ft 6ins by 5ft in patent velvet and described as probably the largest piece ever made on this principle.[52] They also showed what they claimed to be the first large carpet with a centre design made by the patent method, a style usually associated with Crossley and Sons.

Surviving carpets of this type, mentioned before, with a central medallion, borders and corners, were made in two halves. The design, on a quarter of the carpet, turned over four times and each half was a mirror image of the other, which gave a rather kaleidoscopic effect.[53] Several other companies showed carpets made by Whytock's patent Tapestry process in 1851. They included Crossley's, Brinton's, Pardoe and Hoomans, and Smith Turberville Boyle and Co for whom Henderson and Widnell made a velvet carpet in tertiary colours, russet, citrine and olive, called 'Ferns', which was designed by E T Parris.[54] Belatedly, the Kidderminster manufacturers rushed to take part in the rapidly increasing trade which the *Journal of Design* considered in 1850 would certainly continue; 'the realities of artistic beauty, utility and cheapness of production combined, cannot fail to render it (the Tapestry carpet) an article of every day sale'. The journal also noted recent improvements in the printing of the yarns which enabled even minute objects to be introduced into the patterns with great success.[55]

Carpet design in general, however, was criticised by the Great Exhibition jury, who found fault with the elaborate 'wall hanging' style of ornament. The surge in production of printed carpets which had made them cheaper and more widely available was also regretted by Richard Whytock's nephew Alexander. He disliked the prevailing taste for shading, which he claimed gave the painful feeling of walking on an uneven surface and he was particularly critical of the use of architectural detail on floors. Speaking in 1856 of his uncle's patent he commented: 'the downward course of all manufactures in this country has only caused the invention (Whytock's) in great part to assist in gorging the market with carpets for the millions'.[56] This was in part a reference to the introduction of power loom weaving for Tapestry carpets. However, the development of the patent by other companies was of some benefit to Richard Whytock and Co themselves, as their advertisement in *The Scotsman* in May 1849 showed:

RICHARD WHYTOCK & CO
Patentees of the Celebrated Velvet
Pile and Tapestry Carpet
9 GEORGE STREET, EDINBURGH
Beg most respectfully to call the attention of the Nobility, Gentry, and Public to their present Stock of CARPETS, which they have considerably enlarged since their removal to their New Warerooms. It now comprises a beautiful choice of the most elegant Designs of PATENT VELVET SAXONY and TAPESTRY CARPETS yet produced; and from various improvements recently effected in the manufacture, they are enabled to make a considerable Reduction in Price. ENGLISH, BRUSSELS and SUPERFINE CARPETS, together with every other description now in use . . .[57]

At Lasswade, Henderson and Widnell continued to use hand looms, as 'Mr Whytock had a very kind and strong feeling towards the weavers, and believed that its (the power loom) introduction would be to their detriment'.[58] During this period an agreement was made with a leading French carpet company, Jean Jacques Sallandrouze de Larmornais, to teach the warp printing process at Aubusson. A letter dated August 1st 1856, which has survived in the company's papers, set out the terms of the agreement:

We the undersigned, agree to go to France to teach the work people of Messrs Sallandrouze de Lamornais & Co the art of printing warps for weaving carpets etc and setting the same, and to do all in our power to impart to them the knowledge that we possess to enable Messrs Sallandrouze de Lamornais & Co to establish the business, in the terms mentioned below viz

William Lunn	Mechanic	30/- p wk	3 mths
Henry McGowan	Overlooker	30/- p wk	4 mths
	Printers	15/- p wk	6 mths
	do.	15/- p wk	6 mths
	Setter	15/- p wk	6 mths
	do.	15/- p wk	6 mths
William Mirk	Color Mixer	45/- p wk	6 mths

In addition, Messrs Sallandrouze de Lamornais & Co to pay all travelling expenses including living while on the road to Aubusson and back, at the expiration of the respective periods agreed upon. Our weekly wages to commence the day on which we leave Lasswade, and to terminate the day on which we return.

We undertake to behave ourselves respectfully to our employers, and to do whatever may be required of us within the usual hours of work, connected with the branch of the business that we respectively undertake to teach, and in consideration of our doing this to the satisfaction of Messrs Sallandrouze de Lamornais & Co we are to receive the sums attached to our names below in addition to the before named weekly wages as a consideration for the knowledge imparted to their workpeople.

William Lunn and Henry Mc Gowan Ten pound each, and the two printers and setters Two pound ten shillings each, and the expenses to Aubusson of William Mirk's wife to be paid.[59]

It appears that during this period Henry Widnell's son, also named Henry, had taken over one of the two companies run by Henderson and Widnell and in 1859 took over the stock of Henderson and Widnell (which had become bankrupt), forming the company of Henry Widnell and Son.[60] At this point, Henry Henderson may have retired. Printed Tapestry carpets continued to be made by their successors however, until 1958.[61] At the end of World II Henry Widnell and Stewart were the sole manufacturers of printed Tapestry carpet in Britain.

Axminster Carpets Made By Richard Whytock

In 1833, when Whytock and Henderson moved to Lasswade, they manufactured not only printed Tapestry carpets but also Axminster or hand knotted carpets in the Persian and Turkish style. In the Board of Trustees competition that year, Whytock showed a carpet commissioned by the Duke of Buccleuch as well as a patent carpet. Although not described, it was perhaps a Turkey type as the premiums for these had recently been greatly increased. The judges commented:

> The splendid carpet made for the Duke of Buccleuch by Mr Whytock which he obligingly allowed to be hung up for exhibition is a great advance upon anything of the kind hitherto done in Scotland, or perhaps in England; and should have the effect to open the eyes of other Manufacturers to the advantage of far greater attention to beauty and elegance of ornament, harmonious arrangement of colours and the avoidance of those spotty and staring and stiff looking objects to which they have been accustomed.[62]

In his patent of 1833, he had described a method of printing warps for hand knotted carpets which economically avoided colouring the part of the tuft which would not be seen on the surface of the carpet. How practicable this technique might have been or whether it was ever used is not known.[63] It was also pointed out that the printing of Turkey patterns on warp threads in the correct order of selection would allow the weaver to have succeeding colours to hand and thus avoid mistakes. In his pursuit of good design, however, he bought two prize winning original designs for Turkey or Persian carpets from William Hunter in 1833.[64] The following year he exhibited another fine carpet, 44 feet long and 24 feet wide, perhaps another commission as it was not entered for competition. The judges, William Allen, D R Hay and the upholsterer Alex Sclanders recommended a special premium of £50 to be awarded to Whytock 'on account of the beauty and fine taste of the design, the harmonious and skilful manner in which the colours are blendid (sic), the excellence of the fabric and the rich effect of the Toute-ensemble, exceeding anything of the kind hitherto produced in Scotland'.[65] In evidence to the Ewart Select Committee on Design and Manufactures in 1835, Whytock had been commended for the interest he took in design and the training of designers. He employed both William Hunter and an assistant, perhaps a man named James Huchison who trained at the Trustees Academy and lived at Lasswade.[66] James Skene remarked, that in Scotland 'in the circumstances of design and the beauty of execution, I think he stands pre-eminent'.[67] The Board of Trustees were recognized for their encouragement of carpet manufacturing, particularly the introduction of premiums for dyeing and pattern making. Skene stated 'I think the improvements in matters of taste in general has been very remarkable within a few years and in dyes there has been a very great improvement'. In design, 'the improvement has also been obvious, but not so great as yet, because there is no instruction given in it'. But whereas French designers were paid highly and their patterns copyrighted for a year, no such security existed for British designers until the Design Copyright Act of 1839.[68] As has already been noted, the Trustees Academy established pattern drawing classes in Edinbugh in 1836.

Henry Henderson, Whytock's partner, was also credited with making several technical improvements to the manufacture of carpets. In the broad Turkey and Persian types, the weft was shot across by a kind of cross bow, rather than a shuttle being passed from hand to hand.[69] An account of the Lasswade factory written in 1842, stated that the patterns were tied in by boys and that the workmen earned from 20 to 25 shillings a week, but were frequently idle, having to wait six or eight days for webs.[70] In 1838, there were thought to be about 50 looms at work.

One of several carpets woven by Whytock for the newly built Lennox Castle in 1841 included a so-called Scoto-Persian. carpet for the drawing room. D R Hay's estimate for the decoration of this room included the ceiling and cornice heightened with gilding and picked out with ultramarine blue, the walls to be decorated by a gilded sprig to imitate embroidery and woodwork heightened with gilding and picked out lightly with blue. The whole set against five coats 'tinted, flatted and carefully stippled of a warm toned colour'.[71] The Lennox's were clients with views of their own and a letter suggesting that the colours of the carpet border should be changed was swiftly replied to:

Edinburgh 16 December 1840

Sir

Your Drawing Room Carpet is in the Loom and will be commenced in a few days my object in writing is to request Mrs Lennox and your sanction to make the ground of the Border <u>White</u> – this in all our opinions will be a very decided improvement, the Colours in the border with the brown leafy scroll will appear to much greater advantage on the White and it will be. more in keeping with the centre, which is White.

I beg to apologise for not having brought this to your notice when west.

David Whyte

Sir

In answer to your letter relating to the Drawing Room Carpet Mrs Lennox and I are decidedly of opinion that the ground of the Border should be of the Colour formerly fixed – <u>Not White</u> – you will therefore proceed with the Carpet agreeable to the arrangement made by Mrs Lennox.

J. K. Lennox.[72]

In a later letter from David Whyte, a further partner in the company, mention was made of the brown ground of the body of the Scoto-Persian carpet 'which we are happy to say looks extremely well', but there was a problem with a projection into a window bay which Whytock and Co thought would spoil the general effect. The carpet had been designed with a border to lie two feet from the wall at all parts of the room and which would not fit comfortably into the window recess.[73] Like many carpets of the time, this one appears not to have survived, but the Axminster structure, called by Whytock either Scoto-Turkey or Scoto-Persian would have been considerably tougher than the velvet pile type and it is possible that some of them may still lie unrecognized in other houses.

In May 1848 Whytock and Co opened a new extension to their George Street shop, advertising 'a Splendid and entire New Stock of Patent Velvet and Tapestry Carpets of the Lasswade make, also Brussels Carpets of English Manufacture with every description of Carpeting at present in use'.[74] A sale of old stock included a Scoto-Persian carpet of 'exquisite beauty', in size 36 feet by 23 feet. At the end of the year, Whytock and Co wrote to the Earl of Fife at Duff House, Banffshire with details of a square carpet of this size, with a rug, which had been made for another customer.[75] The wholesale price for rug and carpet was £200: 'The party for whom it was made paid Fifty pounds & R W & Co would willingly loose Fifty more as it is not every day such a Carpet will find a purchaser, though very beautiful – It will afford R W & Co great pleasure to hear that it meets with his Lordships approval … A Cypher or arms could be inserted in the centre shield & window pieces of any shape made to match'. Whether this carpet ever found its way to Duff House is unknown.

Their success at the Great Exhibition enabled the company to announce a large addition of magnificent carpets, embracing every variety of style and colour, to their stock in October 1851:

> they would direct particular attention to the important feature of this department, which is, that nearly all their Carpets are of Original and Exclusive Designs, and manufactured of the best materials and most durable colouring, while their scale of price is extremely moderate as compared with what is usually charged for the inferior descriptions, so extensively brought into the market of late years.[76]

In following years Aubusson carpets, Turkey and Masulipatam carpets, real Persia carpets and Koula rugs were added to their range. During the 1850s, Whytock and Co began to expand into other areas, describing themselves as Upholsterers, Decorators and Carvers and Gilders. They also began to stock and manufacture high quality furniture.[77]

Richard Whytock died in January 1857, passing his share of his business interests to his nephews Alexander and James.[78] A highly praised carpet, shown in the International Exhibition of 1862 in London, may have reflected Alexander's taste. This was a Scoto-Axminster carpet for a dining room in the Byzantine style (Figure 7). Illustrated in the official Catalogue, the authors commented: 'This is an example of the much-approved flat, or unshaded ornamentation, in carpet design. The warm neutral colouring is an agreeable advance upon the showy combinations of colour hitherto so much in demand'.[79] Also illustrated was a Wilton carpet in Louis XVI style for a drawing room, 'the first attempt to introduce this style in a quality of carpet within the reach of the general public'. Another carpet of theirs, a bordered Brussels, was illustrated in the *Art Journal Catalogue* alongside the Scoto-Axminster.[80] Whytock and Co also exhibited a pollard oak sideboard which was highly praised and indicated the success of the expansion of the company into furniture making.[81] Alexander Whytock took the Edinburgh cabinet makers Robert and Hugh Reid into partnership in 1876.[82]

Conclusion

It is not widely known that apart from his carpet patent Whytock was involved in the manufacture of other types of fabric. He gained premiums in the Board of Trustees annual competitions for silk and worsted damask, for tapestry medallions for use on chair seats, and for medallions stamped in relief.[83] Early in his career he made decorative fringes for upholstery and soft furnishings. In the 1850s, he patented a process for making fringes mechanically, on a warp lace machine.[84] Called Tressel fringe, it was produced from corded parti-coloured threads, either printed or

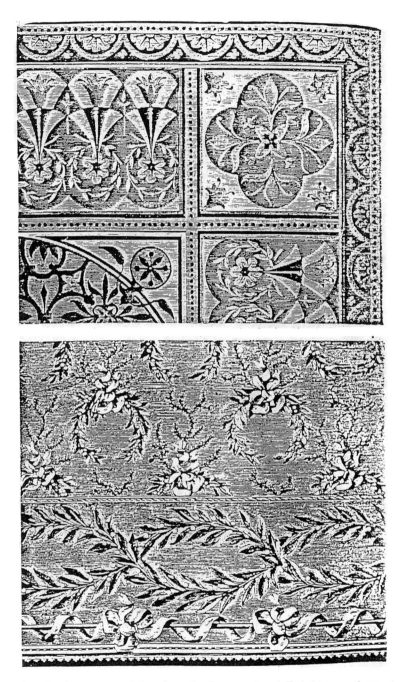

7. Above: a Scoto-Axminster carpet exhibited at the International Exhibition of 1862 by Whytock and Co, but not of their manufacture; below: a Brussels carpet also from Whytock and Co, illustrated in the *Art Journal Catalogue.*

plain, which formed a patterned fringe 5 to 6 inches deep. In 1854, with Thomas Preston of Nottingham, he developed this idea further, to manufacture width fabric on twist lace machinery. In this process two warps were used, a back warp lying vertical and straight, and a front warp, which when printed and laid in a zig zag movement across the back warp, formed a pattern, tied in by bobbin threads.[85] Extra threads might be added to the back warp to give a corded effect and a second pattern warp might also be added to lie behind the back warp. This fabric was used for table covers and advertised as Patent Tressel Table Covers or Tressel Tapestry, part of a stock of rich machine-made table furnishings which characterised the comfortable urban home. Whytock also stocked Aubusson table covers and some made from velvet, tapestry and other embroidered or bordered textiles as well as antique tapestry.[86] Before his death in 1857, he was in the process of setting up the manufacture of a fabric called Arras Ecossais with partners at Dyewood Mill near Greenock, which was a warp printed tapestry also made by Henderson and Widnell.[87] This has not so far been identified, but may have been used for curtains and portières as well as for wall hangings.

The immense popularity of the Tapestry carpet is generally ascribed to the Yorkshire firm of John Crossley and Sons who made improvements to the manufacturing process and introduced steam power to both the printing and weaving sides.[88] A working Tapestry carpet loom was on view at the International Exhibition in London in 1862, exhibited by Tuer and Hall of Bury.[89] But although Scottish production accounted for less than a tenth of total output in 1863, this increased to more than a third by the 1890s.[90] Two employees of Henderson and Widnell, James Sinclair and William Sutherland, established Tapestry carpet factories at Lesmahagow and Stirling.[91] Nevertheless, this type of carpet was generally known as 'Whytock's process', to distinguish it from later carpets printed in the piece and in his hands was designed to be a luxurious floor covering,

originally completely hand made.[92] As it was a true velvet structure, the delicate pile did not wear well underfoot and few complete carpets survive. The portière, also made on this principle, a Victorian glory, has fared better. It is clear that Whytock's successors at Lasswade, Henderson and Widnell, continued to make high quality carpets by hand and that Whytock himself was instrumental in creating well-designed hand knotted carpets, often noted by his contemporaries for his determination to improve design.[93] His career cannot be evaluated without considering his Axminster carpets, which were often made to order and continued a tradition of fine carpet making begun by Germain Havard, a French workman of Thomas Moore's, brought to Scotland by Sir Harry Erskine in 1760 and who worked in Edinburgh for the linen merchant William Cheape.[94] Whytock was one of the first manufacturers in Britain to employ a resident designer, preceding, according to the *Art Union*, even the leading Kidderminster companies, the quality of whose goods he also threatened. By the 1850s the company occupied a prestigious position as house furnishers in the Edinburgh New Town, stocking many of the most fashionable European fabrics – Swiss lace curtains, Lyons silks, Aubusson tapestries and so on. After his death, his nephew Alexander Whytock continued to expand the cabinet making side of the business. The later history of the company, with the partnership of Robert and Hugh Reid, is of interest to furniture historians.[95] An inventor, merchant and manufacturer, the founder, Richard Whytock, who is still remembered in the company name, is buried in the East Preston Street cemetery in Edinburgh, close to the tenement apartments he owned as a young man, to the site of his cabinet works at St Leonard's and to his own villa, Green Park at Liberton.[96] Though other companies successfully developed his process, Alexander Whytock could claim that his uncle had produced 'quite as good and praiseworthy specimens of his own patent carpets as any other manufacturer; neither had the working of the principle been improved since it left his hands'.[97]

Notes and References

1 *New Statistical Account of Scotland*, I (1845), 334: Lasswade.

2 *The Scotsman*, 28 February 1838.

3 *Edinburgh Evening Courant*, 27 October 1806. Richard Barnet Whytock, the fourth of nine children of George Whytock and Margaret Barnet, was baptized in Dalkeith in March 1784. His brother William was baptized there in January 1786. I am grateful to the staff at Whytock and Reid, Sunbury House, Edinburgh for discussions about the founder of the company.

4 *Edinburgh Advertiser*, 31 August 1810.

5 *Edinburgh Evening Courant*, 11 June 1818.

6 National Archives of Scotland (NAS), Board of Trustees for Manufactures, Register of Premiums awarded by the Board, NG 1/42/2.

7 NAS, NG 1/42/2.

8 NAS, Henry Widnell and Stewart Ltd, GD 405/13/1.

9 The partnership was dissolved in May 1829. *Edinburgh Evening Courant*, 5 September 1829.

10 NAS, Hall of Dunglass Mss, GD 206/3/9/2/9.

11 NAS, Skene, Edwards and Garson WS, GD 244 Box 9/1 Bundle 7.

12 'The idea of the Printed Carpet came to Whytock early in the nineteenth century after examining a piece of block printed material. One story states he was examining a piece of printed delaine, while the other story is that while confined to bed with a broken leg he pulled some threads out of a silk tie and this first aroused his interest.' A typescript history of Henry Widnell and Stewart Ltd, NAS, GD 405/11/13. Whytock and his first partner Robert Grieve described themselves as calico printers but there is no surviving evidence that they printed fabrics themselves – although a calico printer was working at Queensberry House in the 1820s.

13 In his specifications, Whytock described the warp printing processes of Bennet Woodcroft, 1827 and Louis Schwabe, 1831, but claimed that his method would produce exact repeating patterns to correspond to a previous and intended design, without using blocks or cylinders. The colour roller revolving in the colour box was referred to as the method established by Whytock in Crossley, Collier and Hudson's later patent.

14 NAS, Chancery Records, Patents, C20/33/3. This includes two large sheets of hand coloured drawings, scale 1 inch to 1 foot, signed by Richard Whytock, 18 January 1833, 'at my House at No 1 Upper Montagu St Bedford Square London'. Drawn by the civil engineer John Farey.

15 Whytock, A. Recent Improvements in Carpet Manufacture, their Use and Abuse; with a Word on Beauty and Deformity in Carpet Design, *Journal of the Society of Arts* IV (1856), 251.

16 NAS, GD 405/11/13.

17 NAS, NG 1/42/2.

18 *Edinburgh Evening Courant*, 3 December 1832.

19 Report from the Select Committee of the House of Commons into the means of extending a knowledge of the Arts and of the Principles of Design among the people ... of the country ... *Parl Papers*, 1835 (598)V, 375, 1836(568)IX,1.

20 NAS, GD 405/11/13.

21 NAS, Melville Castle Mss, GD 51/17/81, RHP 86185 Plate 10.

22 NAS, NG 1/42/2.

23 NAS, NG 1/42/2.

24 NAS, NG 1/42/4.

25 See above, Note 19.

26 *The Scotsman*, 4 July 1838. A triumphal arch with flowers was erected across the road at St Ann's Gate and a large new room in the factory 80 feet long decorated with flowers and evergreens – 'Mr Henderson, with his wonted liberality, gave an excellent dinner to his workmen in this splendid room . . . At six o'clock the company left the room, and formed themselves into the order of procession; each man having received an apron made from a piece of his own weaving, they proceeded with flags and music through Bonnyriggs, Springfield and Loanhead, and having returned to St Ann's, concluded the evening with a ball and a supper. It must be very gratifying to this spirited firm, that the greatest harmony and unanimity prevailed during the whole of this interesting demonstration of loyalty.'

27 NAS, C20/39/107.

28 NAS, GD 405/11/5.

29 National Library of Scotland, Catalogue of the 1839 Exhibition of Arts, Manufactures and Practical Science.

30 Glasgow City Archives, Lennox Castle Mss, T-LX 12/1/2. Lennox Castle later became a mental hospital.

31 Glasgow City Archives, T-LX 12/1/2.

32 *The Scotsman*, 6 January 1843.

33 For example the sale of No 23 Melville Street, furnished by the first manufacturers in Edinburgh (not named), largely during the last two years, which included in the first and second drawing rooms the finest Patent Velvet Carpets, *Edinburgh Evening Courant*, 16 April 1842. The sale of No 1 Inverleith Terrace, which contained two splendid Patent Carpets, 24ft by 15ft 11ins and 18ft 10 ins by 13ft, as well as three couches and vaseback and easy chairs in rosewood and damask, a splendid chimney mirror in an Elizabethan gold frame, gas chandeliers with water joints, Venetian blinds and window curtains in damask with gold cornices, *The Scotsman*, 6 January 1844. Also the sale of furnishings at No 11 Rutland

Square, which included in the dining room, Spanish mahogany dining tables, a large and massive round mahogany table with 18 chairs in ruby leather, a very handsome pedestal sideboard and Whytock's Patent Carpet and Persian Rug. The drawing room included a set of 8 antique richly carved Elizabethan chairs with gilt backs covered with rich crimson velvet and a Patent Carpet and Rugs, *Edinburgh Evening Courant*, 4 April 1846.

34 Bartlett, J Neville. *Carpeting the Millions, The Growth of Britain's Carpet Industry,* Edinburgh, 1978, 19.

35 *ibid.*, 20.

36 Visits to British Manufactories, The Carpet Works of Messrs Whytock and Co, Edinburgh, *Art Union, Monthly Journal of the Fine Arts and the Arts Decorative, Ornamental,* IX (1847), 29.

37 Henry Widnell's name became associated with carpet factories at Bonnyrigg, Roslin and Eskbank.

38 William Hunter lived at Broomieknowe Cottage in Lasswade. In the 1841 Census he was described as 37 years of age with a wife Mary, aged 35 and five children, all girls ranging in age from 12 to 3 months. He died 17 June 1860. His will records that he left £786. NAS, Records of H M Commissary Office, Edinburgh, SC 70/1/105, 343. Richard Whytock bought several designs from Hunter when he was living in Cumberland Street in Edinburgh.

39 NAS, NG 1/3/24, 472.

40 NAS, NG 1/1/37, 11.

41 NAS, NG 1/1/36, 449. Holdway gained several premiums for carpet and shawl patterns from the Board of Trustees. He moved the pattern drawing classes to Glasgow in 1839.

42 *Art Union*, VII (1846), 31.

43 I would like to thank Mr and Mrs F Menotti for kindly allowing me to study and photograph the carpet at Yester House.

44 The orchid is not clearly enough drawn to be identified specifically, but it is possible that the original owner of the carpet may have been a collector of orchids. I am grateful to staff at the Royal Botanic Garden in Edinburgh for their comments.

45 Jacobs, Bertram. *The Story of British Carpets*, London, 1968, 51.

46 NAS, NG 1/3/26, 340.

47 The now defunct company of Coloroll owned five large printed carpets made in two halves of different designs, all in excellent condition.

48 Henry Widnell's son died in 1869 and George Stewart, a warehouseman in Glasgow became a partner of Widnell senior in 1871. The firm was then known as Widnell and Co who were awarded a silver medal at the Exposition Universelle in Paris, 1878, which survives amongst the papers of Henry Widnell and Stewart in the National Archives of Scotland. George Stewart ran the company with his son under the name of Henry Widnell and Stewart,

after Widnell's death. In 1878 a new factory opened at Eskbank under the name of Stewart Brothers, two other sons of George Stewart, and the two companies were amalgamated in 1895 and called Henry Widnell and Stewart. The original factory at St Ann's was demolished in 1867, though the manager's house was left standing for some years afterwards.

49 Henry Henderson was described in the 1851 Census as aged 52, carpet manufacturer born in Dunfermline, married to Christian Henderson, with children Catherine, John, William and Henry. This Census records work people coming to Lasswade from other areas including Kilmarnock, Dunfermline and England.

50 NAS, Register of Sasines, Edinburgh No 1755, 7 January 1852. This land was later built on, and formed the basis for the Bonnyrigg factory.

51 *Art Journal Illustrated Catalogue*, 107. The jury reports commented on the merit of the designs of the patent tapestry carpets, especially the dark grounds which were well executed, 'Reports by the Juries on the Subjects in the Thirty Classes into which the Exhibition was Divided', *Exhibition of the Works of Industry of All Nations, 1851*, London, 1852, II, 1042.

52 *Official Descriptive and Illustrated Catalogue of the Great Exhibition 1851*, London, 1851, II, 567. Henderson and Widnell also showed patent velvet sofa carpets and rugs.

53 Described as, 'The first large carpet of centre design ever made upon the principle of Whytock's patent, showing a very ingenious application of it at a small increase of cost'. Whytock had been working on a method of increasing the depth of the repeat on strip carpeting.

54 *Art Journal Illustrated Catalogue*, An Essay on Taste at the Great Exhibition, xx.

55 Original Papers: Manufacturing Centres &c – Kidderminster, *Journal of Design and Manufactures*, III (1850), 174.

56 See Note 15, 240. A vigorous discussion followed Whytock's paper, led by Francis Crossley and other manufacturers, who were critical of some of his comments on design and of opinions expressed in a letter sent in by J G Crace, who was unable to attend. Crossley felt that Whytock dealt only with those who could afford to pay for a good article and overlooked the wants of the bulk of the population. However, Crossley had brought to the meeting a popular mosaic rug, exhibited upon the wall, 'with a stag in the middle, surrounded by the tartan, and other appendages, and forming a regular Scotch piece. That rug would always sell well, because it was a grand composition, and had something very novel about it.' This was the kind of design that Whytock and others felt to be inappropriate. Crossley's were awarded the Medaille d'honneur

at the French Exhibition in 1855, where some examples of Tapestry carpet woven in Berlin on their patent loom, with the warps printed by Crossley on Whytock's patent process, were exhibited.

57 *The Scotsman*, 19 May 1849.

58 *Journal of the Society of Arts*, IV (1856), 252.

59 NAS, GD 405/11/12.

60 NAS, Register of Deeds, RD/1080, 676.

61 The later history of the company is dealt with in detail in GD 405/11/13

62 NAS, NG 1/1/36, 340.

63 Hefford, Wendy. Patents for Strip Carpeting 1741–1851, *Furniture History*, XXIII (1987), 1.

64 NAS, NG 1/42/5.

65 NAS, NG 1/64/43/32, Premium Reports. The carpets could be manufactured to order, NG 1/64/43/33.

66 NAS, NG 1/1/35, 406. Several designers or pattern drawers are mentioned in the various Census reports for Lasswade. Whytock also bought prize-winning designs from John Whyte during the 1830s who was described as a pattern drawer, a widower aged 71, in the 1871 Census. Also mentioned is a French designer who worked for Widnell and Co for many years, named Pierre Langlade (?), described as a widower aged 54, in 1871.

67 See Note 19.

68 The Design Copyright Act of 1839 gave twelve months protection to all textile fabrics. This was extended to three years, for most classes of textile fabrics in the Designs Act of 1842.

69 *Art Union*, IX (1847), 31.

70 *Topographical, Statistical and Historical Gazetteer of Scotland*, Glasgow, 1842, II, 228.

71 Glasgow City Achives, Lennox Castle, T-LX 12/11

72 Glasgow City Achives, T-LX 12/1/1, Edinburgh 16 December 1840.

73 Glasgow City Achives, T-LX 12/1/2, Lasswade, 13 February 1841.

74 *Edinburgh Evening Courant*, 13 May 1848, 27 May 1848.

75 Aberdeen University Library, Montcoffer Mss 3175/1147/1, Richard Whytock and Co to the Earl of Fife, 18 December 1848.

76 *The Scotsman*, 25 October 1851.

77 *The Scotsman*, 22 April 1854. Whytock's successors opened a cabinet works at St Leonards in Edinburgh.

78 NAS, SC 70/1/95,788.

79 *The Illustrated Catalogue of the International Exhibition 1862*, London, 1862, Class xxii, II, 55. Henry Widnell and Son showed carpets, rugs, table covers, moquettes, velvet and tapestry curtains, 56.

80 *The Art Journal Illustrated Catalogue of the International Exhibition 1862*, London, 1862,168. Two carpets of Whytock and Co are illustrated. The Scoto-Axminster carpet, not made by them, was picked out for special praise by the Journal, which considered that the designer's name had been most unjustly withheld, 90.

81 *ibid.*, 108.

82 NAS, RD/1910, 79. The co-partnership was formed in 1876. Alexander Whytock died 23 November1881.

83 NAS, NG 1/1/36, 20 November 1832, 251.

84 English Patent No 123, 1 October 1852.

85 English Patent No 2686, 20 December 1854.

86 *The Scotsman*, 8 April 1854.

87 NAS, SC 70/1/93, 2.

88 NAS, C20/51/166, Joseph Crossley, George Collier and James Hudson. See *The Art Journal*, New Series, 1895, 237, for photographs of the Tapestry process at Dean Clough Mills, which include 12 feet diameter printing drums, a power loom and two female setters. A printing drum at Henry Widnell and Stewart is illustrated in Jacobs, 38.

89 See Note 79, 101. Clark, D K. *The Exhibited Machinery of 1862*, London, 1862, 101.

90 Bartlett, 72. William Sutherland was described in the 1851 Census as manager of the carpet manufactory. He was born in Dunfermline and one of his children, George, aged 5, was born in England. Subsequent children were born at Lasswade.

91 Bartlett, 27, 72.

92 John Bright and Sons popularised the printing of carpets in the piece using Sievier's terry motion and Burch's method of printing on to the woven fabric.

93 *Art Union*, VIII (1846), 133.

94 National Library of Scotland, Saltoun Mss 17564, f 171.

95 Watt, Margaret. A Firm of Craftsmen, *Edinburgh Year Book 1955*, Edinburgh 1955, 142 shows a photograph of Whytock and Reid's show room in the Robert Adam house in Charlotte Square, now The Georgian House.

96 Richard Whytock lived at Green Park, an early Victorian villa in Liberton, which later became the National Coal Board Scottish Head quarters and has recently been demolished. He is buried in East Preston Street Cemetery. I am indebted to Ian Gow at the National Trust for Scotland for generously sharing his notes on Richard Whytock with me.

97 *Journal of the Society of Arts*, IV (1856), 252.

Horse-racing in Scotland in the Sixteenth and earlier Seventeenth Centuries: Peebles and Beyond[1]

Eila Williamson

A day at the races has proved to be a thrilling experience throughout different epochs. Pliny the Younger, in the first century AD, derided the multitudes who attended the chariot and other races in Rome's Circus Maximus while the Jarrow monk Bede wrote of St John of Beverley's curing of a cleric who had been injured while taking part in horse-racing in the early eighth century.[2] In a later Scottish context an anonymous eighteenth-century would-be poet wrote a ballad (addressed to the Earl of Marchmont) describing his efforts to woo 'the comely Mistress Mary' at a horse race at Leith on 14 October 1717.[3]

The origins of horse-racing in Scotland remain largely obscure but by the sixteenth and seventeenth centuries the records, particularly those of the burghs, become more helpful with regard to the sport. Not only do they provide details of racing in the localities such as courses, numbers of horses, and prizes, but they also identify participants and indicate the geographical radius within which they and spectators were likely to travel to enjoy the recreational activity. This paper is largely concerned with municipal racing and examines the nature of the sport, exploring changes in the period, in particular the greater formalization which occurred in the 1620s and 1630s. In the latter part of the paper the discussion is broadened to analyze horse-racing in a wider cultural context, focusing on its

role in the social sphere through examination of sponsorship and the social status of participants.

The earliest reference to horse-racing in Peebles can be found in one of the burgh's Court and Council books. An entry dated 1 May 1569 requests that John Whiteman restore both a silver arrow and a silver bell to the burgh.[4] Reference to a silver arrow implies that organised archery contests were taking place in sixteenth century Peebles while the silver bell, a traditional prize for horse-racing, indicates that this latter sport served as an entertainment within the burgh. Furthermore, the fact that these items are listed in a passage concerning the restoration of the burgh's common goods suggests that these leisure activities were under municipal control.

Thereafter there is no firm mention of horse-racing in Peebles until 1608 when the Privy Council enacted that the race, which was due to be held in May, be banned for fear of trouble from the 'grite nomberis of people of all qualiteis and rankis, . . . betuix quhom thair being quarrellis, privat grudgeis, and miscontentment . . .' and who would be 'meiting vpoun feildis'.[5] To what extent horse-racing had been occurring between 1569 and 1608 is not apparent especially since continuous burgh records are lacking from the mid-1570s until 1604.[6] The Privy Council act, though, does state that the race 'sall nawyse be haldin nor keipit this 3eir', and that no one should 'assemble yame selffis to the said rais this present 3eir' which perhaps suggests that the race was not an uncommon event. What is clear is that such a race attracted people of all ranks in society and was well attended.

The horse race may not have taken place for a time after this; at least no written proof can be cited until 1623 when the race was won by a black gelding horse belonging to Sir John Stewart of Traquair. The winner of the 1623 race is noted in a description of the 1624 race which was won by the same horse.[7] The bell race, when it was held, took place on the morning after Beltane day, which meant that the date was usually 4 May (or on some occasions 5 May). Traces of horse-racing in the burgh's records indicate that the sport took place annually from 1623 until 1638 inclusive and then from 1640 onwards until 1650, although the bell was not run for every year.

The record of the 1624 race in Peebles is the fullest account of racing there. It describes a field of seven horses, with the names of the owners, of those presenting the horses (whether owners themselves or proxies), and of the riders (two of whom were also owners). Each owner paid an entry fee of one crown of the sun [French gold écu coin depicting the figure of the sun]; the exception being John Stewart lord of Traquair whose horse had won the race the previous year. The riders were weighed and Andrew Hay of Forrest had 'vj pund & ane half of deid weght vi3 ane pair of plet sleivis [intertwined metal rings] and sand'. Three prizes were awarded: a silver bell along with the stakes which had been paid, a saddle, and oats to the first, second and third horses respectively. As seems to have been customary practice in Peebles, a burgess became cautioner for the bell which was to be returned, with an augmentation, to the provost and bailies on the morning of Beltane day the following year.[8] Since the amount of detail in this particular entry is unusual, it remains far from certain how typical these features were of racing in Peebles. Much of the evidence regarding the sport records either purchases of prizes or winners of the bell and their cautioners, as opposed to describing all of the participants. Yet there are similarities between the 1624 Peebles' race and racing in other parts of Britain at this time.

It would seem to be the case that in the 1620s horse-racing was becoming more formalised and was reintroduced in several places. For example, in the north of England at Kiplingcotes, rules covering 'subscriptions, weights, fouls, weighing in and out, and disqualifications' were devised in 1619. Similarly, in the burgh of Paisley, where there had been an unsuccessful attempt to initiate horse-racing in 1608, provision was made in 1620 for annual horse races involving subscriptions, entry fees, weights, and the casting of dice for starting positions.[9] It can be noted too that in Carlisle horse-racing, which had taken place in the sixteenth century, seems to have been discontinued until there was a request in 1619 for it to be restarted. Furthermore, in the Chamberlains' Accounts for 1620–1 there is recorded a payment of six pence for 'parchment for writting the Artickels for the giltinge boule [silver-gilt cup]' and there is also evidence of the use of weights in the 1630s.[10] In 1621 at a race in Cupar in Fife the riders were to be of eight Scots stane weight while in Haddington, in May 1623, a race was to be conducted 'conforme to ye lawis daylie vsit & practised of ye sport of horsruning'.[11]

As with other entertainments and institutions, horse-racing in Peebles evolved over time. The location of the sport changed during the seventeenth century. In the early part of the century the race was from Nether Horsbrugh to the east port of the burgh but by 1644 a new course in Whitehaugh, on land rented from the Tweedie family, was being used. The old way 'fra Eister Horsbruik to the Eist Port' was preferred, however, in 1645.[12] In January 1649 the council were discussing whether or not to abandon racing in Whitehaugh thereby freeing themselves of the annual payment, and by 5 February the provost and bailies were to 'mak intimatioun to the airis and relict of umquhile Thomas Tuedie and uthers haifand entres anent the ourgeving of the hors race upon Quhythauch, and to report the nixt counsell day'. Despite Cromwell's prohibition of horse-racing in 1649, in 1650 the Peebles' race was 'to rin the auld way' but later it reverted to the Whitehaugh course.[13] This is shown by a receipt of payment of ten merks Scots on 12 November 1661, subscribed by Rebecca Vaitche, the widow of Thomas Tweedie of Whitehaugh, who had received the money from the burgh treasurer (on behalf of the provost and bailies) 'for the libertie of ane hors Raice Rwn through ane ordinarie part of my saidis landis at beltane Lastbypast'.[14]

There are few details about the arrangement of the courses themselves. It was not an uncommon feature for races to finish at the gates of towns. The race at Haddington was from Nisbet Loan Head to the west port of the burgh while in Chester it was stated that in 1609 the St George's day race had been established and was run on the Roodee 'from the newtower to the netes, & there torninge to runne vp to the watergate'.[15] Repairs to roads and structural alterations can be exemplified too. In Peebles in 1628 payment was made for mending the 'calsa' [roadway or pavement] at the east port and for taking up stages which would suggest a raised structure, perhaps for viewing the race.[16] In Haddington, on the same day as the council were discussing arrangements for the horse race, it was ordered that all the roads leading to and from the burgh were to be mended so that they would be 'passable for horsis cairtis & waynis [wagons]' – which would not only mean that the race course would be repaired but also that there would be improved access for competitors and spectators. In addition, in Chester in 1624 when the race course was altered – beginning from a point beyond the new Tower and running five times round the Roodee – the new tower gate was enlarged, having previously been 'but a small gate for the rome of 3 horses to run in brest', and the gutters in the Roodee were filled in along with 'the muckhill called pudinghill at the gate'.[17]

When racing in Peebles moved to the new course at Whitehaugh, races took place around 'stowpes' – either three times or twice round the course.[18] These turning posts would presumably be removable since the land for the course was being rented. There is no record of payments for setting up these 'stowpes', however, nor is there evidence for any removal of obstacles or cordoning off of the course for spectators. This can be contrasted with Chester where payments

were made for the taking down and setting up again of 'pales' and at Lincoln where, at a meeting attended by the king in 1617, the course was railed and corded with ropes and hoops.[19] Later, in the Restoration period, in the Rules or Articles for races at Leith in 1666 the final rule states that the spectators 'are to keep themselves within the Stoups, observing the distance of six score from the Horses that are in the Course'.[20]

In Peebles not only were there changes in location but also in the number of races at Beltane. The 1608 Privy Council enactment mentions a single race as does an order issued by the burgh council on 26 April 1624 which required the burgesses, 'euerie man with ane suord at his belt', to attend the magistrates at the time of the Beltane fair and the horse race and at future fairs. By 1643 a similar proclamation ordered the burgesses to attend with swords and staffs on the 'morne efter beltane day athe haill tyme of the horsraces'.[21] It can be noted here that there are parallels with racing at Carlisle when halberdiers were employed to control the crowds.[22] More than one race had been taking place before this time, though. In accounts for 1631 there is payment for a 'skarf' [sash] as a prize for the 'rais' and two bolls of oats as a prize for the 'efter schott' [additional race] while in 1635 there is a payment for a 'skarfe set doun to ye second raice'.[23] When racing moved to Whitehaugh the bell race consisted of running three times round the course while the efterschot race involved a run of twice round.[24] In 1646 not only was there a race run on the Whitehaugh course, but there was also a 'race rune in the Mure' for which the prize was a saddle.[25]

In a summary of developments in English racing before the Cromwellian rebellion, Longrigg mentions the introduction of heat-racing. Seventeenth century Rules for the Newcastle Prize record a system whereby the eventual winner of the prize had to be the winner of two of the three heats (or if no one had won two heats, then the winner of the third heat was the outright winner) and horses which were too far behind at the ends of heats were disqualified.[26] Referring to the period before the advent of the railways in the early nineteenth century, Vamplew attributes the development of heat-racing to the problems of transporting horses and also spectators. For this reason too, few horses took part in races and heat-racing ensured a full day's racing.[27]

There is no direct evidence to suggest that there was heat-racing in Peebles in the seventeenth century. The efterschot race appears to have been a separate race from the main bell race, with a different prize – usually a sash. This secondary race has parallels in Paisley where, in 1620, annual racing was arranged for 6 May. An efterschot race was to be 'fra ane scoir at the sclaittis [slates] of Ellirslie to ane uther scoir at the Calsayheid [top of the road] of the said Burgh of Paislay, be hors of the price of ane hundreth merks money' and the prize was to be a furnished saddle. The bell race, on the other hand, was 'to be start at the Gray Stane callit St Convallis stane, and fra that richt eist to the lytill house at the calsayend [road end] of Renfrew, and fra that the Hie Kingis Way to the Walnuik [corner of the wall] of Paslaye'. Interestingly the bell race was split into two distinct stages: the winning horse at Renfrew was to receive a double angel while the winner at Paisley received the bell and a sum of money (compiled from subscriptions and entry fees) with the exception of a double angel which was given to the second horse.[28] This payment to the second horse is similar to racing at Newcastle where the second horse always retained his stake.[29]

As for the sphere of influence for racing, it is clear that while many competitors were from locations close to the burghs, others travelled from further afield. In Peebles, local lairds such as the Murrays of Blackbarony took part in the races. However, competitors can be found who had travelled a greater distance. For example, the 1635 winner of the bell race was Sir John Seton of St Germains in East Lothian while James Home, victor in 1643, was from Eccles to the north east of Kelso.[30] In horse races in other areas non-local entrants can also be found. One of the Haddington winners was George Rutherford from Dunbar while another was the brother german of Alexander Hume of Manderston in the eastern March.[31] Interestingly, in 1613

John Murray, brother of the Peebles laird of Blackbarony was the winner of Dunfermline's bell race.[32] This suggests that not only was there a family interest in the sport but that members of the family were willing to travel in pursuit of a wider reputation in the sport.

There is also some evidence that the Peebles' races were publicised in a fairly widespread area. In 1632 four missive letters were sent to advertise a new race – the Trinity Cup race. Unfortunately no destinations are given although payment was made to the drummer of Lanark to advertise the cup race there.[33] In 1644, in addition to a proclamation at the burgh's own mercat cross, the race was advertised in Selkirk, Lanark, Lauder and Biggar.[34] Spectators were obviously prepared to travel to enjoy the sport. In the sixteenth century David Hume of Wedderburn is said to have attended horse races at both Peebles and Haddington, staying in each locality for several days.[35] Furthermore, when the Privy Council banned an intended match at Turngate in Annandale in 1611 a proclamation was to made at Selkirk, Hawick, Lochmaben and Dumfries 'charging all and sundry the lieges not to attend the meeting foresaid or any other of the like'.[36]

The records of neither Peebles nor Haddington reveal any information as to the exercising or stabling of the horses before the race. In Paisley the horses were to be present in the burgh for a certain number of days before the race and 'quhatever hors beis not keipit and dyetit [exercised] within the said Burghe the space foirsaid befoir the said day, and led fra Paislaye to the starting place, they sall not be sufferit to runne in tyme cuming'.[37] After the Restoration, at Leith the horses in the cup race were to be kept there for ten days before the race while the horses in the saddle race were required to be in residence for forty-eight hours.[38]

In early seventeenth century Scotland numbers of horses involved in municipal races were relatively small. Apart from the 1624 race in which seven horses ran, no numbers are stated for the Beltane races in Peebles but there were frequent payments for oats for the third horse and, as has been discussed above, there was also a second race.[39] In Dunfermline the numbers of horses taking part in the burgh's racing ranged from three to seven over a non-continuous period from 1606 to 1624.[40] Vamplew mentions a move from matches with two entrants to formalized races with several entrants.[41] Evidence of matches can be found in seventeenth century Scotland separate from and in conjunction with municipal racing. For example, as has been mentioned above, on 22 March 1611 the Privy Council sought to ban an intended match (due to be held on 26 March) between Walter, Master of Buccleuch and Gordon, brother of Sir Robert Gordon of Lochinver.[42] In Haddington, where there was formalized racing from at least 1552 – unfortunately no numbers of competitors are related – there is also evidence of a challenge for a match between two horses in May 1576. On 10 May 1576 John Hume, brother german to Alexander Hume of Manderston had won the silver bell. Two days later Cuthbert Simson was acting as surety for Robert Logan of Restalrig. Logan with his gray horse was challenging Hume to present his black horse and run a race between Nisbet Loan Head and Letham burn on the last day of May. At stake was the silver bell plus ten pounds of money. If Hume did not accept the challenge (provided his horse was alive) he was to give Logan ten pounds plus the value of the bell.[43] Whether or not the race took place is not known. Hume evidently retained the bell as his cautioner presented it to the provost and bailies on 1 March 1577.[44] A definite move away from matches can be seen in the seventeenth century in this burgh, though. By 1623 the Haddington race was to take place 'Provdyng alwayis yair be ma horsis nor tua or thrie at the fewest to rin yairat vyer[other]//wayis ye samen not to be sett vp or run at'.[45]

The prizes for horse-racing varied in different places and at different times. Silver bells were a common prize with the winner usually retaining the bell for a year before returning it – although in Paisley in 1620 it was stated that if a horse won the bell three years in succession then the owner would retain the bell permanently 'conforme to the manner of uthir Burrowes'. In Peebles the bell was to be returned with an augmentation

which often took the form of the addition of a little bell or other object appended to the main trophy.[46] In 1634 the bell was described as being engraved with the names and arms of the earl of Traquair and of Sir Archibald Murray and as having two little bells and a silver plate attached to it. These had been presented by previous winners: the bells by John Hamilton of the Ness in 1628 and John Scott of Hundleshope in 1630 and the silver plate by Robert Pringle of Blindlee (a member of a family which is known to have bred horses in the sixteenth century at least) in 1632. In total the trophy weighed thirteen and one half ounces of silver.[47] By 1645 the bell had two other little bells and eight pendicles attached to it and weighed in total one pound and twelve drop weight of silver.[48]

Around 1630 there was a noticeable change in arrangements for returning the silver bell in Peebles. Although a system of cautioners had been in operation prior to that date, there is no mention in the records of a fine for not returning the bell until 1630. Thereafter until 1641 in the terms of cautionary a fine of five hundred merks money was to be imposed on transgressors.[49] The exception to this was on 26 April 1624 when Archibald Frank as cautioner for the bell was ordered to return it or else pay one hundred pounds.[50] It is possible that the change in procedure was due to the 1626 winner's failure to add an augmentation until 1628. In May 1628 the burgh's provost paid four pounds and nine shillings to the treasurer as the laird of Inchcairny's augmentation to the bell 'wyn be him at beltane 1626'; an amount which the treasurer described as being 'resaweit fra inchkairne his inputt that sowld hawe beine agmentit to the bell'.[51] A monetary payment in lieu of a physical augmentation by the winner became a formal option around this time. In 1630 it was recorded in the Court book that John Scott of Hundleshope, the winner of the bell race, was to present the bell 'Togither with sick vyer augmentatioun as he pleasses augment to ye samyn or els ane Sufficient Staik conforme to ye ordour' on 4 May in the following year.[52]

In Peebles failure to return the bell on time was not a serious problem. In 1640 William Lyell of Bassendean, sheriff-depute of the sheriffdom of Peeblesshire, returned the bell having won it in May 1638. There is no record of a race in 1639 but this is probably due to political strife in the country as a whole rather than to the lack of a bell for a prize.[53] Other burghs operated systems of cautionary such as Stirling, Dunfermline and Haddington. In Stirling in April 1631 Thomas Rollok, as cautioner for John Drummond of Carnock, swore to return, on 1 March 1632, the eight silver bells which weighed in total eight ounces and nine drop weight. Failure to do so would result in a fine of five hundred merks Scots.[54] A penalty of the same sum was also decreed in the terms of cautionary in Dunfermline in April 1610.[55]

In the sixteenth century records of Haddington there is evidence of racing between 1552 and 1559 and then again from 1575 to 1578.[56] Cautioners were employed and in the former period the bell was to be returned on the day of racing. However, by 1575 the bell was ordered to be returned one month before the next race.[57] At the end of both of these periods it can be noted that there were delays in the return of the bell. On 3 May 1558 George Craig, cautioner for Alexander Hume of North Berwick who had won the race in May 1557, was ordered to return the bell upon eight days' warning. It was not until 29 May 1559 that the bell was finally delivered and Craig requested to be relieved of his surety.[58] Similarly on 24 March 1578 George Aytoun, cautioner for Captain David Hume and servants, was commanded to present the silver bell upon fifteen days' warning.[59] Racing did not restart until 1604 (when a new bell was made) and then continued sporadically in the first quarter of the seventeenth century. Cautioners still featured and in 1620 failure to return the bell meant a fine of one hundred pounds. In the Haddington records there is no mention of the addition of little bells or other pendicles to the main trophy but in 1620 the winner was asked to 'cast over & augment the samen ane vyer vnce wecht of fyne siluer'.[60]

While a saddle seems to have been the second prize in the bell race in Peebles before 1646, in Paisley and Haddington a saddle was the prize in separate races. The winner of the Paisley efterschot race received a 'sadill, stok thairof and covering' while the prize for second place was the furnishing of the saddle.[61] On 14 March 1621 the council in Haddington ordered that a horse race be proclaimed the following day for a race to be run on 16 April. The treasurer was 'to caus mak ane sadill of velvet with ane silk & goldin freinȝie [fringe] about the borderis of it to be rvn at ye said day to be tane away fre'.[62] As has been noted above, payments for oats are frequently found in Peebles' accounts and with the exception of 1631 appear to have been the third prize for the bell race. Regular yearly payments were also made for the sash, a non-returnable prize. In April 1627 a new 'skairch' which was ten quarters long with 'perling' [edging] of gold was bought and a payment of six shillings was made for the sewing on of the 'perling' and silk.[63] A payment of six shillings was also made for the sewing and hemming of the sash in 1633.[64] When a place of purchase is recorded, the accounts show that the burgh representative travelled to Edinburgh to make the transaction: in 1628, 1638 and 1640. In 1638 William Melrose, officer, was paid twenty-six shillings and eight pence to go to Edinburgh on 1 May to fetch the 'bend' [sash] and saddle.[65]

In English racing, in the seventeenth century, there was a move towards the award of more valuable prizes such as cups and plates.[66] For example, in Chester in 1623 the mayor sold the three bells which had been previous prizes in order to buy a cup.[67] In Haddington the bell which weighed eight ounces and three drop weight was ordered to be melted down and transformed into a cup in 1616. However, this does not seem to have happened as a bell weighing virtually the same – eight ounces and two drop weight – featured as a prize four years later and there is no record of racing between these dates. It was not until 1623 that a cup had been made and was being raced for.[68] In Peebles in 1632 the burgh paid for a cup to be made in Edinburgh for a new race – the Trinity race – which was to be held on the Tuesday after Trinity Monday. The cup was engraved with the town's arms and 'Peblis' within a shield plus the year.

Aside from information about the actual cup, there are few details of this race. There were two entrants who each paid 'sax dollouris' as an entry fee. The cup may have been a non-returnable prize as neither it nor the race are mentioned in the records again.[69]

Whether the prizes were bells, sashes or cups is not the main issue in the wider cultural context. Those who sponsored and participated in the races reveal more about the role of horse-racing in the social sphere. Members of the Scottish royal family had an interest in horse-racing in the sixteenth and seventeenth centuries. In April 1504 James IV had paid money to 'the boy ran the Kingis hors' in Leith and in May he gave twenty-eight shillings to 'Dande Doule, quhilk he wan fra the King on hors rynnyng' – although it is not clear whether this can be termed a horse race; it is possible that running at the ring is meant.[70] In the following century James VI and I attended racing at Lincoln in 1617.[71] Nevertheless, in comparison with England Scottish racing lacks such a strong connection with royalty and there are no specifically royal race courses such as Newmarket nor notable stud farms such as those at Eltham and Tutbury founded by Henry VIII and Elizabeth respectively. Furthermore, in England there seems to have been greater stratification in sponsorship of the sport: not only were there royal courses but also there were courses of the gentry such as Kiplingcotes distinct from the municipal racing such as at Chester.[72] In addition in the north of England merchant and craft guilds played an important role in sponsoring events. For example, the saddlers in Chester were heavily involved in the organisation of the Shrovetide races while in Carlisle in the 1630s the tanners and merchants contributed money towards the purchase of prizes.[73] In Scotland, however, the nobles and lairds, whilst having private matches, took a keen interest in municipal racing and had a close interrelationship with the localities.

In many Scottish burghs the instigation for horse-racing came from local nobles and lairds, some of whom held important office in the state or in the burgh itself. For example, in Dunfermline the silver bell pertained to Alexander Seton,

earl of Dunfermline (from 1605) and Chancellor of Scotland (1604–22). In 1612 one of his servants was the winner of the bell race.[74] It was the burgh provost, the earl of Abercorn, who was responsible for restarting racing in Paisley in 1620. He can also be found in 1621 making an indenture with lords Boyd and Morton for a race in Cupar in Fife.[75] In Peebles members of the local nobility can frequently be found among the list of winners in the bell race: John Stewart earl of Traquair, who attained the post of Lord High Treasurer in 1636, had his name and arms engraved upon the trophy and won it in 1623, 1624, 1634, and 1646;[76] Sir Archibald Murray of Blackbarony, from a local family of lairds, who also had his name and arms engraved on the bell, carried away the prize in 1625 (the year in which he was member of parliament for Peeblesshire) and his son, Sir Alexander Murray, was the winner of the bell in both 1645 and 1650, and of the saddle and oats in 1646;[77] and members of the Vaitche family of Dawick were recipients of the silver bell prize in 1637 and 1641.[78] In Haddington winners included George lord Seton in 1552, Alexander Hume of North Berwick in 1557, James Borthwick (son of James Borthwick of Lochhill) in 1610 and John Auchtmontie of Scougall in 1616.[79] In 1620 the Haddington bell was described as 'haveing ye armes of the vmquhile lord halyrudehous & of Iames borthwik ye name of the said lord & ye hornes of the gait [*sic*] buk giltit with gold & george leving-toun his armes ingraven vpoun ye said bell'.[80]

Heal and Holmes have discussed the increase in popularity of horse-racing in England in the seventeenth century in relation to its importance to the gentry.[81] In Scotland too in the sixteenth and seventeenth centuries horses were a valued commodity in terms of social status. Writing of the boyhood of James V, the poet and dramatist, Sir David Lindsay, asserted that:

And sum, to schaw thare courtlie corsis [persons],
Wald ryid to leith, and ryn thare horssis,
And wychtlie wallope [vigorously gallop] ouer the sandis;
3e, nother sparit spurris nor wandis [sticks];

Castand galmoundis with bendis and beckis
   [capers with leaps and springs],
For wantones, sum braik thare neckis.

Furthermore, in Robert Wedderburn's mid-sixteenth century *Complaynt of Scotland* the character Lady Scotia complains: '. . . ane man is nocht reput for ane gentil man in scotland, bot gyf he mak mair expensis on his horse and his doggis nor [than] he dois on his vyfe & bayrnis [children]'.[82] In Haddington the horse races were primarily designed for the nobility in the area. When the new silver bell was made in 1604 it was 'to be run at be ye gentill men in ye cuntre' and in 1623 the silver cup was 'to be run at vpoun the twentie day of maij nixt be all noblemen baronis & gentlemen yair horsis'. The saddle race of 1621 was slightly different in that the race was stipulated to be for 'all noblemenis gentlemen & vyeris horssis'; yet the phrasing here implies that the competitors would mainly be of noble rank or affiliation.[83] In the records of Peebles no such stipulations can be found in advertisements for the races, yet there is evidence of competitors being described as gentlemen. For example, in 1634 a payment was made to 'the gentill mane that wane the aittis' while in 1636 a payment of twelve shillings was made for a pint of wine 'to ye gentill man that wanne the bell'.[84] In Peebles it is noticeable too that on a number of occasions the winner of the horse race or his cautioner, sometimes along with their servants, was admitted a burgess and freeman of the burgh. A case in point was in 1637 when James Vaitche of Dawick (the winner of the silver bell) and Alexander Vaitche were made burgesses and freemen on the day after the horse race had taken place.[85] The burgh therefore honoured the competitor by conferring a mark of status on him.

Such stipulations as those at Haddington were possibly not just social class restrictions but also economic ones, for the price of horses precluded ownership to those of lesser means. There was a great demand in Scotland for horses. Maureen Meikle notes that, at the beginning of the seventeenth century, there were complaints in England that the horse trade, which had become one way from England to Scotland by the late sixteenth century, pushed up prices there, reportedly prohibiting ownership to those beneath gentry status.[86] Yet there is an argument that it was ownership of the horse which enabled rise in status. In 1630 there was a case before the Scottish Privy Council in which a merchant from Maybole demanded redress for having been attacked and left for dead and his horse's fore limbs dislocated while on the way to a race meeting at Irvine. The merchant, Alexander Barclay, claimed that he had been used to 'dyet' [exercise] his horse, which was worth twelve hundred pounds, between Maybole and Smithstounburne in preparation for the race at Irvine and that 'by quhilk [which] meanes he hes borne out the ranke of ane honest gentleman these manie yeeres bygane'.[87]

The case is interesting for a number of further reasons. Not only did Barclay claim the status of a gentleman through ownership of the horse, but he also stated that the horse 'wes the best part of his estait and the onelie meanes whairby he lived'. Gambling had been a feature of horse-racing in the sixteenth century. David Hume of Wedderburn was regarded as a master of the sport since often on the eighth day after he had been beaten in a race he would put down double the wager and emerge as the winner.[88] That it was possible to make large sums of money from racing is borne out by an Act of Parliament in August 1621 which prohibited the retention of winnings from gambling (whether it be cards, dicing or horse races) over the sum of one hundred merks. Any excess was to be handed over to the treasurer of the kirk, if the money was won in Edinburgh, or to members of the kirk sessions, if the money was won in the parishes elsewhere. The poor of the parish in which the winning took place were to reap the benefits.[89]

The nature of the attack against Barclay is revealing too. His attacker was Uthrid McDougall, the master stabler of the earl of Cassillis, who bore a 'deadly hatred' towards Barclay. The attack was presented by the victim as being a premeditated one. Barclay claimed that 'Uthrid resolved to make his advantage of this occasioun [ie the dyeting of the horse] and thairby not onlie to kill himselffe bot also to slay his said hors'. McDougall, on one of the earl's coursers, 'ranne at the said compleaner with all his speid' and 'shamefullie strake the compleaner on the head and face with ane hors wand, and than rushed him and his hors to the ground with great violence '. Amongst other injuries, seven of Barclay's ribs were broken.[90] The violent nature of the attack and the fact that Barclay was preparing his horse for racing are strong indications that McDougall (and the earl?) sought the elimination of an opponent to further his own stable's chances of winning in Irvine. Whether or not there was any animosity towards a 'new man' who was not from the traditional ranks of the nobility cannot be determined. However, the possibility that 'new men' were becoming involved in horse-racing may account for Haddington's decision in 1616, when there had been plans to turn the bell into a cup, that the race was to be 'of new rvn at be sic as pleiss' – although, as has been discussed above, a reversion to racing for those of noble rank occurred later.[91]

By the middle of the seventeenth century horse-racing in Scotland had become a widespread municipal sport with reasonably evolved rules for competition. The features of the 1624 bell race in Peebles highlight many of the contemporary developments elsewhere, such as paying of entry fees, use of weights, and employment of a system of cautionary to ensure the safe return of the trophy. The locations and arrangements of the courses may have changed over time, as did the prizes in like manner, but the general trend was one of greater formalization especially in the 1620s and 1630s. In racing throughout the country, an element of municipal control is apparent as it was the burgh officials who organised the publicity for the races and the purchase of prizes. Furthermore, it was they who recorded the terms of cautionary and dealt with issues such as crowd control. In many cases they were responsible too for inaugurating races, such as the Trinity Cup race in Peebles, and for restarting racing, as in Haddington in 1604.

Members of the nobility, though, were particularly prominent in both participation and sponsorship and it is notable that certain families, such as the Humes of Wedderburn and the Pringles of Blindlee, seem to have been especially keen on the sport. This was not only for monetary gain but also for reasons of social status. Nevertheless, there was scope for 'new men' to become involved and accrue the traditional benefits. The 1621 Act of Parliament not only marked official notice of the widespread problem of gambling in society but, with its specific mention of horse-racing, it also recognised the popularity of a sport which was participated in and enjoyed by the different strata of that society.

Notes and References

1 I am grateful to Dr John J McGavin and Dr Maureen M Meikle for helpful criticism of this paper. Dr McGavin must also be thanked for kindly lending his transcriptions of the Haddington material. This paper is the result of research conducted for the Records of Early Drama: Scotland project under the directorship of Dr John J McGavin of the University of Southampton. The current research has been made possible through the award of an AHRB grant.

2 Sherwin-White, A N, ed. *Fifty Letters of Pliny*, second edn, Oxford, 1990, 57–8; Bede. *Ecclesiastical History of the English People*, translated Sherley-Price, Leo, revised Latham, R E, London, 1990, 272–4.

3 The National Archives of Scotland, *Ballad on a horse race at Leith*, GD158/488.

4 NAS, *Peebles Court and Council book*, B58/8/3, fol 83r.

5 NAS, *Registrum Secreti Concilii Acta etc August 1607–June 1608*, PC1/22, 808.

6 There is a Court and Council book which covers the period 1565–73 and contains a few entries for 1578 and 1585. The next volume of Council minutes begins in 1604 (until 1652) while the next extant Court book is for 1623–49; NAS, B58/8/3, B58/13/1, and B58/9/1.

7 NAS, *Peebles Court book*, B58/9/1 (unfoliated), 4 May 1624.

8 *ibid.*

9 Longrigg, Roger. *The History of Horse Racing*, London, 1972, 40–1; Metcalfe, W M, ed. *Charters and Documents Relating to the Burgh of Paisley*

1158-1665 and Extracts from the Records of the Town Council 1594–1620, Paisley, 1902, 284, 287–9.

10 Douglas, Audrey & Greenfield, Peter eds. Records of Early English Drama *Cumberland Westmorland Gloucestershire*, Toronto, 1986, 26, 98, 116, 121.

11 Fittis, R S. *Sports and Pastimes of Scotland*, Wakefield, 1975, 114; NAS, *Haddington Council book*, B30/13/4, fol. 56r, 25 April 1623.

12 NAS, *Peebles Court book*, B58/9/1 (unfoliated), 4 May 1625; *Peebles Council book*, B58/13/1, fol. 126v; *Peebles Court book*, B58/9/1 (unfoliated), 5 May 1645. Use of Whitehaugh as a location for horse-racing concurs with Burnett's thesis that haughs [river meadows] provided one of the suitable sites for the sport; Burnett, John. The Sites and Landscapes of Horse Racing in Scotland before 1860, *The Sports Historian*, 18 (1998), 55–75. I am grateful to Mr John Burnett for providing me with a copy of this article.

13 Renwick, Robert. *Gleanings from the Records of the Royal Burgh of Peebles, 1604–52* Peebles, 1892, 287–8; Longrigg, 1972, 44–5.

14 NAS, *Peebles Accounts* 17th century, B58/17 Box 18 (unnumbered), 12 November 1661.

15 NAS, *Haddington Council book*, B30/13/4, fol. 56r, 25 April 1623; Clopper, Lawrence M, ed. Records of Early English Drama *Chester*, Toronto, 1979, 354.

16 NAS, *Peebles Accounts*, B58/14/2, 1627–8 (unfoliated). The payment of xviij s was 'gewine at comand of the cownsell to James haldine and his tua soneis for mending the calsa at the eist port and taking vp the stagis'. The entry is not dated but appears amongst others relating to Beltane so there is good reason to presume that there is a connection with horse-racing.

17 NAS, *Haddington Council book*, B30/13/4, fol. 56r, 25 April 1623; Clopper, 1979, 360–1.

18 NAS, *Peebles Council book*, B58/13/1, fol. 126v; Renwick, 1892, 287.

19 Clopper, 1979, 275, 286–7, 307, 314; Longrigg, 1972, 40.

20 National Library of Scotland, *Rules or articles for the horse-coursing at Leith, / erected and established by The Right Honourable, The Lord Provost, Bailies, and Councel of Edinburgh; as followeth* (1665) J.133.c.3 (55), rule XIII.

21 NAS, *Peebles Council book*, B58/13/1, fol. 19r, 121r (1 May 1643).

22 Douglas & Greenfield, 1986, 26, 112, 116, 122.

23 Craigie, Sir William A, et al, eds. *A Dictionary of the Older Scottish Tongue from the twelfth century to the end of the seventeenth*, vol I–, London, 1931–. gives one of the definitions of 'scarf' as a 'military scarf or sash' and also cites a reference to the sport of shooting of the papingo at Irvine at which the winner received 'ane benne or scarff', *DOST*, Part XLIII, 210; NAS, *Peebles Accounts*, B58/14/2, 1629–31 (unfoliated) 1 May [1631], 1634–5 (unfoliated).

24 NAS, *Peebles Council book*, B58/13/1, fol. 126v.

25 NAS, *Peebles Accounts*, B58/14/2, 1645–6, page 8.

26 Longrigg, 1972, 40; NAS, *Rules for horse race for Newcastle prize, 17th century*, GD26/15/14, rules 4, 7.

27 Vamplew, Wray. *The Turf. A social and economic history of horse racing*, London, 1976, 17–18.

28 Metcalfe, 1902, 287–9.

29 NAS, GD26/15/14, rule 6.

30 NAS, *Peebles Court book*, B58/9/1 (unfoliated), 5 May 1635, 6 May 1643.

31 NAS, *Haddington Court book*, B30/10/10, fol. 158r, 15 May 1620; *Haddington Court book*, B30/10/4, fol. 18r, 10 May 1576.

32 Shearer, Andrew, ed. *Extracts from the Burgh Records of Dunfermline in 16th and 17th Centuries*, Dunfermline, 1951, 96.

33 Payments were made for the writing and carrying of the missive letters and a separate payment was made to James Robesone *alias* Thack to carry a letter to Lanark; NAS, *Peebles Accounts*, B58/14/2, 1631–2.

34 NAS, *Peebles Council book*, B58/13/1, fol. 126v.

35 Hume, David. *Davidis Humii de Familia Humia Wedderburnensi Liber*, (Abbotsford Club), vol 15 1839, 51.

36 Masson, David, ed. *The Register of the Privy Council of Scotland*, vol IX AD 1610–1613, Edinburgh, 1889, 153.

37 Unfortunately there is a gap where the number of days should be given; Metcalfe, 1902, 288–9.

38 NLS, *Rules or articles for the horse-coursing at Leith*, J.133.c.3 (55), rules IV, X. The cup races were held in March and June while a saddle race took place in each of the other ten months.

39 There are references to the purchase or presentation of oats in the years 1624, 1625, 1627, 1628, 1629, 1631 (although the oats are stated to be for the 'efter schott'), 1632, 1633, 1634, 1635, 1636, 1637, 1638, 1640, and 1646. In 1624, 1627 and 1628 a third horse is specifically mentioned in relation to the oats; NAS, *Peebles Accounts*, B58/14/2, 1624, 1625, 1626–7, 1627–8, 1628–9, 1629–31 (1 May 1631), 1631–2, 1632–3 page 5, 1633–4 page 5, 1634–5, 1635–6, 1636–7, 1638, 1639–40 page 6 (payment is dated 27 May), page [33], 1645–6 page 8.

40 There were seven competitors in 1606, three in 1607, 1609, and 1610, five in 1611, three in 1612, and four in 1613, 1620, and 1624; Shearer, 1951, 58, 74–5, 86, 96, 125, 144. It should be noted that as this volume is one of extracts these figures may be merely selective.

41 Vamplew, 1976, 17.

42 Masson, 1889, 152–3.

43 NAS, *Haddington Court book*, B30/10/4, fol. 18r-v. John Hume was undoubtedly John Hume of Tinnis, a tenant of Lord Hume and 'King's Master Hunter'; Paul, Sir James Balfour, ed. *The Scots Peerage*, vol III, Edinburgh, 1911, 283; Thomson, J M et al, eds. *Registrum Magni Sigilli Regum Scotorum*, 11 vols,

Edinburgh, 1882–, vol VI, no 137. I am grateful to Dr Maureen M Meikle for providing me with this identification and these references.

44 NAS, *Haddington Council book*, B30/13/1, fol. 89r.

45 NAS, *Haddington Council book*, B30/13/4, fol. 56r.

46 Metcalfe, 1902, 288–9. Other Scottish burghs which had races for silver bells included Stirling, Haddington, Dumfries, Dunfermline, Perth, and Lanark. The silver bell of Lanark, which has been calculated to have been made c1608–10, is still extant. Four inches high (excluding the handle), 1628 is the date of the earliest badge which is attached to it. For a description and illustration of the Lanark silver bell, see Brook, Alexander J S. Notice of the Silver Bell of Lanark, a horse-racing trophy of the seventeenth century, with some references to the early practice of horse-racing in Scotland, *Proceedings of the Society of Antiquaries* XXV 1890–91, Edinburgh, 1891, 174–88. I am grateful to Mr John Burnett for this reference. The practice of the augmenting of a trophy by an annual winner 'stems from continental shooting guilds'; Burnett, 1998.

47 NAS, *Peebles Court book*, B58/9/1 (unfoliated), 5 May 1634. The silver plate bore the inscription 'Win be me Robert pringle of blindlie 1632'. For Robert Pringle, tutor of Blindlee, as a horse-breeder in the sixteenth century, see Meikle, Maureen Manuel. 'Lairds and Gentlemen: A study of the landed families of the eastern Anglo-Scottish borders c1540–1603', PhD, University of Edinburgh, 1988, 315–16.

48 NAS, *Peebles Court book*, B58/9/1 (unfoliated), 5 May 1645.

49 NAS, *Peebles Court book*, B58/9/1 (unfoliated), 4 May 1630, 4 May 1632, 5 May 1634, 5 May 1635, 4 May 1636, 5 May 1637, 5 May 1638, 4 May 1641.

50 NAS, *Peebles Council book*, B58/13/1, fol. 19r.

51 NAS, *Peebles Council book*, B58/13/1, fol. 43v, *Peebles Accounts*, B58/14/2, 1627–8. There is no direct reference to the bell race in 1627 but there were payments made for a new sash and for oats (for the third horse); NAS, *Peebles Accounts*, B58/14/2, 1626–7. There is no record of the terms of cautionary for 1628 although the winner of the race is recorded in the description of the bell in 1634; NAS, *Peebles Court book*, B58/9/1 (unfoliated), 5 May 1634.

52 NAS, *Peebles Court book*, B58/9/1 (unfoliated), 4 May 1630. In previous years no mention had been made of providing stake money instead of an augmentation. However, a virtually identical statement appears in the record for 4 May 1632.

53 The Covenanting forces were in open rebellion against the king at this time: Lynch, Michael. *Scotland. A new history*, London, 1993, 270–1; Donaldson, Gordon. *Scotland. James V – James VII.* (The Edinburgh History of Scotland, vol 3), Edinburgh, 1987, 322–4.

54 Renwick, R, ed. *Extracts from the Records of the Royal Burgh of Stirling A.D. 1519–1666 With Appendix AD 1295–1666* (Sons of the Rock Society), Glasgow, 1887, 166.

55 Shearer, 1951, 74–5.

56 NAS, *Haddington Court book*, B30/9/2, fol. 219r, 259v; *Haddington Court book*, B30/10/1, fol. 88v, 129r, 154r, 156r; *Haddington Court book*, B30/10/3, fol. 91v; *Haddington Court book*, B30/10/4, fol. 18r-v; *Haddington Council book*, B30/13/1, fol. 89r; *Haddington Court book*, B30/10/4, fol. 84r.

57 For example, the silver bell which had been won on 10 May 1552 was to be returned on 3 November 'to be run for ye said day' while the winner of the bell on 22 June 1575 was to 'deliuer & present ye samyn ane monecht afore ye said monecht of may': the race was to be held on 1 May; NAS, *Haddington Court book*, B30/9/2, fol. 219r; *Haddington Court book*, B30/10/3, fol. 91v.

58 NAS, *Haddington Court book*, B30/10/1, fol. 88v, 129r, 154r.

59 NAS, *Haddington Court book*, B30/10/4, fol. 84r.

60 Arrangements were being made for a new bell in April and it had been completed by 26 October 1604; NAS, *Haddington Council book*, B30/13/3, fol. 18r, 21r. In 1620 the bell weighed eight ounces and two drop weight of silver; *Haddington Court book*, B30/10/10, fol. 158r.

61 Metcalfe, 1902, 289.

62 NAS, *Haddington Council book*, B30/13/4, fol. 44r.

63 NAS, *Peebles Accounts*, B58/14/2, 1626–7.

64 NAS, *Peebles Accounts*, B58/14/2, 1632–3.

65 NAS, *Peebles Accounts*, B58/14/2, 1627–8, 1638, 1639–40, page 5.

66 Longrigg, 1972, 40.

67 Clopper, 1979, 361.

68 NAS, *Haddington Court book*, B30/10/10, fol. 30v, 158r; *Haddington Council book*, B30/13/4, fol. 56r.

69 The race was to be held on 29 May; NAS, *Peebles Council book*, B58/13/1, fol. 65r. The cup weighed twelve and one half ounces with each ounce costing three pounds and eight shillings. The total value was forty-two pounds and ten shillings; *Peebles Accounts*, B58/14/2, 1631–2.

70 Paul, Sir James Balfour, ed. *Compota Thesaurariorum Regum Scotorum*, vol II AD 1500–1504, Edinburgh, 1900, 428, 430. On 4 May a payment of nine shillings was made to 'Watte Turnbull to send for gray Gretno to ryn'; *ibid*, 432.

71 Longrigg, 1972, 40.

72 *Ibid.*, 28, 30.

73 Clopper, 1979, 41, 209, 236, 275, 286, 314, 368, 373; Douglas & Greenfield, 1986, 27, 113–15, 117–18, 120.

74 Shearer, 1951, 58, 75, 86, 96. The winning horse in 1612 had a bell on his forehead.

75 Metcalfe, 1902, 287; Fittis, 1975, 114.

76 NAS, *Peebles Court book*, B58/9/1 (unfoliated), 4 May 1624, 5 May 1634; Renwick, 1892, 287. In the description of the bell in 1634 the name and arms of the earl are described as being for the year 1634.

However, the description appears in the terms of cautionary for the winner of the May 1634 race – James Hamilton of Boiges. It is possible that there has been an error; however, two of the other three names of winners where the years are also given can be confirmed elsewhere in the Court book. The bell is described in May 1635 when '1634' is also stated along with the name and arms of the earl. However, this description has evidently been copied from that of the previous year as there are noticeable errors; NAS, *Peebles Court book*, B58/9/1 (unfoliated), 5 May 1634, 5 May 1635. For a summary of the career of John Stewart, earl of Traquair, see Paul, 1911, 402–5. Traquair is situated to the south-east of Peebles.

77 NAS, *Peebles Court book*, B58/9/1 (unfoliated), 4 May 1625, 5 May 1645; Renwick, 1892, 288; NAS, *Peebles Accounts*, B58/14/2, 1645–6, page 8. For biographical information concerning Sir Archibald and his son, see G E C [George Edward Cokayne], ed. *Complete Baronetage*, vol II 1625–1649, Exeter, 1902, 352–3. Blackbarony or Darnhall is situated to the north of Peebles.

78 James Vaitche, son of William Vaitche of Dawick won the bell in 1637 while Robert Vaitche, brother german to Sir John Vaitche of Dawick was the 1641 winner; NAS, *Peebles Court book*, B58/9/1 (unfoliated), 5 May 1637, 4 May 1641. Dawick is situated to the south-west of Peebles.

79 NAS, *Haddington Court book*, B30/9/2, fol. 219r; *Haddington Court book*, B30/10/1, fol. 88v; *Haddington Council book*, B30/13/3, fol. 66v; *Haddington Court book*, B30/10/10, fol. 30v.

80 NAS, *Haddington Court book*, B30/10/10, fol. 158r.

81 Heal, Felicity and Holmes, Clive. *The Gentry in England and Wales, 1500–1700*, London, 1994, 309.

82 Lindsay, Sir David. The Complaynt of Schir David Lindesay, lines 177–82. In Hamer, Douglas, ed, *The Works of Sir David Lindsay of the Mount 1490–1555*, vol I: Text of the Poems (Scottish Text Society third series 1), Edinburgh, 1931, 44–5; Wedderburn, Robert. *The Complaynt of Scotland (c1550)*. In Stewart, A M, ed. (Scottish Text Society fourth series 11), Edinburgh, 1979, ch xvii, 123. The latter quote may refer to the use of horses for hunting; nevertheless, it indicates the value of ownership of horses in terms of social status.

83 NAS, *Haddington Council book*, B30/13/3, fol. 18r; *Haddington Council book*, B30/13/4, fol. 56r, 44r.

84 On 4 May 1634 a payment of twelve pounds, thirteen shillings and four pence was made to the winner of the oats before one of the bailies of the burgh; NAS, *Peebles Accounts*, B58/14/2, 1633–4, page 5. The gentleman who won the bell in 1636 was John Dalyell of Newton; NAS, *Peebles Accounts*, B58/14/2, 1635–6, *Peebles Court book*, B58/9/1 (unfoliated), 4 May 1636.

85 NAS, *Peebles Court book*, B58/9/1 (unfoliated), 5 May 1637. See also *ibid.*, 5 May 1634, 6 May 1643.

86 Meikle, 1988, 437–8. For some examples of prices of race-horses, see *ibid.*, 316.

87 Brown, P Hume, ed. *The Register of the Privy Council of Scotland*, second series vol III 1629–1630, Edinburgh, 1901, 607.

88 'Ipse etiam ejus artis tantus magister, ut saepe superatus cum esset, octavo post die duplum deponeret, ac victor evaderet'; Hume, 1839, 51.

89 Thomson, T, ed. *The Acts of the Parliaments of Scotland*, vol IV 1593–1625, Edinburgh, 1816, 613–14.

90 Brown, 1901, 607.

91 NAS, *Haddington Court book*, B30/10/10, fol. 30v.

Note: all contractions have been expanded

Grangemouth Children's Day, Bo'ness Fair and Lanimer Day at Lanark

John Burnett and Malcolm MacCallum

Introduction

> one of the most remarkable phenomena in twentieth century Scotland is the reflorescence of local patriotism in the form of festivals and pageants.[1]

The local holiday is such a widespread phenomenon, and has been in existence for so many centuries, that it may seem trite to define it. It is a day, or series of days, on which the people from one specific place give up much of their work and enjoy themselves collectively. The eating of more food than usual, and of special foods, the drinking of alcohol, often to excess, are common, though on some religious holidays fasting may be the norm. Special dress is often worn.

Within these broad outlines there is a host of variables. The holiday may be religious or secular, and if the latter it may recognise a figure of power – the monarch or local magnate – or it may involve a leader chosen from the people. It usually includes the decoration of the place where it is held, and of the items such as horses which take part in it. A procession is common, either on the model of a pilgrimage to a specific place, or around the town or district. The nature of the clothes worn, and the food and drink consumed, differ from one place and one time to another. Some elements of some festivals are carried out according to written rules, such as religious rites or the commemoration of those killed in war. These festivals tend to be quite similar from year to year. Others may vary in their practice from one year to another, depending on the state of trade, weather, and other circumstances. Finally, holidays differ in the special events that may be incorporated in them, such as a walk to a healing well, or a sporting event.

The local holiday is distinct from the fair and the market, whose original purposes were commercial. It is different from the holidays of individual trade groups such as soutars or gardeners, which were primarily for those groups, and not for the whole community. The local holiday is also separate from the local manifestation of the national holiday, whether secular, like the monarch's birthday, or religious, like Christmas.

Scotland has only a limited tradition of local summer holidays, unlike the rest of Europe. The celebration of saints' days and other religious holidays was abolished at the Reformation. Some survived because they were also fairs, such as Marymas (the Feast of the Assumption) at Irvine, or Johnsmas at Lerwick. Indeed, the fair became the commonest occasion for a summer holiday, and *fair* has been used in Scotland, at least since the nineteenth century, to mean a local summer holiday. Consequently the local holiday, as a pure holiday, had to be reinvented. At Lanark, this was done by reconstructing an old holiday, and at Bo'ness, a holiday for a single trade was expanded into one for the whole community. Grangemouth Children's Day, in contrast, is an example of a new invention.

1. The statue of William Wallace on Lanark parish church, with a garland of flowers on his head. The crowning of the Lanimer queen took place on a stage beneath the statue. Scottish Life Archive, SLA 5. 19899.

Lanimer Day at Lanark

Lanark is in upper Clydesdale, about 25 miles southwest of Glasgow. It was made a royal burgh by David I in 1140, and the murder of the sheriff of Lanark by William Wallace in 1297 is often taken to be the start of the Wars of Independence. The cotton mills at New Lanark, one of the most important sites of the early Industrial Revolution, are just outside the town. When, after 1820, coal mining and the iron industry grew rapidly in north Lanarkshire, Lanark itself was a few miles outside the mining area, and so it remained a market town.

Lanimer Day at Lanark has several origins. The obvious one, indicated in its name, is the annual checking of the boundaries of the parish, and confirming that boundary markers were in place. *Lanimer* comes from the Old Scots *landimere*, a boundary. In England, the boundaries of country parishes were beaten at Rogationtide, the Monday, Tuesday and Wednesday before Ascension, with the purpose of seeking a blessing on the crops.[2] One hesitates to associate this too closely with the Scottish practice for which there is evidence only in burghs, and not in the countryside.[3] It is possible that the practice was followed all over Scotland, and survived the Reformation only at burghs where its secular side, the checking of the ownership of land, could be emphasised.

At Lanark there is also an element of 'bringing in the May' or 'bringing in the summer.' The practice of bringing birch boughs into a town is recorded at Dumfries in the seventeenth century,[4] and there is no reason to doubt that it had been going on for centuries. Indeed, a legal dispute in 1840–47 with a nearby landlord, over the cutting of branches on the morning of Lanimer Thursday, implied that the custom was of long standing. There was a powerful popular conviction that access to the woods was a right.[5] At Lanark the boughs were always of birch: the procession was 'a moving forest of birks' (1892), or was made up of 'birks, bouquets, designs' (1894).[6] The plants used for English May garlands varied. Hawthorn and sycamore were common, though birch was usual in Wales and the Welsh Marches.[7]

Lanimer Day may owe something to Corpus Christi. This festival was instituted in 1317 on the Thursday after Trinity Sunday, and in England it had become a showpiece for town guilds by the middle of the fourteenth century.[8] In particular, the guilds performed religious dramas. When information about Lanark starts to be available in 1816, the trades were still in the Lanimer procession.[9] By 1894, to give examples from one year only, there was a lorry carrying a working loom from the mills at New Lanark, another with a model railway provided by the Caledonian Railway at Carstairs, and a third with stocking-knitting machines from a factory at Kirkfieldbank.

There is a compelling body of evidence which points to a period of 'revivals' of summer or 'May Day' festivals, particularly in England, throughout the nineteenth and into the early twentieth centuries.[10] These 'revivals' seem partly to have resulted from persistent contemporary worries within many industrial and industrializing towns regarding the weakening of social bonds and the perceived idea of a loss of 'community'. A movement of 'romantic antiquarianism', led by literary figures such as Sir Walter Scott (1771–1832) and William Wordsworth (1770–1850) advocated a return to the values of the Middle Ages, a time that was generally considered one of greater social order and cohesion. The revival of the May Day celebrations and the associated 'Merrie England' ethos had the intention of bonding together people of the same town or village: 'whereas Christmas was essentially redefined as the supreme festival of the family, the May games were viewed as an expression of the community.'[11]

In England, the practice of appointing Queens of the May was revived in Lancashire and Cheshire in the 1870s and 1880s.[12] F. Marian McNeill pointed to May Queens in Scotland in the sixteenth century, and indicated an improbable continuity from there to the 1890s, despite absence of evidence.[13] May Queens came from England to Scotland, and Lanark was

probably the first Scottish town to have one, in 1894. Transferred to June, she became simply a Queen, but the debt to England was recognised by a local poet:

> The noble Lord Tennyson, laurell'd and
>   famed,
> Sang sweetly o'er England's fair, lovely
>   May Queen,
> But the June Queen's o' Lanark are fairer
>   by far
> Than any wha had in auld Albion been seen.[14]

The poet is referring to Tennyson's lines 'You must wake and call me early, call me early mother dear . . . / For I'm to be Queen o' the May, mother, I'm to be Queen o' the May'. They had been published in 1832, and thus pre-date the late-Victorian revival of May customs.

The year before instituting the Lanimer Queen, Lanark had brought children to the forefront of their celebrations. This *seems* to have been derived from English May festivities, but the inclusion of children in a parade is not a sufficiently specific practice to make the inference of an English link certain.

Having sketched out the origins of Lanimer Day at Lanark, we now move on to look at some aspects of the celebrations that reflect contemporary concerns. Foremost was the model of a Queen and her courtiers, a gesture of loyalty and perhaps even affection towards Queen Victoria. It is difficult to look with complete seriousness on a court of lords and ladies in waiting, a guard of honour including a knight in armour, and the Queen's heralds preceded by Little Boy Blue and Little Red Riding Hood – all of them Lanark schoolchildren – without remembering W.S. Gilbert's 'Regular Royal Queen' in *The Gondoliers* (1889). A lorry carrying Britannia, surrounded by children representing various colonies and the pipe band of the Cameronian Regiment represented imperialism. These components should not be given too much weight: this was a civic occasion, not a monarchic or imperial one. Yet Lanark saw itself as part of a larger picture. When the local newspaper set out the arguments for and against change from one year to the next, it ended:

2. David Hughes, not only father of the Lanimer Queen, but also the Lord Cornet for 2001. His Right Hand Man is behind him. Scottish Life Archive, SLA 5. 19900.

> . . . it should be remembered that new generations are entitled to introduce new features so long as they remain true to THE PATRIOTIC SPIRIT which moved their fathers in observing Lanimer day.[15]

Britannia and the Queen pointed to a British patriotism, but Lanark was also proudly Scots. It had a life-size statue of William Wallace, who was said to have been living in a house in the Castlegate when he killed the sheriff and began his rebellion. From the year it was unveiled, 1820, 'Scots wha' hae' was sung each year at the Cross.[16] In 1894 the provost paid for the statue to be fitted with a kilt on Lanimer Day.

Lanimer Day has always been a celebration of civic pride. As one of the Royal Burghs created by David I, it was proud of its age and status. The burgh's procession took place before, and separately from, the one for the Queen. The council led the men bearing birks, and then came representatives of the trades and the lorries that represented different kinds of work. The child-Queen processed with children, but the council marched with the menfolk.

Finally, by the 1890s, Lanimer Day included figures from national, and even international, popular culture. The figure of Ally Sloper was in the procession in 1893, stemming from the mass-market weekly comic, *Ally Sloper's Half Holiday*, which had first appeared in 1884. Present too, was Tom Thumb, indirectly echoing the figure in a sixteenth-century nursery rhyme, and directly referring to the General Tom Thumb (1838–83) who had worked for the great circus proprietor Phineas T. Barnum. And in 1894 Buffalo Bill himself was at Lanark, the original William Frederick Cody (1847–1917), once a cowpuncher, now a showman, and soon to become a pioneer aviator.

Lanimer Day at Lanark was thus by the 1890s a large and complex assemblage of practices with various origins. Many of them related to the

3. The home of David Hughes, Lord Coronet for 2001 and his daughter Aileen, the year's Lanimer Queen, with a garland over the door. Lanark decorations are less elaborate than those in Grangemouth. Scottish Life Archive, SLA 5. 19901.

burgh, either to its own social structure, or to the way its people saw themselves as part of British and Scottish life. Compared to other local holidays, the Lanimers are unusually complex: Grangemouth Children's Day was simpler and more typical.

Bo'ness Fair

At the start of the twentieth century, town and village communities throughout Central Scotland were establishing, or in many cases re-establishing or re-inventing, a local festival. Whilst towns like Carnwath, Irvine, Kilbarchan and Lanark were already celebrating increasingly successful festival days, smaller towns situated closer to Grangemouth, like Polmont and Lauriston, were also enjoying a local fair. More directly important for Grangemouth, her near neighbour along the River Forth, Bo'ness, had spectacularly re-invented her summer festival day.

In order to understand Grangemouth Children's Day we must first examine the development of the Fair at the nearby, and much larger, town of Bo'ness. From 1799, when an Act of Parliament freed colliers from bondage, a festival day of sorts had been celebrated in

4. One of the 2001 pageants at Lanark was 'The Jewel in the Crown'. Spectacular and colourful dress is a prominent feature of the Lanimer procession. Scottish Life Archive, SLA 5. 19902.

5. A caveman in the Lanimer procession, 2001. He was part of a 'Flintstones' pageant, a popular cartoon, transferred from television to the streets of Lanark. Scottish Life Archive, SLA 5. 19903.

6. Drinkers outside 'The Wee Mans', Castlegate, Lanark, 2001. On Lanimer Day, the pubs are filled to overflowing. Although there are 'Irn Bru' cans on the ground, most of the group are drinking something stronger. Scottish Life Archive, SLA 5. 19904.

7. The Royal Carriage at Lanark, 2001. Queen Aileen is obscured by a member of her guard. She is passing in front of the statue of William Wallace at Lanark parish church. Scottish Life Archive, SLA 66/1/8.

Bo'ness. To celebrate their release, the miners marched round the town; in doing so an annual fair day, exclusive to the miners, was born. The focus of this celebration soon became blurred by the miners' tendency to over-indulge in alcohol and gambling. Each year the chaotic procession was interrupted by stops for whisky, the day ending drunkenly with horseracing along the shore.[17]

The Bo'ness Fair originally belonged to the miners, but by the mid-nineteenth century, a gradually widening group of working men from the town was being included in the day's events. From the 1850s, the iron foundry workers, woodyard workers and pottery workers were represented in the annual procession, each trade dressed in their working clothes and carrying symbols of their occupation. [18]

Concerns over heavy drinking and rowdiness ensured that not all Bo'ness townsfolk approved of the fair. By the last decade of the nineteenth century the festival was, if not moribund, then certainly in a steep decline. A substantial revamp was needed to involve the wider community and therefore gain their support. In 1894 the miners invited the local police commissioners to join their parade. The inclusion of the commissioners, who acted as town councillors in Bo'ness in the days before local politics took shape as we recognize it today, brought pageantry and an injection of previously absent civic pride. In 1894 the parade looked as it had never done before with the Miners' Deacon, Provost and Police Commissioners making their way round the town in decorated horse-drawn carriages, with regally dressed outriders and standard bearers displaying the town's coat of arms.

Three years later, at Queen Victoria's diamond jubilee, the Bo'ness Fair completely reinvented itself. In 1897 the first Bo'ness Fair queen, Grace Strachan, was crowned, her coronation taking place in front of her court of regally dressed schoolchildren. While the coronation of a schoolgirl Queen at Lanark echoed that of the May Queens of England, the first coronation at Bo'ness in 1897 seems more obviously to have been influenced by the diamond jubilee of the 'real' Queen Victoria in that same year. For the first time the town's children became the focus of the overhauled celebration, as was increasingly the case at Lanark's Lanimer festivals of the 1890s.

Grangemouth Children's Day

The town of Grangemouth was founded by Sir Laurence Dundas, who in 1777 established a small number of houses for workers employed in the construction of the nearby Forth and Clyde Canal. As the trade and industry generated by the river and canal gradually increased, the town grew up on the surrounding flat farmlands on the southern shore of the River Forth. By 1874, the population of Grangemouth had reached about 3000 and the docks and a port of some repute had been established. From 1881 to 1901 the population of the town continued to spiral from 4560 to 8386, but 'apart from its trade and manufactures' it was said to be a 'place of little note'.[19]

The original consideration in the establishment of the fair at Grangemouth, seems to have

been exclusively for the children of the town. The first Children's Day was held, not at the start of summer, but 'immediately after the school holidays' in August.[20] Not until the following year of 1907 did the date for the town's festival day move to a more 'traditional' summer's day in June. Rather than any original emphasis on a 'bringing in the may', the event was simply referred to as a 'method of entertainment for the young folks' or even 'a day of mirth and cessation from scholastic labours'.[21]

Like many summer festivals across Scotland, special dress played a key role in the day's events in Grangemouth. Visible on that rainy first day in 1906, however, were not the robes of office of local dignitaries, nor the working dress of the trades as seen in Bo'ness and Lanark, but school colours and new items of specially bought or made clothing worn by the children. The *Grangemouth Advertiser* reports that two thousand 'gaily and artistically dressed schoolchildren' each carrying a coloured ribbon denoting which school they attended marched proudly along the streets.[22] The acquiring of new clothes for the Children's Day soon became a tradition and by 1919 local shops were advertising 'Girls Summer Dresses for Gala Days and Victory Celebrations'.[23] On 17 June 1922, a Falkirk Herald reporter stated 'the gas iron and other laundry implements will be busily employed this forthcoming week [before Children's Day] not to mention mother and her needle and shop assistants where they sell blazers and shoes and school colours.' The following year, the drapers of the town were said to be 'all ready for the rush, with stocks of ties and belts and ribbon and school colours and white dresses.'[24]

Grangemouth was not unique in the holding of a festival day with its emphasis entirely on children. In Bathgate, 'Newland Day' had been celebrated since 1843. This annual festival commemorated the generosity of John Newland, a Bathgate man who made his fortune as a planter in Jamaica and bequeathed a large part of his estate to form a free school, Bathgate Academy. On 17 April each year, the children of Bathgate marched from the school to the church to celebrate Newland's Birthday.[25] The festival

8. Queen Laura's house at Beancross Road, Grangemouth. The Queen's arch is generally the most spectacular in the town, and this one takes its theme from the popular recent Walt Disney film, '102 Dalmations'. Scottish Life Archive, SLA 66/1/14.

9. The Dunfermline Accordion Band at Abbots Road, Grangemouth. They are heading, with the rest of the bands, children and decorated floats towards Zetland Park for the crowning of the Queen. Nine bands took part in the Children's Day procession of 2001. Scottish Life Archive, SLA 66/2/7.

was subsequently moved to June and although the wider community of Bathgate became increasingly involved, the focus of the day remained on the young folk of the town.

Unlike festivals such as the miners' fair at Bo'ness, or others which may have exclusively involved members of the Town Council, the Incorporated Trades or Friendly Societies, the Grangemouth festival, partly due to the way it was originally funded, was very much a socially inclusive day for all the community to enjoy. 'Although the entertainment is especially provided for the children, parents and others will be made heartily welcome to follow the procession and witness the proceedings', reported the *Grangemouth Advertiser* on 11 August 1906.

With no financial support from the local Council, the Grangemouth Children's Days were funded by public subscription, initially in the form of a door to door collection and from 1921 onwards, a 'Flag Day'. Although a figure of fifty or sixty pounds was needed for the day to progress smoothly, the townspeople seemed eager to make the day a success. A month after the collections had started, it was reported that 'the collectors had been so well received throughout the town that they now had sufficient funds to ensure that the Children's Day would go on.'[26]

The inclusive nature of Grangemouth Children's Day must be seen as a consistently prominent feature of the festival and remains so till this day. The motion for the inaugural Children's Day was proposed to the Grangemouth and Bothkennar School Board by Father Birnie, a Catholic priest, but the day itself was entirely secular in outlook, or rather excluded no branch of any particular religion practised within the town: 'the children, irrespective of denomination or creed, are assembled together for the purposes of enjoyment.'[27]

The emphasis on providing entertainment for the children continued for the duration of the day; the early Children's Days had 'Punch and Judy' shows, swingboats and 'merry-go-rounds', while each year 'a large bag of pastry and sweets and bottles of lemonade' or 'milk and bags of chocolate' were distributed to the children.

Towards the end of the day, games and sports, consisting largely of sprinting races and football, took place.[28]

During the inaugural Children's Day sports of 1906, only successful athletes were awarded for their efforts leaving many with no prize to take home. This contradicted the inclusive ethos of the festival and resolutions were made to increase the townspeople's contributions for the next year so that every child taking part in the games would receive a prize. A local journalist later reported: 'it was rather pitiful last year to see a child coming away with a doll valued about three shillings, and two or three dozen other children empty handed and consequently disappointed. One penny would have made the children happy.'[29] Again we see that this was to be a day for all the children of the town, regardless of the school they attended, their religion, social background or even athletic ability.

Soon the festival in Grangemouth began to take on the characteristics of a traditional May Day celebration. As early as 1907 there was talk of introducing maypole dancing and from 1909, with Nancy Baxter from Grangemouth High School, the crowning of a Children's Day queen took place.[30] In 1910, the schoolgirl monarch was being described as a 'May Queen' and soon 'May Day songs' were being sung at the coronation ceremony.[31]

Echoing evidence that we have already seen for Lanimer Day in Lanark of the 1890s when boughs of birch were brought into the town, the children of Grangemouth in 1920 'carried half hoops, in the form of intertwining wreaths of natural marguerites and ivy, with roses and ribbons'.[32] In the following year, the children wore 'daisy crowns and walked under a flowery bower of ivy and marguerites, while others carried flower baskets filled with natural greenery and roses.'[33]

Arches and Other Decorations

In the years following 1906, the Children's Day festival gathered momentum. The streets and houses of Grangemouth were decorated with increasing vigour, creating a 'public expression'

10. A patriotic arch! This house in Hazel Road is home to the Grangemouth Children's Day Herald, Dean Wilson. The house and garden have been decorated with a 'Braveheart' theme. The Wallace Monument can be seen behind the 'castle' in the front garden.

of celebration.[34] In 1910, a local newspaper report describes the town thus: 'Flags and buntings were used in many parts to great advantage, festoons adorned the exterior of numerous buildings, and a triumphal arch was erected over the entrance of the Zetland School'.[35] The building of arches is an imitation of events along the River Forth at Bo'ness. During the Bo'ness Fair Day, the miners, once the principal focus of the festival, had not been entirely forgotten as they competed with each other to build large and increasingly spectacular floral and boxwood arches. In 1905, a boxwood arch adorned with greenery was built, spanning the entire street, at the Snab rows.[36]

Throughout the 1920s, the arch-building and street decoration in Grangemouth became increasingly spectacular, notably involving houses belonging to the elected Queen and members of her retinue. In 1922, 'the Queen's residence [was

said to be] adorned with a very effective floral arch',[37] while in 1924 'the entrance to the home of the Queen-elect was a bower of flowers. A deep arch of rhododendrons and greenery above the entrance trailed off artistically in streamers of marguerites, and there was not a ledge of the building upon which flowers were not heaped, while all manner of flags and embellishments transformed the place'.[38] By 1927 it was reported that 'many houses throughout the town were gaily decorated with flags, bunting, flowers and evergreens. A magnificent floral porch distinguished the residence of the Queen in Kerse Road with a large crown suspended on it'.[39]

The tradition of arch building and house decoration continues to this day, with the Queen's arch generally still remaining the most spectacular. Today arch building incorporates themes of Disney Cartoon characters, popular music, film, sports stars or television favourites.

Arches and house decorations built with a specific theme are not, however, necessarily a modern innovation. As early as 1923 the Day Queen's house in Grangemouth was said to be a 'bower of beauty, the pergola and real Japanese lanterns attracting much attention from the public'.[40] The Queen herself incorporated the theme into her dress by wearing 'a very beautiful robe of Japanese silk with exquisite bead design.'[41]

The Grangemouth Children's Day held on 28 June 1919 was a particularly spectacular affair. Celebrating the declaration of peace following the Great War, themes of celebration, imperialism, identity and community ran vividly throughout the day. These same themes can be seen replicated in the summer festival days of towns and villages across Scotland and Europe at this time.

The pageant that passed through the town in 1919 was made up of seven decorated lorries, each depicting a historical tableau. First came 'Queen Elizabeth' and her court, with luminaries from British history such as Sir Walter Raleigh (who was said to have looked particularly convincing!) and William Shakespeare. Then followed the 'Dominion of Canada' with the Pilgrim fathers and Red Indians on board, the 'Indian Empire' with Jessie of Lucknow amidst others, the 'Commonwealth of Australia and New Zealand' the 'African Possession' including the Zulus, the 'Outlying Dependencies' with Malta and the Arctic regions prominent, and finally came 'Britannia', an enduring symbol of Britishness and Empire.

The procession showed loyalty to the Monarchy, Britain and the Empire, but local and civic loyalty was not forgotten. The Children's Day Queen, Miss Alison Porter, was also acknowledged, arriving in a 'flower decked carriage' with her ladies in waiting, escorted by a company of the Boys' Brigade. Songs sung on the day included 'When Britain of Old' but also 'God Bless our May Day Queen', whilst there was Morris dancing there was also an identifiably Scottish feel to the event with pipe bands and 'schottische' dancing as part of the celebrations.

As part of the coronation ceremony of 1924, the Herald addressed the Queen Dowager: 'Your Majesty it is now twelve months since you were elected Queen of our Children's Empire. The laws of our Empire declare that your successor take your place on the throne, but before the crown and sceptre, the symbols of your Royal office, pass into her keeping, we desire to assure you of our continued loyalty and obedience. The wish of your subjects is that you may live long and happy, and that for long you may look upon your reign as a pleasant memory'.[42] Within this simple speech we see the words 'children', 'empire', 'loyalty' and 'obedience' and with it, the spirit of the Grangemouth Children's Day is neatly encapsulated.

Conclusions

One of the elements in Grangemouth Children's Day is reaction to war. It took two forms. First, the Children's Day was established after the Boer War (1899–1902). Many men had been rejected as army recruits because they were not sufficiently healthy, and the question arose that if there was difficulty in recruiting for a small war, where would Britain stand in the event of a major one which required general mobilisation? Part of the response was that healthy babies would mean healthy soldiers, so child welfare became a matter of national concern.[43] In addition, there is a widespread practice of valuing children after a war, because they are the future of the community. Festivals of this kind, which started in Germany after the Thirty Years' War (1618–1648), are still held, for example at Dinkelsbühl and Lindau.[44] The second kind of reaction to war appeared in 1919, when the festival became both a commemoration of the dead and a celebration of peace, as well as continuing to have its established function as a celebration of community. This phenomenon can be seen in other Scottish summer holidays, which typically start with the laying of a wreath at the war memorial.

If we look at the ways in which festivals change over time, we can recognise three types.

First, there are festivals that are celebrated according to rules that are imposed by author-

11. At 8.50 a.m. on Lanimer Day, 2001, a group of men marched up Lanark High Street dressed as characters from the television series 'Dad's Army'. 'Captain Mainwaring' ordered them as their next manoeuvre into the 'Horse and Jockey'. Scottish Life Archive, SLA 5, 19905.

ity, such as Easter. These festivals tend to be unchanging over long periods, or at least to change only slowly. They may change quickly, or be abolished, especially if the powerful institution behind them is challenged. Two obvious examples are the church during the Scottish Reformation, and the French Revolution.[45]

Next, there are festivals that are means of handling conflict. One example is the *fête des fous*, in which the minor clergy showed their antagonism to their superiors.[46] Another is Carnival, which stands in opposition to Lent, and for the opposition of licence to discipline. Although the forms of these festivals vary as the concerns of the participants vary from year to year, their nature may remain constant for centuries because they are based on a fundamental opposition.

Finally, there are festivals whose only function is to celebrate the local community, or some aspect of it. They are highly flexible because they have no rules as such, merely conventional forms such as floats, costume, decorations and processions. They can change very quickly, and respond to other forms of popular culture, including in the twentieth century film and television. Grangemouth Children's Day is obviously an example, but most other Scottish local holidays, even if they had some distant religious origin, have now joined this category. The only large group, which are notably different at the beginning of the twenty-first century, are the Border Ridings. All of these festivals constitute an area of popular culture worthy of further investigation.

Notes and References

1 McNeill, F M. *The Silver Bough* 4 vols, Glasgow, 1957–68, iv, 15.

2 Hole, Christina. *A Dictionary of British Folk Customs*, Oxford, 1995, 251.

3 Banks, Mary McLeod. *British Calendar Customs – Scotland* 3 vols, London, 1937–41, i, 97–8.

4 McDowall, William. *History of the Burgh of Dumfries* 2nd edn, Dumfries, 1873, 308.

5 Reid, Thoma. *Lanimer Day, Lanark, 1570 to 1913*, Lanark, 1913, 36–46.

6 Unless otherwise noted, the material on the Lanimers of 1892–4 comes from the *Hamilton Advertiser*.

7 Hutton, Ronald. *Stations of the Sun*, Oxford, 1994, 230.

8 Hutton, 304.

9 Reid, 28.

10 Hutton, 295–7.

11 Hutton, 29.

12 Hutton, 297.

13 McNeill, iv, 41.

14 *Hamilton Advertiser*, 2 June 1894.

15 *Hamilton Advertiser*, 9 June 1894.

16 Reid, 34.

17 For a fuller overview of the origins and development of the Bo'ness Fair, W.F. Hendrie, *The Morn's the Fair*, Linlithgow, 1982, is invaluable.

18 Hendrie, William Fyfe. All the fun of the Fair, *Scots Magazine*, 146 (1997), 611–5.

19 Groome, Francis H. *Ordnance Gazetteer of Scotland* new edn, Edinburgh, 1901, 771–2.

20 *Grangemouth Advertiser*, 9 June 1906.

21 *Falkirk Herald*, 24 June 1905 and 26 June 1907.

22 *Grangemouth Advertiser*, 18 August 1906.

23 *Falkirk Herald*, 14 June 1919.

24 *Falkirk Herald*, 16 June 1923.

25 The 17th of April was actually his baptismal date. A fuller account can be found in McNeill, iv, 49–52.

26 *Grangemouth Advertiser*, 7 July 1906.

27 *Falkirk Herald*, 26 June 1907.

28 *Grangemouth Advertiser*, 20 June 1907, *Falkirk Herald*, 28 June 1922.

29 *Grangemouth Advertiser*, 8 June 1907.

30 *Grangemouth Advertiser*, 18 August 1907.

31 *Falkirk Herald*, 22 June and 3 July 1920.

32 *Falkirk Herald*, 3 July 1920.

33 *Falkirk Herald*, 2 July 1921.

34 Jarman, Neil. The Orange arch: creating traditions in Ulster, *Folklore*, 112 (2001), 1–22, 3.

35 *Falkirk Herald*, 22 June 1910.

36 Jarman notes that a similar arch building competition took place within Protestant communities in Ireland from 1880–1914, with groups trying to built higher, better and more spectacular 'Orange' arches during the 'marching season'.

37 *Falkirk Herald*, 28 June 1922.

38 *Falkirk Herald*, 25 June 1924.

39 *Falkirk Herald*, 22 June 1927.

40 *Falkirk Herald*, 30 June 1923.

41 *Falkirk Herald*, 30 June 1923.

42 *Falkirk Herald*, 25 June 1924.

43 Jones, Helen, *Health and Society in Twentieth-Century Britain*, London, 1994, 21–3.

44 Petzoldt, Leander. *Volkstümliche Feste*, Munich, 1983, 154–6, 171–2.

45 Hutton, 25–8, Michel Vovelle, *Les Métamorphoses de la Fête en Provence*, Avignon, 1976.

46 Heers, Jacques. *Fêtes des Fous et Carnavals*, Paris, 1983.

The Great Highland Famine of 1846: The Lack Of Medical Aid

Morrice McCrae

In August 1845 an *Act for the Amendment and better Administration of the Law relating to the Relief of the Poor in Scotland* became law. For some three centuries responsibility for the administration of the Poor Law in Scotland had been devolved to the Kirk and almost nothing had been spent on medical aid even for paupers on the Parish Rolls.[1] Under the new Act the state set up Parochial Boards in every parish to 'have and exercise all the Powers and Authority hitherto exercised by the Heritors and the Kirk Sessions.' Unlike the Poor Law (Amendment) Act introduced for England in 1834, the Scottish Act required that the provisions for the welfare of paupers must include personal medical care. It has been claimed, wrongly, that this innovation benefited the whole working population of Scotland since it led to the establishment of a resident doctor in parishes 'where otherwise there would have been none.'[2]

From the beginning the leading social reformers in Scotland recognised that the provisions of the new Act were inadequate. For over a decade they had argued that state support should be given, not only to those who had been forced by circumstances into pauperism, but also to those able-bodied poor who found themselves, for whatever reason, unable to support their families. In little over a year the case for such support became all too clear. In 1846 the potato blight spread to Scotland and, in the years that followed, the destruction of the crop on which the people of the Highlands and Islands chiefly depended, caused widespread poverty and destitution. In

this 'Great Highland Famine'[3] suffering was made worse by a lack of medical services for the sick. In the winter of 1850–51, those with the immediate professional responsibility for the welfare of the people of the Highlands and Islands, the parish ministers and the local medical practitioners, wrote of 'the lamentable condition' of their people and reported that the great majority of the sick in their parishes 'certainly cannot procure the services of a medical man.'[4] In correspondence with the Royal College of Physicians of Edinburgh, ministers and medical practitioners alike, urged that medical aid must be provided for all the impoverished people of their parishes, including the able–bodied. Since this could not be financed from local resources, they looked to central government. They put forward proposals that anticipated the expansion of state medical services that was to take place in the next century. In the 1850s, however, their proposals were incompatible with the ideologies of the time and they met with only dismissive silence.

Yet, in the nineteenth century, the need for some new provision for the poor had become compelling. The remorseless industrialisation of Britain had destined to poverty an ever-growing proportion of the population – the new overworked, poorly paid and badly housed urban industrial workforce. In the years of economic depression that had followed the Napoleonic Wars, the poverty and discontent of the working poor deepened further. Thomas Carlyle wrote of a general feeling in the country that 'the condition and disposition of Working Classes is a rather ominous matter at present; something ought to be said, something ought to be done, regarding it.'[5] Parliament responded to this increasing public anxiety in 1834. A Poor Law (Amendment) Act was passed for England and Wales, based on the Utilitarian ideas influential in England at that time. The greatest good of the greatest number was to be achieved by reducing the threat that pauperism and its attendant evils presented to the general public and by containing the financial burden that increasing pauperism forced on the productive and self-supporting majority.

Since Elizabethan times, the Poor Laws in England had determined that anyone who had fallen into absolute poverty and opted to surrender the normal privileges of citizenship in order to become officially designated as a pauper, was entitled to support from the local community. In 1834 Edwin Chadwick, the Benthamite architect of the new Act, aimed to contain the rising cost of the ever-increasing numbers being maintained under the old laws. Relief was to be administered with greater economic efficiency and the year on year increase in the number entitled to relief was to be halted. Chadwick identified the diseases and disabilities of the working poor as the chief cause of the decline of so many into destitution and pauperism. He was persuaded by the belief, then common in England, that the chief cause of the pauperising diseases of the poor was miasma, the noxious effluvium from urban filth. He was confident that by eliminating miasma from the country's towns and cities by a program of sewerage and drainage, the chief cause of pauperism would be removed. Not only would the numbers, and therefore the cost, of the paupers be contained but the slums which harboured the urban poor would no longer be the breeding grounds of disease and the source of a constant threat to the health of the community at large. However, the English Act of 1834 made no provision for the personal medical care of paupers, even where their pauperism was due to sickness.[6] Chadwick looked only to prevention of sickness; doctors were 'necessary evils not likely to last,' who would ultimately become redundant as his sanitary measures took effect.[7]

In 1834 it was the government's intention that these measures should be extended to Scotland but for over a decade there was well-argued resistance led by the medical profession north of the border. Opinion in Scotland was unconvinced by Utilitarian ideology and the medical profession discounted miasma as a significant cause of pauperism. The accepted model of the relationship between disease and poverty was an inversion of that held in England. For over a century,[8] physicians in Scotland had held that poverty – through poor diet, inadequate clothing and shelter, overwork and overcrowding – led to 'debility'. In the nineteenth century, medical students at Glasgow and Edinburgh were taught that it was the 'debility' of poverty that was at the root of the diseases of the urban working class.[9] Led by W P Alison, then the Professor of Medicine at Edinburgh University, social reformers in Scotland argued that any new Poor Law must include support for the able-bodied poor so that, when deprived of employment for whatever reason, the worker and his family would not necessarily be reduced to destitution, debility, depression and disease.[10] Equally, the sick poor must have access to the medical treatment that might restore their fitness to work and to provide for their families.

The resistance in Scotland was only partially successful. Since the sixteenth century, the Poor Law in Scotland had not required parish authorities to provide for the able-bodied and that ancient principle was continued in the Poor Law (Amendment) Act in 1845. The Act did not extend the reponsibities of the new Poor Law to include the able bodied; 'poor', in this context, continued to mean only 'pauper'. Although the new legislation did nothing to prevent the able bodied from falling into pauperism, it did offer those pauperised by sickness some assistance to recover their ability to work. In the Bill presented to Parliament, Parochial Boards were to be obliged to raise 'Funds for the Relief of the Poor' from within the parish either by voluntarily offerings or by assessment and were required, out of these funds, 'to provide for Medicines,

Medical Attendance, nutritious diet, Cordials and Clothing for such poor and in such a manner and to such an extent as seem equitable and expedient.'

In the House of Commons, Scottish members continued to object that this proposed enabling legislation did not go far enough. They demanded that the Poor Law must ensure that every parish had the services of a resident medical officer and that, to provide the necessary funds, assessment should be made compulsory. The Home Secretary, Sir James Graham, agreed that 'general assessment must be desirable but considering the difference of opinion he thought it infinitely more wise to leave the public of Scotland, by a voluntary act, to adopt assessment themselves rather than by an enactment to make it compulsory'.[11] The Prime Minister, Sir Robert Peel considered that the provision of a paid medical officer in every parish was impractical and that Scottish members were being over ambitious. 'He entertained a strong objection to giving the people of Scotland a positive assurance that the poor should at all times be supplied with medical relief. He thought there should be caution in how they excited expectation which could not be realised. Everything that was possible ought to be done but fallacious hopes should not be raised.'[12]

Nevertheless, after the Act was passed, Scottish pressure continued[13] and in 1848 the government offered a compromise. An annual grant of £10,000 was made to the Board of Supervision of the Poor Law to finance a subsidy for any parish that agreed to finance the appointment of a medical officer. Sir John McNeil, the Chairman of the Board, was confident that, with this inducement, a full complement of medical officers would be recruited throughout Scotland.[14]

On introducing his Poor Law (Amendment) Bill in 1845, the Lord Advocate had referred to the problem of increasing poverty in the towns and cities to which there had previously been 'perhaps some indifference – or rather a want of attentive observation.'[15] He also drew attention to the very different, but equally pressing, problems of poverty in the Highlands and Islands.

In many districts a great change of circumstances has been occasioned by the alteration in the system of management of land. Small farms have been thrown together into large farms and the consequence is that there are fewer people able to contribute to the relief of the poor now than formerly. Then again in some extensive locations along the coast the entire annihilation of kelp manufacture has thrown many persons out of employment and while the means of the contributors has decreased the fund for relieving the poor has become lessened. The poverty and misery of the labouring classes has naturally increased.

It was appropriate that the people of the Highlands and Islands, who made up little over 10 per cent of the population of Scotland, should have special consideration. Although communications by sea had recently improved with the introduction of steamboat services from the Clyde, the Western Highlands and Islands were still remote from the main body of Scotland. In 1850, the way of life and the usual language of the people, as much as geography set the community apart and its social problems were its own.

Since the seventeenth century the old military Gaelic society and its clan structure had been disintegrating. For centuries the clans had presented themselves as 'families' although their people were not necessarily all of the same blood. In theory the lands occupied by the clan were communal, gained by conquest and held by military power with the clan chief as the chosen military leader. In practice, the clan was ruled by a hereditary military aristocracy and lands could be acquired or lost by marriage as well as by force. The economy of this military and ruler-owns-all society was supported by the rearing and exporting of cattle and its people were sustained by the communal farming of scattered and intermingled holdings and open grazings, a system common in the Europe of the Middle Ages.

The destruction of this military society was purposefully accelerated by government fiat after the suppression of the Jacobite rising in 1746.[16] In the process of change, it was at last seen that the tradition of common ownership of the clan lands had long been a myth. Clan chiefs were now recognised as landed gentlemen, legal owners of vast estates that were grossly overpopulated and burdened by an obsolete agricultural economy. Many estates were soon bankrupt and almost all urgently required new investment to make them commercially viable. A number of the old aristocratic families were able to raise the necessary funds by selling part of their estates; others sold out completely, usually to men who had made fortunes overseas or in the new industries of the south. This new generation of commercially minded owners introduced modern agricultural practices to the best of their arable ground and gave over other vast acres to profitable sheep runs. In this restructured agricultural system there was a place only for the landowners, their large tenants and a limited agricultural workforce. Employment could only be found for the few; the great majority of the population of Highlands and Islands was now redundant. A few of the minor gentry became large tenant farmers but most found that they could only maintain their life style by moving away. Numbers of the ordinary people – those who could find the means – also moved away, emigrating in the hope of a new and better life in the south or in North America. The unwanted mass of the population that remained was displaced from the inland glens to peripheral coastal land and settled on crofts too small to provide a livelihood for a family. In the early years of the nineteenth century almost every crofter had to rely on additional income from employment in the local kelp industry or from the earnings of those of his family who could find seasonal work in the fishing fleets operating from the east coast or temporary employment in the industrial south.[17]

The Highlands and Islands made their contribution to nineteenth century Britain by supplying wool for the expanding industry in the south, labour for the expanding economy and, as ever, manpower for the country's armed forces. But the society that had emerged in the nineteenth century was not one in which a professional middle class could flourish. There were few people of substance; the overwhelming majority of the people now belonged to a crofting community that was poor almost by definition and as its numbers continued to increase during the first half of the century so also did its poverty.

In giving particular attention to the Highlands and Islands in 1845, the Lord Advocate was recognising that the poverty and misery of the crofting community had increased even further since the end of the Napoleonic Wars. A sharp fall in cattle prices had made the crofters' few beasts almost worthless, the collapse of the kelp industry had closed their chief opportunity for local employment, and a failure in herring fishing and the general recession in Scotland had made it more difficult to find work elsewhere. Few crofters could see any prospect of prosperity in Scotland and many, perhaps a majority, were 'inspired with the spirit of emigration. Nothing but the reluctance to part with their scanty stock of cattle, at present at very low prices, seems to retard the emigration of a great many people.'[18] The crofters could contribute almost nothing to the economy of the estates and most were allowed to remain on the land ' by humanity alone.'[19] But they remained in dire poverty, badly housed and poorly clad. 'Their domestic economy is frugal beyond conception. The produce of foreign soil, as tea, coffee and sugar, and the common conveniences of art, as knives and forks &c. are to them altogether alien. Their ordinary food consists of oat and barley meal, potatoes and milk, variously prepared.'[20]

A year after the introduction of the new Poor Law, the people of the Highlands and Islands were further 'blasted by providence.' The potato blight that had been devastating Ireland since 1845 spread to Scotland and for a decade the people of the Highlands and Islands were unable to grow the crop on which they chiefly depended. Meal had to be brought in by relief organisations and paid for by the people in whatever cash they possessed or, when that was exhausted, by their labour. In Ireland during these years the structure and functioning of society was undermined, 20,000 died of starvation and a further 193,000 died from typhus.[21] In the Highlands and Islands social order was maintained and enough meal was shipped in to prevent deaths from starvation. Typhus, which had been a continuing scourge in Ireland since the great epidemic there in 1816–19, never reached epidemic proportions in the Highlands and Islands. [22] The Great Highland Famine was not a cause of death but a cause of deep poverty and destitution.

After four years of general distress and misery, Dr John Coldstream drew attention to the great lack of medical aid. Coldstream, a friend and former colleague of Charles Darwin, had abandoned a career in natural history to return to Edinburgh to practice medicine and to take part in the missionary work of the new Free Church of Scotland.[23] The Free Church had been one of the principal agencies delivering relief to the Highlands and Islands during the Highland Famine and, in July 1850, Coldstream reported on conditions there in a paper to the Royal College of Physicians of Edinburgh. He attributed the difficulty in finding assistance for the sick poor to the very small number of medical men practising in the region.[24] Since he could give no exact figures, the College applied to the Board of Supervision 'for such information as it happened to be possessed of, regarding the supply of medical aid in the northern districts of Scotland.'[25] On being informed by the Chairman of the Board that the relevant information 'was not to be found,' The College appointed a committee to assist Coldstream in conducting an inquiry 'to determine the proportion which the Practitioners bear to the whole population and to ascertain whether there be much complaint on the part of the people of the difficulty in getting medical aid.'[26]

A questionnaire was sent to 'the Ministers of Parishes and some others resident in the counties of Argyll, Bute, Inverness, Ross, Sutherland, Caithness, Orkney and Shetland to the number of 320, in 170 parishes'. The Ministers were asked to give the names and addresses of all doctors in each parish, to state whether the number of doctors was increasing or decreasing, to assess the extent of the inadequacy of medical aid in their districts and for suggestions for improvement. A questionnaire was also sent to the only 71 doctors known by the College to be practising in the region at that time.[27]

Almost all the questionnaires were returned and many of the ministers and medical practitioners took the opportunity to set out, at much greater length, their assessments of the situation and their proposed solutions. There were then 370,000 people living in the 14,000 square miles of the Highlands and Islands and in the winter of 1850 there was little to distinguish paupers from the general population. The small numbers of paupers (2–4 per cent of the population)[28] entitled to medical care under the Poor Law had hardly changed since the Famine began. Yet one typical parish 'contains upward of 2000 of a very scattered population who, except for six families are in a pauperised condition.'[29] From another parish, Dr MacLean reported that although he was 'paid by the Boards only to attend the paupers of two parishes, I have out of my own pocket to physic and attend a population of 3000 who are unable to pay a medical man.'[30]

In all, the parish ministers of the Highlands and Islands were able to identify a total of only 133 medical men in the whole region and not all were regarded as reliable. In many cases it was suspected that the practitioner had no proper training or qualification. In 1852, it might have been discovered from the first Scottish Medical Directory that 34 had no recognised qualification, 63 had qualified as surgeons (for the most part licentiates of the Royal College of Surgeons of Edinburgh or the Royal Faculty of Physicians and Surgeons of Glasgow) and 36 had university degrees in medicine (MD). Although all 133 made themselves available to treat anyone in urgent need of attention, not all were in full time practice as doctors. Four parish ministers and seven large farmers had medical degrees and gave assistance when required but took no income from medical practice. Ten practitioners were in semi-retirement from service in the Royal Navy, the Hon East India Company, the Hudson's Bay Company or from the army.

The distribution of the 133 medical practitioners bore little relation to the parish structure of the region. No fewer than 92 parishes had no resident doctor although several reported that, if absolutely necessary, they could call on the services of a doctor from a neighbouring parish. As many as 41 parishes, mostly in Ross, Sutherland and the Islands, were 'never visited by any regular practitioner and may therefore be regarded as destitute of medical aid'.[31] Although, in 1850, many were receiving a 'salary' under the new Poor Law, medical practitioners did not necessarily base themselves on the parishes that employed them. The practice of medicine was an entrepreneurial business and those medical men who were entirely dependent for their livelihood on the practice of their profession based themselves in the market towns or in those villages which had a few shops, a post office and some promise of commercial activity. For the majority of the people of the more landward areas these commercial doctors were remote and their services were neither immediately available nor affordable.[32]

Medical men could not make a living from private practice among the people in the more remote districts. In Skye, the population being 'so much scattered' and, in normal times 'the health generally so good,' Dr Ferguson found that even a single practitioner could not find reasonable living; there were few prosperous tenant farmers, no middle class and the 'people, being so poor, are unable to pay either for attendance or medicine.'[33] In the Highlands and Islands, earnings from fees were seldom more than a few pounds a year and income had to be supplemented from some other source. Most combined medical practice with 'small' farming and, for some, farming was their chief employment. In a very few parishes, the medical practitioners could depend on an annual salary, varying from £6 to £20, from a scheme of 'Mutual Insurance'[34] organised by the local tenants.[35] On some great estates the proprietor lent financial support. On his vast estates in the north the Duke of Sutherland employed district surgeons on an annual salary of £40, which, with their other earnings made them among the most financially secure medical practitioners in the Highlands. However, few proprietors were so wealthy or so careful of the welfare of their people. Many estates were 'in the hands of a Trustee – a poor proprietor with a poorer tenantry'.[36] After 26 years in practice, one dispirited medical man wrote

> It has been a life of labour but not an age of ease. Owing to the miserably inadequate remuneration I could not afford, after supporting my wife and family, even to insure myself or make any provision for myself or for them. As my family increased, I was obliged to give up a medical periodical and I could scarce afford to give my family the common rudiments of an education.[37]

Over the years many well-qualified medical men had attempted to establish themselves in the Highland and Islands but, finding too few patients able to pay for their services and unable to find other financial support, had been forced to leave. Now, as poverty increased in the years after the Wars, even some of those who had seemed well established began to drift away.

When, in 1846, the arrival of the potato blight in the Highland and Islands turned poverty into destitution, that drift increased. Almost every practitioner complained that 'the poverty is so great that few can afford to pay a medical man for his services although on all occasions they insist on prompt attention for which, generally speaking, they are quite unable to pay.'[38] 'All the tenants, crofters and cottars, except those farmers who hold sheep alone, are in a state of, or bordering on, bankruptcy and not able to pay their rents since the failure of the potatoes and the depression of the price of black cattle.'[39] When tenants could no longer find the means to meet their rents, some previously benevolent landowners withdrew their support for the local medical practitioner.

> In South Uist, Col. Gordon generously guaranteed my salary on behalf of his tenants for which I attended their wants. The condition of the people having come to such indigence of late the proprietor could not find it possible to extract rents far less his other land taxes including the doctors salary so that last term day he withdrew this and now I cannot count on anything.[40]

While a few practitioners discriminated in their attendance on patients – 'now resolved not to attend to their wants except in cases where a remuneration may be accepted'[41] – the great majority continued to be 'the humble servant of everyone night and day'[42] attending those unable to pay and bearing the cost of medicines and travel from their own resources. For almost all, medical practice became both commercially impossible and personally oppressive.

> I cannot see how efficient medical practices can be supported in this place. Some of us expend a large . . . sum on medicine for the people in indigent circumstances who, though not in receipt of parochial relief, cannot afford to pay for medical attention. And further the discomfort a medical man endures by being obliged to ride or drive eight or ten miles in severe weather and then forced to remain for many hours in a miserable hovel without warmth and almost invariably without food, is unknown to those who have not experienced it.[43]

The demands were particularly severe on practitioners in the remote coastal districts. There the daily round could be dangerous as well as financially unrewarding.

> Take for instance a bad case of midwifery and a coarse night journey of 20 to 30 miles crossing arms of the sea. It may be very inaccessible to get to and to hire any conveyance or means of shifting that is safe and dry is out of the question. And after all that fatigue and expense I am sorry to say that not more than three out of ten can pay anything. So in a pecuniary point of view, I would be much better stopping at home had it not been for the suffering of humanity.[44]

The suffering from lack of access to medical help was most severe on the small islands.

> When the case is critical and the doctor must be sent for they have to cross the distance separating this island from Sanday in a small open boat. At certain time of the year a fortnight, or even longer, may elapse before the attempt can be made with safety. In some islands, death has ensued before his arrival. In many cases his advice has only been sought at the eleventh hour when his services are unrewarding.[45]

As the repeated failure of the potato crop deepened widespread poverty into destitution, medical practitioners continued to leave the Highlands and Islands. The measures introduced in 1845 by the Poor Law (Amendment) Act, even when strengthened by the subsidy added in 1848, did little towards reversing that trend. In 1851, together the ministers in the Highlands and Islands reported to Dr Coldstream the loss of a further 35 medical practitioners from their parishes. Five had died and had not been replaced. Four had emigrated – two to the Hon East India Company and two to Canada – and one had joined the army. Five had remained in the Highlands but abandoned medical practice for full-time farming. All the others had left to practise in the Lowlands or in England.

While the exodus continued, a total of 15 new doctors had come to the Highland and Islands but of these three, although qualified to practise medicine, had come to the Highlands principally as farmers. Of those who, encouraged by the promise of support under the new Poor Law, had come expecting to make a living from medical practice, four had become disillusioned by 1851 and were already looking for employment elsewhere. Of the 200 parish ministers who replied to the College's inquiry, the great majority (141) reported that the new Poor Law had brought no improvement in medical services in their parishes and 32 reported that the number of medical practitioners available to their people had continued to decrease.

In general the reputation of the medical practitioners who continued to practise was enhanced during the difficult years of the Highland Famine. There was 'no class of men more extensively and actively charitable than the Medical Practitioners in the Highlands.'[46] However, in spite of their individual efforts, the service they were able to deliver was far from satisfactory.

The medical men of the Highlands are usually humane and in every instance inadequately remunerated, but at the same time the difficulty of procuring their services and affording any remuneration for them are so great that it is only in very extreme cases that medical aid is usually sought by the poorer classes. In such cases, especially when we consider that his stay is necessarily so short that his visits, if repeated at all, are so only at distant intervals and that his prescriptions, if administered in his absence, are given unsatisfactorily and partially under much injudicious treatment calculated to counteract their efficiency, the medical attendant can be of little service and hence, without regard to these circumstances the people have but too generally lost due confidence in medical aid, and thus from day to day we, the Clergymen of the Highlands, who are necessarily conversant with their condition see what appears at the outset but a simple ailment, assuming by neglect, inattention and unskilful treatment the aggravated form of the dangerous and it may be fatal illness. In cases of childbirth the poor females of the Country are usually subjected to the most ignorant treatment, left dependent as they generally are on female attendants of their own class who have rashly assumed a calling in the nature of which they never had one hour's instruction. Indeed I am fully persuaded that due inquiry on this point, while it would lead to surprise that so few lives are sacrificed, would at the same time unfold details of the most trying and lamentable nature. [47]

A number of ministers took the opportunity not only to comment on the general deficiency in medical aid but to express disappointment in the qualities of the medical officers recruited since 1845. From Gairloch, the Rev John Mackay complained that 'Charles Robertson, surgeon and little farmer, was procured for the paupers and crofters on the Gairloch property and for other inferior purposes. It seems to be an increase numerically speaking but we are worse than wanting a medical man from all I know and hear.'[48] From the parish of Bressay the Rev J

M Hamilton reported that 'it would almost be better to have none at all than an ignorant half educated person.'[49]

In other cases it was not only professional competence that was found wanting. 'Some of them, I regret to say, have yielded themselves to habits of intemperance.'[50] In Westray a resident doctor had been recruited but the minister, the Rev James Brotchie, 'found it necessary to have no intercourse with him.' From Kildalton, the Rev Alexander Mackenzie wrote of his local practitioner: 'Let it suffice to say that he is employed by no respectable family in the district nor by any of them that can possibly avoid it.'[51]

Some new appointments, though eminently successful and greatly valued by the parishioners, seemed unlikely to last. From Helmsdale, Rev John MacDonald reported that Thomas Rutherford 'was the only Medical Practitioner of standing and respectability who has resided for any length of time in this place.' The parish was

> . . . a most important place for a qualified medical practitioner not only on account of the largeness of the population but on account of its being one of the principle [sic] herring fishing stations on the coast. Many flock to it from all parts of the country during the fishing season, many of them poor people who are exposed to accidents, on sea and on land, of which there have been many since I became connected with the place. Among such a multitude of people accidents must happen, sometimes severe ones in consequence of mishaps and the upsetting of boats, so much so that, unless medical help were at hand, life would be in the greatest danger.[52]

However the heritors of the parish were making no effort towards 'keeping a respectable medical practitioner in the place.' In 1850, overworked and underpaid, Dr Rutherford was already planning to leave.

Five years after the passing of the Poor Law (Amendment) Act, and in spite of the subsidy offered to the Parish Boards in 1848, the number of medical practitioners was even more inadequate than before. There were fears that even more medical men would be forced to leave. Many could not afford to stay without an income from their small farms and farming was in recession. For the minister on Barra this was a particularly pressing problem. 'Supposing the medical men residing in this parish transferred their agricultural capital elsewhere the deficiencies in supply of medical aid could not be relieved.'[53] Deficiencies could only be made up by attracting new medical practitioners 'but there is little likelihood at present of anyone making the experiment.'

By 1850 it was clear that the implementation of the medical provisions of the Poor Law (Amendment) Act, and in particular the Treasury grant, had not been well managed. The primary intention had been to provide medical care for the paupers on the Poor Roll in every parish in Scotland. For the Highlands and Islands there was an important second intention; it was hoped to improve the medical care available to all the working poor indirectly by encouraging an increase in the total number of medical practitioners in the region. As Sir John McNeil wrote in a letter to the College of Physicians in Edinburgh, it was intended that 'more particularly in the remote parishes' the Treasury grant would 'doubtless exert a direct influence on the actual supply of medical aid to the mass of the people'.[54]

In the event, the scheme only succeeded in slowing the drift of medical practitioners form the region. Even with the subsidy offered by the Treasury, parochial boards found it difficult to appoint a medical officer since the Treasury grant had to be matched by an equal contribution from parish funds. In an exceptional arrangement, the parochial boards of Creich and Lairg in Sutherland and Kincardine in Ross and Cromarty found it possible to employ Alexander MacEwan as an additional practitioner for their three parishes by pooling their resources. More typically, the Treasury grant only made it possible for the parish to persuade an existing practitioner to stay. Dr Fenton of Bowmore, for example, reported that 'without the £35 from the Parochial Board I should been compelled to leave.'[55]

However, in many cases the Treasury grants were neither taken up nor used so effectively. Across the region, parochial boards were often arbitrary and inconsistent in their use of the subsidy and some chose not to apply for it. In Orkney, parochial boards may have been persuaded by one of the long established medical practitioners to reject the offered grant. Dr Duguid, already grieved that 'druggists interfere very much with the emoluments of the professional man', resisted the recruitment of even more competition. 'I regard the Orkney Islands as abundantly supplied with medical men … tho' no doubt some of the islands suffer inconvenience at times from stormy weather preventing them from sending boats across the ferry.'[56] The offered grant was refused, leading a less influential surgeon to complain:

> The islands of Walls, Hoy, Fara, Cava and Flota have no medical aid. I am often called there and detained from bad weather. The boats they send are often very bad and, were funds allowed, a good one could be got. I have to land on the barren shore far from the houses and remain until daylight, not being able to trust the boat. If I could get a good boat I could visit them oftener.[57]

The Rev Joseph Caskey agreed that an opportunity had been lost.

> There is no one here who pretends to medical skill with the exception of a retired schoolmaster and the sick nurse and it is doubtful how far their pretensions could be trusted. There are no heritors resident in the parish and, in general, the inhabitants are not wealthy but, with a view to obtaining a suitable doctor, I think between the Parochial Board and the inhabitants the sum of thirty pounds might have been depended upon. A doctor is very much required here and, with aid from some other quarter, he could have a comfortable living.[58]

Paradoxically, it was in the poorest and most badly served parishes that the offered Treasury grant was most often rejected. It was a condition of the grant that the parish must provide an equal sum. In many parishes this sum could not be found and the grant had to be refused. In more prosperous parishes, where the need was less pressing, the grant was invariably accepted. As we have seen, the parishes that made up the Duke of Sutherland's estate were already well served by the practitioners employed on a salary from the Duke. One of them, John McLean was able to report that, with the additional sum from the Treasury grants, he was financially secure:

My salary from the Duke of Sutherland	£40
Surgeon to the Parochial Board of Edderachyllis	£15
Surgeon to the Parochial Board of Assynt	£20
For attending farmers	£20
	with a house £100

In many parishes, where the grant was accepted, its distribution became a cause of resentment and even anger. The Parochial Board of Kilcalmonell received a grant of £25 but allocated the greater part to a practitioner who did not live or practise in the parish. The resident surgeon, John MacKeller, complained: 'Only four lousy pounds for advice and medicine to the paupers in a parish 16 miles in length and containing 100 paupers. So much for justice.'[59] On Arran, both parishes – Kilmorie and Kilbride – allotted the whole of their grants to Andrew Stoddart, an unqualified practitioner based in Brodick. Charles Cook, the surgeon at Lamlash, complained that Stoddart

> . . . is upwards of 18 miles from many of the paupers and he is not able to attend them all. Often I have to give advice and medicine without any remuneration. There are only two medical men on the island. If the salary of two parishes were divided, as he lives in Brodick and I at Lamlash, the north would answer to him and the south to me. I am sure the poor would get better justice.[60]

Neither Charles Cook nor Andrew Stoddart had any proper registerable qualification. In 1850, few parochial boards distinguished carefully between qualified and unqualified practitioners in appointing medical officers. This added

further to the dissatisfaction in many parishes that the Treasury grant had not been used rationally or fairly. Even where the grant was used to the best effect, it often proved insufficient to relieve the almost overwhelming financial pressure on the local medical practitioner. Colin MacTavish, a surgeon on Islay complained:

> Although the medical practitioners of this place are allowed thirty pounds and some odd shillings for attending the paupers on the roll, some of us have to expend a large proportion of that sum on medicine for the people in indigent circumstances who, though not in receipt of parochial relief, cannot pay for medical attention.[61]

By 1850 it was apparent that the Poor Law (Amendment) Act, even with the addition of the annual Treasury grant, had not succeeded in ensuring the provision of adequate medical care in what was the poorest community in the country. Although the measures allowed by the Act had not been carried out fully in every parish and the best use had not always been made of the funds made available by the Treasury, these were not seen as the main causes of the scheme's failure in the Highlands and Islands. The fundamental problem was the overwhelming extent and severity of the poverty. The few paupers, whose care was directly financed by the state, made up far too small a proportion of the total number of those who were too poor to pay for medicines and medical attention. In many prosperous regions in Scotland, medical practitioners could earn enough in fees from those who could afford to pay to allow them to provide services *gratis* to that manageable proportion of their patients who could not. In the Highlands and Islands those who could pay were too few to support the parish medical practitioner; by providing medicines and service *gratis* to all those who required it he faced financial ruin. In many cases the practitioner was only saved from being overwhelmed by the restraint of the great majority of poor. 'The people seldom think of calling a medical man until there is manifest danger and often cases are too far gone before advice is had.'[62] Fortunately, throughout the Highland Famine the population remained 'generally healthy.'[63] A small number of people from Canna, returning from an unsuccessful attempt to find work in the industrial south, brought smallpox with them causing three deaths.[64] Typhus was 'lurking on the islands'[65] and, in 1849, caused a number of deaths on North Ronaldsay. The medical practitioners were in constant fear that 'were any serious epidemic to visit, the mortality will inevitably be painful in the extreme,'[66] but the great epidemic that was then causing the deaths of so many thousands in Ireland did not descend on the Highlands and Islands. Nevertheless, during the years of scarcity 'things were sufficiently bad' and in their distress 'the bulk of the people were not able to get proper medical attention.'[67]

In 1850, the poverty that was at the root of the problem in the Highlands and Islands was not seen as a passing phenomenon and was not related specifically to the years of failure of the potato crops. In the 232 reports received by John Coldstream, the parish ministers and medical practitioners seldom mentioned the potato famine. Without exception they saw the problem of poverty as endemic and set to continue indefinitely. Many described the situation as hopeless. It was agreed that there could be no improvement in medical services while such poverty continued.

A few believed that the chronic poverty could be relieved by new legislation that would force every tenant in the Highlands to introduce modern agricultural practices. Individual landowners had attempted to rationalise the management of their estates but often in haphazard and crudely conducted 'clearances' that were inevitably resisted by many of the small tenants. Properly conducted modernisation of the agricultural economy was seen as the only answer and, if its potential was to be fully exploited, it was seen as imperative that access to the region should be opened up by extension and development of the new steamboat services.

These were long-term and unexceptionable ambitions. However, a number of Coldstream's correspondents made proposals for more radical measures, proposals that were remarkable at a time when Victorian philanthropy was 'widely thought to the most wholesome and reliable remedy for the nation's ills'[68] and when government was committed to a policy of *laissez faire*. Every one of their constructive proposals called for increased state intervention

It was proposed that the new Poor Law scheme should be made more effective by additional legislation to make assessment of parishes obligatory, to increase the Treasury grant and to oblige Parochial Boards to accept it. In addition the Treasury should underwrite the cost of medicines for those who could not afford them, medical practitioners' travel expenses when attending the poor, and free vaccination services for the whole population. To ensure continuity of service the Treasury should also fund the employment of locums for medical practitioners whenever necessary. One correspondent, possibly mindful of the Medical Bill then under discussion, suggested that the position of medical practitioners should be protected by legislation to prohibit the activities of those quacks, parish ministers and other unqualified 'persons who injure the profession by visiting and prescribing, not only among the poor but among those who are able to pay.'[69]

Most medical practitioners felt that, without state support in some form, they would remain insecure and undervalued.

> Owing to the dependent circumstances in which all of us are placed in consequence of our small incomes, we cannot hold the status in society to which out profession entitles us. We are often looked down upon, even treated disrespectfully and contemptibly, by people who are our inferiors in every sense. We are in fact slaves of many masters. In this parish is a population of 3000 and for a trifling contribution to my small income I must be the humble servant of every one of them night and day. Superhuman labour is attendant on our professional avocation yet a mechanic in the south is a much more independent man than a district surgeon can aspire to here. Medical practitioners in these remote quarters ought to be on the same footing as the parish clergymen.

Their labour is a thousand times more valuable in the eyes of the community; their education is equal if not superior and their experience greater than that of a clergyman.[70]

Most parish ministers and medical practitioners were agreed that improvement in the income and status of medical practitioners could only be achieved as part of a radical reform of medical services. It was clearly anomalous that the state should provide those few parishioners permanently on the Poor Rolls with free medical care while the great majority in every parish, the working poor, had no guarantee of medical aid even when, in times of particular hardship, they could not find the funds to buy it for themselves and their families. It was imperative that there should be free medical treatment 'in the case of any family such as a tradesman or workman, previously supporting himself and his family but now laid upon a sickbed' and this could only be achieved by creating some new form of service.

It was implicit in every suggestion for the future of medical services in the Highlands and Islands that reliance on philanthropy must be abandoned. Rev Alexander Shand of Nesting spoke for all: 'I cannot see what philanthropy can do.' Philanthropy must be set aside and so also must the government's policy of *laissez faire*. It was accepted that nothing worthwhile could be achieved without government intervention. The more cautious proposed that government should introduce new legislation to oblige parishes to combine in small groups [larger local authorities] and be required, with Treasury support, to employ salaried medical officers to provide free services for all those in need.

More innovative schemes called for new services to be provided directly by central government:

The simplest and cheapest plan to give medicines and medical aid to tens of thousands living in the Hebrides would be to employ a few sober men of good character and energy, provided with medicines and instruments and a small steamboat (as the Marquis of Salisbury has done for Rum) to move constantly about among the people when they could conveniently assemble to be cured of their diseases. By this plan [salaried medical practitioners] would more economically and efficiently be brought into contact with the sick and the maimed than by the establishment of stationary practitioners.[71]

From the mainland parishes it was suggested that an 'association' should be organised to appoint an adequate number of salaried medical officers in service for every district. This new service, financed by the Treasury, could be staffed by the 'many of our own Army and Navy surgeons, unemployed and inadequately provided for.'[72] It was further suggested that, because of 'the filth and wretchedness of the hovels' in which the people lived, local hospitals should be established 'containing 10 to 20 beds.' This, in itself 'the best, and at all events the most practicable, scheme for the improvement of the chief evils to which the poor are exposed in cases of sickness,'[73] would also provide local centres for the proposed domiciliary medical services.

In 1850 these were radical proposals. They proceeded from the experience and pragmatic judgements of those with immediate professional responsibility for the welfare of the people among whom they lived. However they ran counter to the prevailing ideologies of those who directed the governance of the nation. At the Reformation, Scotland had adopted a religious ideology. The Kirk had become 'the real State in Scotland'[74] taking on important areas of collective responsibility, including the welfare of the education and welfare of the people. At the Union, the Kirk lost some of its authority but had come under little pressure to relinquish these responsibilities. After the split caused by the Disruption of 1843, the diminished Established Kirk had to accept that its parishes could no longer command the financial resources to provide for their poor. However, its Moderate leadership remained tied to the Union and was inhibited in promoting radical independent initiatives for Scotland. The new Free Church, led by the evangelical Thomas Chalmers, was more vigorous but insisted that the church, not the state, must retain responsibility for the welfare of its people.

The Royal Commission that had prepared the ground for the new Poor Law was much influenced by Chalmer's philosophical outlook[75] but its members had also recognised that, most clearly in the growing urban centres created by industrialisation, there was a 'new order of things.' The parish structure and organisation that had served mixed rural communities for centuries could not be successfully replicated in the new urban communities, especially in those parishes populated almost entirely by the new industrial poor. The Royal Commission recommended that responsibility for the Poor Law should no longer be left to the church.

But the industries which had created these new communities owed their success to free trade and a government policy of *laissez-faire*. Political economists had provided the intellectual arguments for a minimal role for government and, whenever possible, the avoidance of state intervention. Scotland's Samuel Smiles, in his phenomenally successful book, *Self Help*, would soon to be at the forefront of the promotion of moral improvement, personal initiative and personal responsibility as the only way to success. The Royal Commission did not advise an extension of state support to the able bodied; it ruled that 'if a man will not work, neither should he eat'.

Any calls for state aid for the poor and economically redundant could expect little sympathy and in the 1850s calls from the Highlands and Islands could expect no sympathy at all. Majority opinion in England and in Lowland Scotland had turned against the people of the Highlands and Islands. The arrival of the potato blight in the Highland and Islands in 1846, and the hunger and destitution visited on the people, had initially provoked widespread and generous concern but it had also attracted critical attention. *The Times* expected a 'substantial calamity'[76] in Scotland comparable with that in Ireland. Aid must be provided but, at the same time, the *Glasgow Herald* thought it must

. . . press upon the public attention . . . that no time may be lost in inquiring into the condition and prospects of the population who are thus deprived of their chief, and in the majority of cases, their sole means of subsistence.[77]

That inquiry brought down the judgement of both press and public. For five years observers commissioned by the nation's leading journals examined the causes of the endemic poverty in this distant part of Britain. They concluded that the explanation for their poverty lay in the people themselves. 'They preferred their habitual mode of life, their few days of desultory labour intermingled with weeks of lounging gossip, their half clad condition, to regular well paid toil.'[78] Even the Scottish press decided that 'the great cause of the destitution is not the failure of the potato crop but the intense and abominable idleness of the inhabitants.'[79] Due to a 'lack of energy, persevering vigour, enterprise and commercial spirit,'[80] no middle class had emerged to challenge an outdated patriarchal society made up of a few landlords and an ever-increasing number of poor.

When it had first become obvious that the potato crop had failed, schemes of relief had been quickly organised, principally by the Relief Committee of the Free Church of Scotland and by the Relief Committees set up in Edinburgh and Glasgow and a Central Board London. The system of relief was conducted according to the principles of the time. To give assistance to the able-bodied without demanding work in return was to encourage idleness and moral degradation. Meal must be paid for 'in the shape of labour.'[81] Over the next four years the relief schemes were successful in that there were no deaths from starvation and no deaths from 'famine fever.' But the Highlanders' reluctant and dilatory response to the demand for labour in exchange for meal brought disappointment and anger. The potato blight had attacked crops in almost every part of the British Isles but it had only caused destitution among the Gaels of Ireland and the Western Highlands and Islands of Scotland. These Celtic people, it was said, had 'submitted year after year to the visitation of famine, have folded their arms and prayed for better times, but to put their shoulder to the wheel, to know that Providence helps those who help themselves, is a lesson which they have yet to be taught.' It was said of the Highlanders, as of the Irish, that 'morally and intellectually they are an inferior race.' 'The whole wealth of the Lowlands, if it were now poured into the Highlands, would wither away, as if under the judgement of Heaven, among the idle hands of this people.'[82]

In advancing schemes for the improvement of medical services for their people, the parish ministers and medical practitioners of the Highlands and Islands were as voices crying from the wilderness. They were appealing on behalf of a distant and alien race whose predicament was the 'fruit of their vices.'[83] Help was being demanded from the industrious people of Britain, and to give such aid would be against, not only the popular principle of self-help, but also the successful government doctrine of *laissez faire*.

The Royal College of Physicians of Edinburgh was well aware of the views of the public. But it was sympathetic with the principles behind the proposals made by the ministers and medical practitioners of the Highland and Islands. In his book *Observations of the Famine of 1946–47*,[84] W P Alison, a prominent Fellow and former President, insisted that in spite of the many prejudices that had been expressed, the plight of the working poor in the Highlands was essentially no different from that of the working poor elsewhere in Scotland. In 1852, the Council of the College was of a mind to promote the idea that there should be state intervention to correct 'the evils of deficiency of medical aid' and particularly the 'anomaly of the very poor, who are recipients of parish aid, receiving more attention than those who are in comparatively independent circumstances, although unable to pay for medical aid'.[85] However, after some weeks of consideration, the strength of both public and government opinion was admitted and 'keeping in mind that the College should never aim at any object which they are unlikely to obtain'[86] it was decided to let the matter drop for the moment. The College was already deeply engaged in a campaign that seemed more urgent and more promising of success. Its President, Sir James Y Simpson, along when many others in the profession in Scotland, was concerned that doctors were being 'admitted to the honour of that name without learning.'[87] Along with other medical bodies the College was pressing for the reforms soon to be embodied in the Medical Act of 1858. The College gave first priority to ensuring that the public in Scotland would be able to rely on the competence of their medical practitioners but did not lose sight of the need to make competent medical services available to those who urgently required them.

In August 1852 the College published a *Statement Regarding the Existing Deficiency of Medical Practitioners in the Highlands and Islands* setting out only the statistics gathered in the inquiry inquiry. The radical proposals for some form of state medical service for the working poor, the great majority of the people of Britain, were not included and John Coldstream's correspondence was consigned to the College Archive. In 1852, proposals for state intervention, to provide essential medical care for those for whom it would otherwise be unaffordable, were out of their time. But in 1913 the same ideas reappeared in the creation of the Highlands and Islands Medical Service, the first comprehensive and free state health service in Britain and the forerunner of the National Health Service thirty-five years later.

Notes and References

1 Levitt, I and Smout, T C. *The State of the Scottish Working Class in 1843*, Edinburgh, 1979, 217.

2 Hamilton, D. The Highlands and Islands Medical Service. In McLachlan, G, *Improving the Common Weal*, Edinburgh, 1987.

3 Devine, T M. *The Great Highland Famine*, Edinburgh, 1988.

4 Rev John Keiller, letter to Dr. Coldstream, 2 December 1850. RCPE Archive.

5 Carlyle, T. *Chartism*, London, 1839.

6 Hodgkinson, R. *The Origins of the National Health Service*, London, 1967, 3.

7 *Ibid.*, 639.

8 Wm Cullen 1710–1790, Professor of Medicine, University of Edinburgh; Buchan, Wm. *Domestic Medicine or the Family Physician*, London, 1769.

9 Robert Cowan, Professor of Medical Jurisprudence and Police, Glasgow University; W Alison, Professor of Medical Jurisprudence and Professor of Medicine, Edinburgh University.

10 Alison, W. *Observations on the Management of the Poor in Scotland*, Edinburgh, 1840.

11 *Hansard* ixxxi, HC 12 June 1845, col 425.

12 *Ibid.*, col 1477.

13 Alison, W. *Remarks on the Report of Her Majesties Commissioners on the Poor Laws of Scotland*, Edinburgh, 1844.

14 Sir John McNeil, letter quoted in a Report of a Committee of the College, 3 February 1852. RCPE Archive.

15 *Hansard* ixxviii, HC 2 April 1945, col. 1399.

16 Richards, E. *The Highland Clearances*, Edinburgh, 2000, 32.

17 *New Statistical Account of Scotland*, vii, (1845), 185.

18 *New Statistical Account of Scotland*, xiv, (1845), 169.

19 *New Statistical Account of Scotland*, vii, (1845), 185.

20 *Ibid.*, 147.

21 Kiple, K F. *Cambridge World History of Human Disease*, Cambridge, 1993, 161.

22 Alison, W. *Observations on the Famine of 1846–47 in the Highlands of Scotland and in Ireland*, Edinburgh, 1847.

23 V. Cecil, great-great-granddaughter of John Coldstream. Personal communication.

24 Minutes of the Royal College of Physicians of Edinburgh, 16 July 1850.

25 *Ibid.*, 5 November 1850.

26 *Ibid.*, 2 July 1850.

27 There was no Medical Register until 1858.

28 Levitt and Smout, *op. cit*, Table 8A

29 Rev John MacIntyre, Delting. Royal College of Physicians of Edinburgh Archive. Coldstream Inquiry RCPE CI/149

30 John McLean, MD, Badcall. RCPE CI/511

31 Report of a Committee of the Royal College of Physicians of Edinburgh, 3 February 1852. RCPE Archive.

32 A single visit at a distance of a little over ten miles might command a fee of 30 shillings.

33 John Ferguson, surgeon, Dunvegan. RCPE CI/535.

34 Robert Clark, surgeon, Harris. RCPE CI/539

35 Donald Kennedy, surgeon, Lochalsh; John Fenton, surgeon Kilchoman; Robert Clerk, surgeon, Harris.

36 Colin MacTavish, surgeon, Kilarrow. RCPE CI/477.

37 *Ibid.*

38 *Ibid.*

39 Daniel Livingston, surgeon, Duror. RCPE CI/533

40 Roderick Maclean, MD, South Uist. RCPE CI/543.

41 *Ibid.*

42 Robert Clerk, *op. cit.*

43 Colin MacTavish, *op. cit.*

44 Daniel Livingston, *op. cit.*

45 Rev John Keillor, North Ronaldsay. RCPE CI/407.

46 Rev John Macleod, Morven. RCPE CI/135.

47 *Ibid.*

48 Rev John Mackay, Poolewe. RCPE CI/287

49 Rev J M Mamilton, Bressay. RCPE CI/423

50 Rev Coll MacDonald, Lochshiel. RCPE CI/123.

51 Rev Alexander MacKenzie, Kildalton. RCPE CI/99.

52 Rev John MacDonald, Helmsdale. RCPE CI/237.

53 Rev Henry Beaton, Barra. RCPE CI/339.

54 Sir John McNeil, *op. cit.*

55 John Fenton, surgeon, Bowmore. RCPE CI/473.

56 Alexander Duguid, MD, Kirkwall. RCPE CI/549

57 William Ballenden, surgeon, Stromness. RCPE CI/557.

58 Rev Joseph Caskey, Stronsay. RCPE CI/417

59 John McKellor, surgeon. Kilcalmonell. RCPE CI/463.

60 Charles Cook, surgeon, Lamlash. RCPE CI/467.

61 Colin MacTavish, *op. cit.*

62 Rev. Allan Gunn, Watten. RCPE CI/275.

63 *Ibid.*

64 Coll MacDonald, *op. cit.*

65 Rev John Keillor. North Ronaldsay. RCPE CI/407.

66 Rev Alexander Shand, Nesting. RCPE CI/453

67 Coll MacDonald, *op. cit.*

68 Porchaska, F K. Philanthropy. In Thomson, F M L, ed, *The Cambridge Social History of Britain*, iii, Cambridge, 1996, 357.

69 Daniel Cormick, surgeon, Beauly. RCPE CI/513

70 Robert Clark, *op. cit.*

71 Coll MacDonald, *op. cit.*

72 Rev John MacLeod, *op. cit.*

73 Rev Archibald Clerk, Kilmallie. RCPE CI/305.

74 Harvie, C. *Scotland and Nationalism*, London, 1994, 85.

75 Levitt I and Smout, C. *The State of the Scottish Working Class in 1843*, Edinburgh, 1979, 173.
76 *The Times*, 8 September 1847.
77 Quoted by Fenyö, K. *Contempt, Sympathy and Romance*, East Linton, 2000, 54.
78 *The Glasgow Herald*, 9 June 1845, quoted *ibid*, 48.
79 *Fyfeshire Journal*, 11 February 1947.
80 *Ibid.*, 56.
81 *Inverness Courier*, 10 February 1847.
82 *Scotsman*, 10 February 1847, quoted Fenyö, *op. cit*, 61.
83 Fenyö, *op. cit*, 64.
84 Alison, 1857, *op. cit.*
85 Report of a Committee of the Royal College of Physicians, 3 February 1853, *op. cit.*
86 Minutes of the Royal College of Physicians, 4 May 1852.
87 Duns, J. *Memoir of Sir James Y Simpson*, Edinburgh, 1873, 382.

The Unsung Heroines of Victorian Feminism: The Executive Committee of the Edinburgh Hospital for Women and Children, c1885–c1920

Elaine Thomson

Women's entry to the medical profession has received a good deal of attention from historians.[1] Their studies have tended to focus on the feminist politics of the struggle, or on the larger-than-life personalities of individual campaigning women. The political and professional success of the early medical women was, however, certainly in the Victorian period, dependent on local networks of committed supporters and sympathisers. Yet despite the importance of these local networks, the women who constituted them have been sadly neglected by scholars in their pursuit of what have been regarded as more high-profile historical subjects and personalities. The local context of grass-roots feminist support remains an unexplored, but essential, background to any full historical appreciation of the nineteenth-century women's rights' movement. To throw some light on the constitution of local feminist networks, the middle-class women of Edinburgh who lent their support to the foundation and operation of the Edinburgh Hospital and Dispensary for Women and Children – the first hospital in Scotland to be founded and run by women – provides an instructive case study. This essay will build up a profile of the political interests of those women who worked on the Executive Committee of the Edinburgh Hospital, and highlight their personal involvement with various national and local women's rights campaigns, societies and institutions.

The Edinburgh Provident Dispensary for Women and Children was the first medical institution to be established by a female physician in Britain outside London.[2] It was founded by Sophia Jex-Blake, charismatic leader of the campaign for the medical education of women, at 73 Grove Street in September of 1878, the year after her return to the city as a qualified medical practitioner. Primarily established to serve the interests of women doctors in the city, in 1885 the tiny Dispensary transferred to 6 Grove Street and was expanded to become a cottage hospital containing six beds. This venture was such a success that the Hospital moved once again to larger and better equipped premises in 1900. Although the *de facto* founder of the Dispensary (and in 1885 of the Hospital), it is clear that Jex-Blake could not have succeeded in the venture without the help of a group of enthusiastic, like-minded local women. These women backed the establishment of the Dispensary and Hospital and went on to make up its Executive Committee. Over the years, their close involvement with the day-to-day running of the Hospital and Dispensary meant that they were crucial in ensuring its success and in giving it its unique character.

The first volume of minutes from the Executive Committee meetings is wanting, as are the Annual Reports of the Edinburgh Hospital and Dispensary from 1878 to 1899. The earliest we can join the Committee, therefore, is 1884, the year before the Dispensary expanded to become a small hospital. During these early years, the main Committee members were: Miss Margaret Orr; Mrs Elizabeth Pease Nichol; Miss Dick Lauder (all three resigned in 1884[3]); Miss Ursula Du Pre; Mrs Dora Burn Murdoch; Mrs Emily Jackson; Mrs Emma C Beilby; Mrs Hugh Rose; Mrs M H Urmiston; Miss Alexina Edington; Miss Isabella Spring Brown; Mrs E H Sheills; Mrs Annette Haldane; Mrs Sibbald and Mrs Alexander Russel. Between 1890 and 1899, due to the resignation of some of the above, eight new members were appointed: Miss C H Elliott Lockhart; Lady Chalmers; Mrs Somerville; Miss Stodart; Mrs Kirkwood; Mrs Wilson; Miss Sarah Elizabeth Siddons Mair and Miss Margaret Houldsworth.[4]

Of these ladies, three were close personal friends of Jex-Blake, and had supported the campaign for the medical education of women from its outset: Miss Du Pre, Miss Orr and Mrs Burn Murdoch.[5] Four more had been original members of the Committee for Securing a Complete Medical Education for Women, which was founded in 1871 during the height of the campaign in Edinburgh (renamed the National Association for the Medical Education of Women in 1879.[6]): Mrs Nichol, Miss Mair, Mrs Rose and Miss Edington.[7] Two had begun to study medicine themselves, but had not completed their training: Mrs Alexander Russel, and Mrs Somerville. The former had been one of Jex-Blake's group of seven pioneer women medical students, but had given up her studies to marry the editor of the *Scotsman* – a keen supporter of the medical women – in 1871. Although Mrs Somerville also failed to complete her professional training as a doctor, she remained dedicated to the cause of medical women, becoming treasurer of Jex-Blake's extra-mural medical school for women, and remaining an active member of the

Hospital's Executive Committee until 1935.[8] One committee member, Mrs Sibbald, was the wife of a doctor.[9]

Many of the women on the Committee also had connections with the women's movement, both on a local and a national level. Indeed, between them, this group of committee ladies embody the ideological links between the earliest feminist movements in the 1820s, the campaigns for higher education in the 1870s, and the first successful conclusion of the campaign for women's suffrage in 1918. They include activists, campaigners, and suffragists, those who joined groups, attended meetings, gave speeches, or simply donated money.

The most distinguished member of the committee was Elizabeth Pease Nichol (1807–1897), who was one of the earliest and most vocal supporters of Jex-Blake's campaign for the medical education of women.[10] Mrs Nichol was the daughter of an English Quaker manufacturer, who was closely involved in the abolition of slavery. She became involved in this work, first as her father's secretary, and then as a member of the Women's Abolition Society of Darlington. She corresponded with the leaders of the American anti-slavery movement, and became the most influential women in the British abolitionist group. In the 1840s and 1850s she attended various international congresses on issues such as abolition of slavery and world peace. She was also active in the campaigns for Catholic emancipation, the abolition of the Test Acts, and Free Trade. The feminism which she became involved with from the 1860s onwards was only one aspect of her general concern for human rights; other causes which she supported included Chartism, the Anti-Corn Law League, Italian unification, and the RSPCA. She was on friendly terms with Richard Cobden, John Bright, William Lloyd Garrison and Wendell Phillips. In 1853 she married John Pringle Nichol, Regius Professor of Astronomy at Glasgow University and himself a vigorous advocate of social reform, and moved to Scotland. (This caused a breach with the Society of Friends, as she had married outside the Quaker circle.) On the death of her husband in 1859 Mrs Nichol moved to Edinburgh and during the 1860s her interest in woman's rights grew from sympathy to activity. She was close friends with Duncan McLaren MP and his wife (who was John Bright's sister), both of whom strongly supported the medical women (their daughter, Agnes, was one of them), and were also high profile activists in the movement for women's suffrage. In 1871 Mrs Nichol was one of the founder members of the Committee for Securing the Complete Medical Education of Women in Scotland. She was also a member of the Committee for Women's Suffrage, which had been set up by Mrs McLaren, and was one of the earliest members of the Scottish Suffrage Society, appearing at numerous meetings and demonstrations for this cause throughout the 1880s.[11] She was an executive committee member of the Ladies National Association for the Repeal of the Contagious Diseases Acts, and was well acquainted with Josephine Butler. At the same time she lent her support to the Edinburgh Ladies Education Association (ELEA) and the Edinburgh Association for the University Education for Women (EAUEW), being a member of the former from 1868, and one of the first to donate money for the foundation of Masson Hall, the hall of residence for women at Edinburgh University, in 1893–4.[12] She retired from a lifetime of active campaigning at the same time that she resigned from the executive committee of the Edinburgh Dispensary for Women and Children, in 1884. Her last recorded public appearance was at the age of 77, as a delegate at the Scottish National Demonstration for Women in 1884.[13]

Given the lifelong commitment of Mrs Nichol to radical causes, it is perhaps not surprising that she supported the medical women and was a member of the committee of their hospital in Edinburgh. The length and diversity of Mrs Nichol's activities illustrates the extent to which 'the nineteenth century feminist movement was bound up with a wider movement for social reform'.[14] They also reveal the fundamental humanitarian concerns which underlay the different strands of nineteenth century feminism. Mrs Nichol herself implied such a common cause in a letter to Jex-Blake giving her written support to the medical women's campaign after the Royal Infirmary elections in January 1870. 'You, and the struggle you are carrying on' she wrote, 'remind me so forcibly of the contest which the band of women in America so nobly waged against the demon of Slavery.'[15] The claim of the medical women for equal opportunities, in terms of both their right to higher education and their need for better employment opportunities through access to the professions, was linked to the same equal rights philosophy which, as a part of the intellectual legacy of the Enlightenment, had inspired many of the early nineteenth century social reforms with which Mrs Nichol had been involved. Mrs Nichol's distinguished presence on the Committee embodied the intellectual continuity between the humanitarian causes of the early nineteenth century radical reformers and the movements for women's rights during the later nineteenth century.

Few members of the Hospital committee could boast such a list of diverse, yet worthy, causes in which they were, or had been, involved. However, most had definite links with other feminist groups, interests, and institutions. Many, for instance, had either attended classes, or where involved with the running of the ELEA. For example, Emily Jackson was registered for, and passed, classes in Logic and Mental Philosophy in the academic year from 1882–3, and Moral Philosophy in 1884; and Mrs Hugh Rose attended classes in Geology in 1889–90 and 1891, Latin in 1890–91 and Physiology in 1886–87.[16] In the Annual Reports for the ELEA and EAUEW from 1968, and throughout the 1870s and 1880s, as ordinary members and Executive Committee members we find Miss Dick Lauder, Miss Spring Brown, Miss Edington, Miss Stodart, Miss Houldsworth and Miss Mair.[17] By 1900, the Association boasted Miss Houldsworth, Miss Edington and Miss Dick Lauder as members,[18] whilst life membership was granted to Miss Edington, Miss Houldsworth and Miss Mair.[19] Among the first list of donations to the 'Masson Hall Fund' in 1893–4 were those received from Miss Houldsworth, Miss Mair, and Mrs Hugh Rose.[20]

Two Ladies who joined the Hospital Committee in 1898 and 1899, Miss Sarah Elizabeth Siddons Mair and Miss Houldsworth, were well known throughout the city, and were closely involved with the ELEA. Miss Mair (1846–1941) became one of the leading figures on the Hospital committee from 1898 to 1922 (at which point she left the Executive Committee and became Vice President, a position she held until 1940). Although always non-militant, from the age of 19, she was involved in almost every group in the city which was concerned with the advancement of women's rights. In 1865 she founded the Edinburgh Essay Society, which became the Ladies Edinburgh Debating Society in 1872, and which met in her front room every Saturday morning for 70 years. Rae credits the Society with being the first in the country to discuss the question of extending the franchise to women.[21] Sarah Mair also helped to edit the *Ladies Edinburgh Magazine* (1875–1898), previously called *The Attempt* (1869–75) – a journal which grew out of her debating society and discussed feminist issues, such as the extension of the suffrage, and the right of women to paid employment and higher education.

From the 1860s, both Miss Mair and Miss Houldsworth were prominent figures in the local movement for the university education of women. Their names appear regularly on the class registers and members lists of the ELEA and EAUEW,[22] and during the 1870s and 1880s both ladies created bursaries to enable women to study in these organisations.[23] By 1879, Miss Houldsworth was Vice President of the Association, and by 1900 Miss Mair was Honorary Treasurer.[24] Both ladies were also amongst the founders of St George's School for Girls in 1888 – a college set up by the ELEA specifically for women students to further their teacher training – and were members of its committee of management for many years.[25] Sarah Mair was also Honorary Treasurer at Masson Hall during the 1890s.[26]

Margaret Houldsworth, although committed to the ELEA and EAUEW, was a more reserved woman than Miss Mair. Rosaline Masson remembered her as a quiet figure, who remained in the shadow of more vigorous personalities in

the Association, 'never coming out to the open, but generous with help in money or kind, both to the Association and to the students'.[27] Indeed, Miss Houldsworth was one of the most generous contributors to the cause of women's education in the city, establishing bursaries at the ELEA, St George's School, and Masson Hall.[28] On her death in 1909, she left a bequest of £3,000 to the Edinburgh Hospital for Women and Children and The Hospice (from 1924 the Elsie Inglis Memorial Maternity Home) for the purpose of developing these institutions further for the teaching and training of medical women in the practice of gynaecology and midwifery in Edinburgh.[29]

A number of the women on the committee of the Edinburgh Hospital for Women and Children were only involved with feminism on this specific, local level – simply attending classes at the ELEA. As Olive Banks has observed, 'active involvement in the women's movement was, even for the most conservative of feminists, a conscious and deliberate act of revolt, even if it was only a revolt against the current belief that intellectual pursuits were harmful and inappropriate for women'.[30] However, the connection between the members of the Hospital Committee and the movement for women's rights was not entirely restricted to their involvement with the local campaign for women's higher education, although this was a distinctive feature of its composition. A number of the Committee women were also involved in national feminist campaigns, such as the campaign for the extension of the suffrage. Mrs Emma C Beilby, for example, who devoted over fifty five years of her life to committee work at the Edinburgh Hospital for Women and Children (as did her sister, Mrs Sheills[31]), was a keen supporter of the campaign for women doctors, and for women's rights in general.[32] Unfortunately, public evidence of Mrs Beilby's support for women's rights – aside from her involvement with the women's hospital – is limited to her name on the Annual Report of the Scottish University Women's Suffrage Union in 1918.[33]

Emma Beilby was one of Jex-Blake's earliest patients,[34] and was committed to the success of the medical women and the development of their institutions. This interest and dedication, however, was not restricted to Edinburgh, as is made clear by the large sums of money which she bequeathed to six women's hospitals throughout Britain, all of which she had been involved with, through donations of money, for many years. The Edinburgh Hospital for Women and Children, and the South London Hospital for Women and Children received the largest bequests; with the Elizabeth Garrett Anderson Hospital in London, the New Sussex Hospital for Women and Children, the Clapham Maternity Hospital and Bristol Private Hospital for Women and Children receiving smaller sums. She was also involved with charities for the prevention of cruelty to children and animals, leaving generous contributions to the RSPCA and the NSPCC. Furthermore, her belief in the importance of higher education for women was confirmed by further substantial donations to Somerville College, Oxford and Bedford College in London.[35] These bequests reveal a commitment to a number of women's institutions throughout the country. Although, as far as we can tell, remaining out of the limelight of the feminist campaigns, Mrs Beilby was, clearly, none the less deeply sympathetic to the causes they espoused.

The most co-ordinated and widely supported feminist campaign was that for the extension of the franchise to women. Although the issue of votes for women had been simmering since the 1860s, it emerged more forcefully in the 1880s and 1890s, and was the last major feminist cause of the nineteenth, and early twentieth century.[36] Of the Hospital's most long serving Committee members, one Sarah Mair, became increasingly involved with the campaign for women's suffrage. She attended many meetings on the subject, and was a delegate at the Scottish National Demonstration for Women in 1884.[37] She was the president of the Edinburgh Women's Franchise Association – a non-party and non-militant body – and, after the extension of the franchise in 1918, of the Edinburgh Women's Citizen's Association.[38] She was also a member, along with Margaret Houldsworth, of the Edinburgh National Association for Women's Suffrage,

and the Scottish Churches' League for Women's Suffrage.[39]

Despite the limited sources available on the suffrage movement in Scotland,[40] there is evidence that a number of the ladies on the Committee were involved with, or at least lent their support to, this campaign. Mrs Nichol and Mrs Beilby have already been mentioned in connection with this aspect of the women's movement. In addition, however, Mrs Somerville and Lady Chalmers were delegates at the Scottish National Demonstration for Women in 1884, which was held 'on the subject of extending the franchise to women householders'; and at similar meetings in 1882 and 1894 we also find Mrs Hugh Rose.[41]

It is clear, therefore, that many of the women on the committee of the Hospital actively took part in the various feminist campaigns of the period. Biographical sketches of the older and longer serving members of the committee reveal that there are definite strands of continuity and solidarity between the different women's rights activities throughout the nineteenth century. In particular, the recurrence of the names of the same women in a number of separate campaigns reveals that Victorian, or 'first wave' feminism was based on a series of social networks, linked often by personal friendships, and strengthened by the commitment and interaction of the same individuals to the different causes. From this, feminism derived a special nexus of support and solidarity in which it was able to flourish.

Clearly, the Edinburgh Hospital for Women and Children was crucial as a focus in the city for women who had a common interest in women's rights. Furthermore, in addition to training women doctors it provided the Executive Committee with the opportunity to gain leadership skills as well as the secretarial, accounting and general administrative expertise essential to women if they were to enter professional life. Indeed, traditionally excluded from the administration of hospitals, the Executive Committee of the Edinburgh Hospital was unique in the city in that it provided the first opportunity for Victorian women to explore the possibilities of hospital administration. By the early twentieth-century, the significance of the Edinburgh Hospital in these terms was still being remarked upon by the Secretary of the Executive Committee. 'In themselves', remarked Mrs Johnson, Secretary to the Hospital in the 1920s, '[hospitals staffed entirely by women] offer a chance of medical service and development which is proving of great value not only to medical women, but to the whole question of hospital administration'.[42] As members of the Hospital's Executive, these local women were an active part of the movement for the involvement of women more widely into public life, whilst their involvement with the medical women's Hospital was just one aspect of their dedication to the extension of women's rights

Notes and References

1 For example, Wilson, D C. *Lone Woman (Elizabeth Blackwell)*, Boston and Toronto, 1970; Ross, I. *Child of Destiny (Elizabeth Blackwell)*, New York, 1949; Manton, J. *Elizabeth Garrett Anderson*, London, 1965; Roberts, Shirley. *Sophia Jex-Blake: A Women Pioneer in Nineteenth-Century Medical Reform*, London, 1993; Todd, Margaret. *The Life of Sophia Jex-Blake*, London, 1918; Balfour, Frances. *Dr Elsie Inglis*, London and New York, 1918, Lawrence, M. *Shadow of Swords: A Biography of Elsie Inglis*, London, 1971; Blake, Catriona. *The Charge of the Parasols: Women's Entry to the Medical Profession*, London, 1990; Moberly-Bell, E. *Storming the Citadel: The Rise of the Woman Doctor*, London, 1953; Lutzker, Edythe. *Women Gain a Place in Medicine*, New York and London, 1969; Lovejoy, Esther Pohl. *Women Doctors of the World*, New York, 1958.

2 The New Hospital for Women had been founded by Elizabeth Garrett Anderson in London in 1872. Blake, *op cit*, 217.

3 Edinburgh Hospital for Women and Children (EHWC) Executive Committee Minutes, vol 2, 11 Nov. 1884, 22. (Lothian Health Board Archives, Bruntsfield Hospital Papers (LHB8), Edinburgh University Main Library (EUML))

4 Bye Laws of the Edinburgh Dispensary for Women and Children, 1883; Executive Committee Minutes, vol 2 (LHB8, EUML).

5 Todd, *op cit*, 221–3, 106, 110 and 229.

6 *Ibid*, 509–510. Blake, *op cit*, 191.

7 Todd, *op cit*, 510.

8 EHWC Annual Report 1953, 5 (LHB8, EUML)

9 Todd, *op cit*, 340–341 and 525; EHWC Annual Report 1900–1901 (LHB8, EUML).

10 Todd, *op cit*, 300 and 303.

11 See, for example, *Englishwoman's Review* (1882), 131; *The Scotsman*, 24 March 1882; *The Scotsman*, 14 October 1884.

12 Edinburgh Ladies Education Association (ELEA) Annual Report Members List, 1868, also Edinburgh Association for the University Education of Women (EAUEW) Annual Report 1893 (Edinburgh University Archives, EUML).

13 *The Scotsman*, March 24 1884. See Stoddart, Anna. *Elizabeth Pease Nichol*, London, 1899; Obituary in *Englishwoman's Review*, 15 April 1897; Banks, Olive. *Biographical Dictionary of British Feminists, Vol 1, 1800–1930*, Brighton, 1985, 140; Blake, *op cit*, 130–131; Todd, *op cit*, 302–303; Annual Reports and Calendars of the ELEA and EAUEW 1868–1900.

14 Banks, *op cit*, 140.

15 Todd, *op cit*, 303.

16 ELEA and EAUEW Class Registers, 1882–1888. Elsie Inglis attended the classes in Moral Philosophy, and Physiology in 1886–7, and English Literature in 1884–5.

17 ELEA Annual Reports and Calendars 1868–1880.

18 EAUEW Annual Report 1900.

19 EAUEW Annual Report 1899.

20 EAUEW Annual Report 1893–4.

21 Milne Rae, Lettice. *Ladies In Debate: Being a History of the Ladies Edinburgh Debating Society 1865–1935*, Edinburgh, 1936; Hamilton, Sheila. 'Women and the Scottish Universities, c 1896–1939', PhD, Edinburgh University, 1987, 25.

22 ELEA and EAUEW Annual Reports 1868–1900; ELEA and EAUEW Class Registers 1882–1888.

23 Hamilton, *op cit*, 173; ELEA Annual Report 1884.

24 ELEA Annual Reports 1879–80 and 1900.

25 Hamilton, *op cit*, 104–105.

26 EAUEW Annual Report 1893–94; Hamilton, *op cit*, 163; Boog-Watson, E. The First Eight Ladies, *University of Edinburgh Journal*, 23 (1970), 227–34.

27 Letter to Miss Elspeth Boog-Watson from Miss Rosaline Masson, 1948, (Edinburgh University Archives).

28 Hamilton, *op cit*, 173.

29 EHWC Annual Report 1909. Biographical details on Mair and Houldsworth are from Rae, *op cit*; *The Scotsman*, Monday 17 Feb 1941; *The Scotsman*, Wednesday 19 Feb 1941; *The Scotsman*, Saturday 19 Feb 1941; Edinburgh Women's Citizen's Association Souvenir Coming of Age, Edinburgh, 1939; Hamilton, *op cit*, chapters 1 and 2; In Memoriam: Sarah Elizabeth Siddons Mair, EAUEW Papers; Annual Reports and Calendars of the ELEA

and EAUEW 1868–1900 (Edinburgh University Archives).

30 Banks, Olive. *Faces of Feminism: The Social Origins of First Wave Feminism*, Oxford, 1981, 9.

31 Mrs Beilby was one of the original committee members of the Dispensary in 1878, and she remained on the executive committee up to her death in 1935. Mrs Sheills was on the executive committee from the early 1880s to 1934. EHWC Annual Reports 1934 and 1935 (LHB, EUML).

32 Correspondence with Mr O J Beilby.

33 From the Scottish University Women's Suffrage Union, 7th, 8th, 9th and 10th Annual Reports. Mrs Beilby was also the 'Glasgow delegate' for the Women's Suffrage Society in London in 1917. Letter from Mrs Beilby to Mrs Johnson, 2 February 1917 (LHB8, EUML).

34 Todd, *op cit*, 525.

35 Beilby private papers.

36 Banks, *Faces of Feminism*, 46.

37 *The Scotsman*, Wednesday 13 October 1884; *English-woman's Review* (1894), 25; *The Scotsman*, Monday 24 March 1884.

38 Edinburgh Women Citizens Association Souvenir Coming of Age, *op cit*.

39 Hamilton, *op cit*, 274.

40 *Ibid*, 358. The main work on the movement in Scotland is a pamphlet by King, Elspeth. *Scottish Women's Suffrage Movement*, Glasgow, 1978; reprinted 1985. See also *idem*, 'The Scottish Women's Suffrage Movement', in Breitenbach, Esther and Gordon, Eleanor, eds. *Out of Bounds: Women in Scottish Society, 1800–1945*, Edinburgh, 1992, 121–150.

41 *The Scotsman*, Monday 24 March 1884; *Englishwoman's Review* (1882), 131; *Englishwoman's Review* (1894), 25.

42 Letter from Mrs J C Johnson to Mrs F M Huxley, (n d) (LHB8, EUML).

Analysis of Some Aspects of New Noth, Aberdeenshire Farm Diary, 1801–1850

Susan Storrier

This Aberdeenshire diary covers the period from 1746 to the twentieth century. Early entries are, however, concerned with the affairs of Lady Aroundall and not with Noth itself. The farm is first mentioned in 1801, in connection with the lands of Achairn, Binhall and Reidfold. By 1803 New Noth appears alone, although areas of unnamed grass lets are also noted. The first reference to Old Noth is in 1837 and it seems that sometime in the 1820s or 1830s the two farms were taken under the same management. We do not know the exact date of amalgamation as rent entries often do not state the properties concerned. However, in 1827 there occurred a jump in Noth's rent from £39. 15/- to £53. 10/-, and it may assumed be that this was the year of Old Noth's inclusion.

The information presented in this diary is frequently fragmentary in nature and this has greatly hampered analysis. For a number of years there is no information available; 1810, 1814, 1816, 1819, 1820, 1823–28, and 1837–43 all fail to have entries. It is possible, however, that further study of the diary will fill in at least some of the gaps. Entries do not appear to have always been made in chronological order and the writer, when examining the document in 1989, did not have the time to look beyond the main block of 1850 entries. It may be that some of the missing information will present itself amongst the later material.

New Noth farm diary offers a wide range of information within the 1801–1850 period. Cash labour costs were focused on as these were particularly amenable to quantitative analysis. These were examined in relation to the general picture of New Noth's income and expenditure.

Income

Income for New Noth was largely derived from the farm's locally exported produce – both arable and pastoral – and from the kind and cash rent payments of sub-tenants. A very small proportion of the income came from bank interest and from the boarding of artisans and day labourers. Occasionally there are references to New Noth borrowing money, either from other farmers or from his own sub-tenants. On 27 August 1827, for example, he borrowed £2. 0/- from sub-tenant John Ord.

The destination of the bulk of the farm's produce was the sub-tenantry themselves or the markets at Rhynie, Huntly and Clatt. In 1828 sub-tenant Heugh Dallas bought 'Meall Beaff and Potatoes and 4 load of fire from the hill' from New Noth at a price of £3. 15/-. There is also evidence of commodities being occasionally transported to Aberdeen. Arable produce consisted of oats, bere, barley (sold mainly to the local distilleries), peas, potatoes, turnips and seeds. Pastoral equivalents were cheese, butter, beef, mutton, hides, tallow and feathers, plus livestock consisting of pigs, sheep, cows, bulls, marts, calves and horses.

Rents were paid to New Noth for farms, smaller holdings and grazings, and very occasionally for small patches of land used by fee'd farm servants. Most entries in the diary referring to sub-tenants' rents list only one person. This may have been simply for reasons of convenience, but it is more likely that joint tenancy was rare. There is, however, one instance of two brothers – or perhaps father and son – sharing a tenancy, Charles and George Dawson in 1847. Occasionally sub-tenants are female. In 1834 Ann Dey paid £0. 17/- for an unspecified holding. In 1844 Ann Henry paid £0. 10/- for grass, while Miss Jean Russel paid £72. 0/-, Mrs Russel £100. 0/-, and Mrs MacGrigor the impressive sum of £300. 0/- (the highest rent paid by any sub-tenant, though she may well have been paying arrears). The majority of cash rents paid by men were less than £10 a year.

Considerable proportions of the sub-tenants' rents were paid in kind. James Steuart in 1822 entered into a seven-year agreement with New Noth whereby he would have three and a half acres of land in return for £2 an acre plus four bolls of meal and two days' work a year. It was impractical in the time available to record the amount of produce received by New Noth in the 1801–1850 period and thus gauge the importance of rent in kind in relation to cash rents. However, the significance of oats and livestock as a means of payment was apparent.

Expenditure

New Noth's expenditure can be divided into four categories: labour; rents, leases and taxes; commodities; and miscellaneous expenditure. The cost of transportation, postage, entertaining and charitable donations are included in the latter category, as are loans to other farmers or, as was more often the case, to sub-tenants. Sub-tenant John Pittendreich received £1. 10/- on 27 August 1827, the same day as New Noth himself was borrowing from sub-tenant John Ord.

Commodities bought by New Noth fall into two groups: produce and goods bought from other farms and holdings; and goods bought from nearby market centres. From neighbours and sub-tenants came oats, clover, bere, unspecified fodder, calves, horses, foals, marts, sheep, lambs, pigs, meat, wood, oil, and tar. At the town, New Noth purchased flour, salt, fish, tea, honey, porter, whisky, tobacco, clocks, a barometer, a perspective glass, papers, almanacs, maps, books, a pack of cards, ribbon, napkins, bonnets, clothes, cloth, lint, furniture (a dresser, chest of drawers, tables and chairs), powder and shot, nails, locks, ropes, canvas, tar, tools (ploughs and harrows), carts, seeds (clover and ryegrass), iron, coal, lime (there was an account with Ardonald), and a share in the North of Scotland Life Assurance Company.

Taxes to be paid included turnpike dues, church tithes, cess, horse tax, house tax, window tax, road tax and road building contributions (the road from Huntly to Keith is mentioned on several occasions), and mill taxes (for corn and lint until such time as New Noth built his own mill). Contributions also had to be paid for school carriage and to the wives and families of the militia. On one occasion £40. 0/- was paid to a stand-in for the militia. Rents were paid for Old and New Noth, Achairn, Binhall and Reidfold. A nineteen year lease of New Noth was purchased for £100. 0/- in 1804 and a grassum for New Noth was paid to the Duke of Gordon in 1845. It was of £350. 0/-. Money was also paid for grazings separate from the main farm, as in 1837 when £12. 15/- was paid for 'pasture grass in the hill moss'. The main rents appear to have been fairly stable at £17. 0/- in the 1801–1803 period, £39. 15/- in 1805–1817 (for New Noth alone), and £53. 10/- from 1827 onwards (it is presumed for Old and New Noth together).

Rents, leases, and taxes accounted for a considerable proportion of New Noth's total cash expenditure, but more money was spent on employing labour (£2263. 19/4 as opposed to £1769. 19/1 ½). The total rent received from sub-tenants, however, rarely covered New Noth's own rent, and so it must be assumed that the farm was largely reliant on the sale of its produce to provide cash income. This reliance increases throughout the fifty-year period while rents from sub-tenants become less significant.

Labour was paid for not only in cash. Board and lodging and other forms of payment in kind seem to have sometimes been used to pay certain employees. Likewise many sub-tenants would labour for New Noth as part-payment for their holdings. The cash labour picture, then, is very far from the total labour story.

Five categories of labour can be discerned in this diary: farm labour employed by the term (fee'd labour); harvest labour; artisan and specialized non-professional services; professional services; and a miscellaneous category (often consisting of labour paid by the day or piece workers).

Farm Labour Employed by the Term (Fee'd Labour)

This was by far the most important form of labour employed on the farm, at least in terms of the amount of cash spent. Some 61 per cent of the total sum spent over the fifty year period on labour was assigned to paying fee'd workers (£1376. 1/3 from a total of £2263. 19/4).

The importance of fee'd labour seems to have increased throughout the period under consideration. Both in terms of numbers of people involved and sums spent on wages the situation in relation to male workers is the more significant and grows increasingly so through time. Female wage levels and numbers, although also increasing through time, do so at a far lesser rate. The total spent on female fee'd labour during the half-century amounted to only 20 per cent of the total fee'd labour cost. Wages for female workers appear to have been much more uniform than those of male workers, although a greater range of wages was in general being paid out to both men and women through time. This might indicate greater specialization in work and stratification of workers, along with a widening of the range of jobs to be done on the farm. Certainly there are occasional references throughout the fifty years to paying herd-boys, cattlemen and horsemen.

It should be remembered that these observations have been made on the basis of incomplete and at times ambiguous data, the more so for female workers. Some payments are noted merely as 'wages' and it is impossible to know the type of labour they cover. Where fee'd labour is clearly identified, it has sometimes been necessary to calculate averages on the basis of just one or two figures, permitting anomalies to be retained. The length of a fee is not always stated and it is impossible to ascertain if variant spellings in Christian names and surnames indicate different people or simply inconsistency on New Noth's behalf (displayed elsewhere). It may also be the case that children's wages are included in their parents' fees. New Noth made a note of paying James Grant's herding fee to his mother, but could have failed to record similar instances. In a number of cases he states that a payment is only part of that due to an individual and fails to record if the rest of the fee was paid or, of it was, when it was paid.

Harvest Labour

Harvest labour accounted for approximately seven per cent of the total labour expenditure over the fifty year period (£148. 14/9 from a total of £2263. 19/4). This surprisingly low figure may be the result of harvest wages being entered in the diary simply as 'wages', as outlined above. In addition much of the harvest work may have been paid in kind, especially board and lodging.

72 per cent of the total sum spent on harvest labour was paid to male workers. Although rates of pay seem to have been higher for males than for females for every year except 1850, the disparity between both groups' wages was on the whole much less significant than that of the fee'd workers. Indeed it seems that a woman could often earn as much, or even more, at the harvest than she could from six months' fee'd work. At the start of the nineteenth century men could also earn as much at the harvest as they could in six months, but as time passed fees rose to be considerably higher than harvest wages. For both sexes harvest wages appear

to have been relatively stable, despite short-term fluctuations.

Twenty-three women were employed over the fifty years at harvest-time as opposed to thirty-eight male workers. There was a trend to employ more male harvesters as time progressed whilst female numbers remained more or less constant. However Old Noth's inclusion has to be considered again, and it may be that there was in fact a decline in the real numbers of female New Noth harvesters.

With harvest labour costs there are the same problems of poor quality data. Averages were calculated on very few figures (again this was especially the case in regard to female labour). In addition, a sum was occasionally said to cover both harvest fee and payment for some unspecified form of labour.

Artisan and Specialized Non-Professional Services / Professional Services

Professional services were used very infrequently by New Noth and consisted of medical services, undertaking, sewing and dancing instruction, and the work of lawyers, writers and sheriff's officers.

The artisan and specialized non-professional services used on the farm encompassed blacksmithing, farriering, saddlery, shoemaking (New Noth had accounts with a saddler and with a shoemaker, George Cran, both paid twice yearly), weaving, carding, wright work, masons' work, thatching (although this was sometimes carried out by fee'd farm labour), tailoring, dyeing, bookbinding, castrating, watch repairing, gardening, and mole-catching.

There was a 99.8 per cent male contribution to these two combined categories of labour. The amount spent on such work varied from year to year although a gradual overall increase can be discerned throughout the study period with an accelerated rise between 1845 and 1850.

The two categories together accounted for around 16 per cent of the total labour costs of the fifty year period (£353. 10/4 out of £2263. 19/4). Seven trades accounted for roughly 72 per cent of this.

Percentage of total sum spent on
Artisan and Specialized Non-Professional
Services / Professional Services

Blacksmithing and Farriering 27.9%
Shoemaking 14.6%
Saddlery 9.2%
Masons' Work 7.5%
Weaving and Carding 3.9%

As far as blacksmithing and farriering are concerned, there appears to have been a substantial increase in the amount of cash spent on them in the years 1846 and 1847, perhaps indicating an expansion of the use of horses on the farm.

Miscellaneous Labour

This category, which more or less accords with day labouring and piece work, accounted for roughly 16 per cent of the total sum spent on labour during the half century (£367. 14/1 out of £2263. 19/4). Of that, 92 per cent went to pay male workers. There was a considerable increase in spending on male labour of this kind in the late 1820s. A rise occurs again in the late 1840s, but this time the increase applies to both male and female workers. The inclusion of Old Noth seems an unsatisfactory explanation for all of this. Certainly there was a particularly close recording of spending in the years 1827 and 1828 which is itself significant and might affect the figures, but it is reasonable to assume that there was some real increase in this type of work carried out on the farm. New Noth was certainly undertaking a growing number of 'improvements' on his lands. Draining, ditching, dyking, mill-building and various upgradings of and modifications to the farm buildings are all attested to, with such entries appearing more frequently as the diary progresses. Employing more piece workers seems to have been a favoured strategy for providing the necessary labour for such activities and it is interesting to note that many of these workers appear to have come from the sub-tenantry. A sample entry for 23 May 1836 goes as follows:

> Received from Wm. Fraser his rent and sundries
> at the same time paid him for casting 412 ells

at 11 per ell and 23 days work at ½ per day
£3. 5/1.

Male workers were employed to build dykes,
ditch (these two activities were particularly
important), thatch, herd, assist with building,
slaughter, glaze, cast peats, construct roads, cut
grass, drive, transport and undertake general
odd-jobbing. Women earned money by setting
peats, hoeing, drawing straw and racking.

Conclusion

In this analysis of the cash labour information in
New Noth farm diary, 1801–1850, a quantitative
approach has been taken throughout. The data
is far from ideal, and the time available to the
writer limited. Nevertheless it has been possible
to make a number of tentative statements.

The cost of employing labour on the farm
seems to have been New Noth's greatest cash
burden, which the income from sub-tenants' cash
rents did not in any way cover. Five categories
of labour were paid for with money: labour
employed by the term (fee'd labour), harvest
labour, artisan and specialized non-professional
services; professional services; and a miscellaneous category largely amounting to work
carried out by day labourers and piece work. Of
these, fee'd labour is by far the most significant.
Through time there is discernible a general
increase in the number of employees. Accompanying this is not only an increase in the total sum
spent on labour on the farm, but also an increase
in the average wage paid to each worker (though
this varies between and within categories of
labour). There are indications also of increasing
stratification of workers.

The Journal of Donald Sinclair, Schoolmaster, Islay, 1835–71

Susan Sinclair

This Journal, which has been transcribed by Susan Sinclair, was in the possession of her late father-in-law, the Rev Donald Sinclair, who was descended from the writer. It throws much light on the harshness of everyday life in Islay in the second half of the nineteenth century. This note is intended to draw attention to it, in the hope that it may yet be published in full.

Times were far from easy in Islay. Starting with the top, the laird Mr W F Campbell 'abandoned' the place in November 1847. The young laird, John Campbell 'took away the young family by the Portellen way on Friday the 19th of Nov. 1947 to be conveyed to their Parents'. This was a sad loss to the country people, who 'greatly grieved for Mr Campbell and family Especially Mr John the young Heir of Islay'. The island fell into the hands of the Royal Bank of Scotland, and was managed by a Trustee from Edinburgh, a Mr Brown, and by Mr William Webster, Dial. 'A deplorable time for distress and hardship prevail in the place'. In November 1852, Mr William Webster was out of the factorage of the estates of Islay, and a Mr Henderson was appointed as factor for Mr Morrison, Esq., of Islay, though 'the island is nothing better in regard of goodness towards the benefits of the poor'. Details of changes in ownership and factors and their activities, however, must be filled out from other sources. Here, we present an outline of the life of Donald Sinclair and of his family, which was hard enough in all conscience, and conclude with data on his school teaching activities, as a contribution to the history of education in Scotland. [Editors]

Donald Sinclair and his Family Life.

The writer, Donald Sinclair, was probably the son of Peter Sinclair and Ann Kirkland, who were living at Ballitarsin in 1792. He was born on 27 February 1792. From the Journal, a certain amount can be gleaned about his personal life. In 1835, he was already described as schoolmaster, and on 10 September he entered into possession of the second land of Ballitarsin and so worked a farm also. But he was unlucky. He lost a cow on 22 March 1836 – drowned in a bog – as well as a heifer and half his crop. In view of these heavy losses, he gave it up and removed to his mother's house.

His wife Margaret Campbell fell ill of the fever on 8 February 1838 and died nine days later. Expenses during her illness were 19/-, and funeral expenses amounted to £2.10/-. He had to borrow £1.10/- to cover the costs, which included 2 gallons of whisky.

In philosophical mood he wrote on 24 February 1838:

And you my Chosen friends and neighbours good when I am to be buried, I wish you will bury me in the Same Grave where my beloved Spouse is Interred May the Lord reward those who Sympathised with me in my trouble I am not rich in worldly riches, but my Soul is full of love to my God, my Saviour and my Sanctifier the Holy Trinity to whom be the praise now and forever Amen.

His financial state was put on paper on 12 February, when, fearing the worst, he made a brief inventory of his concerns and personal debts. He had a five year old cow in calf and a heifer out to fodder with John Campbell, Mulindra; one fifth of seat No 18 in the west gallery of Bowmore Church, for which he had paid £1.7/- in 1828; wages of £3 for the school winter quarter were due from several persons; wages of £1 and 10/- were due to his sons Alexander and Peter for herding; he owed Mr John Simson, Bowmore, £1.6/- for meal; £5.7/- was paid on a bond to Mr John Campbell, late Kilinala; 10/4 was paid to John McKay, Bowmore; and he had paid sums of 3/- and 9 or 10/- to two other individuals. This was not high living.

In 1841 he had the job of working with Mr Laughlan, the surveyor, in measuring the line of the new road from Bridgend to Portellen, measuring it in numbers of pegs placed 500 feet apart, and some 400 feet, making a total of 10 miles and 70 feet.

In the same year, he got married again, in a very businesslike way:

Remained a Widower three years and Sixteen days.

I saw a widow woman in Truidernish whose Name is Mary Campbell to whom I send Message in Feby. 16th and on the 27th agreed with her, Married her on Thursday 4th March 1841 at the age of 48 years She is 34. My Expenses about that Marriage is Five pounds Sterling. On the 8th She came home. She remained here one week returned home with her Brother Neil and Staid with him till the 31st of March when she came home accompanied by Jannet McLee carrying a live hen & a dead one with them. On the 8th of April I took home her Chist and Spinning Wheel, a . . . Chair two Stools and a water Stoup which her Brother Neil left in the house of John Campbell Kiletearnain.

Saturday May the 8th I accompanied her to her Brothers house when I left her on . . . She

came home the 15th . . . Carrying her Daughter Margaret Cameron on her back by Porthillin & Bowmore. This Margt. Cameron is the daughter of Donald Cameron Piper & Sailor by her first husband unconsented brought to my House. She is two years and nine Months old, is ill with the Chincough. Bot. Biscuits, loaf & Sugar . . . provision for her and in Bridgend bt. Castor Oil Candie & Lozenges @ 3d. Continuing time by my wife Consuming of Butter milk & Eggs and the time of my wife attending her is considered at 7d per day. Recovered Augt. 1st 1841.

Sabbath Feby. 6th 1842. Delivered of a Daughter at noon Mary Campbell my Spouse, Baptized by the Revd. Mr Achd. McTavish of Kildalton in the House of Doctor McTavish Spring Bank, Agnes our first Child 7 Days Old. . . .

Nov. 10th. Great Struggle in our Church between Mr Campbell Esq., of Islay and An Advocate of her Majesty Queen A. V. for The Patronage of . . . 37 of the Communicants Sided the Crown Patronage and 35 Adhered to Mr Campbell's Scheme. The Minister Mr Alexr Stuart for the Crown . . . Mr Hector McNeil Rejected by the most Part of the Parishioners. This Caused Great variance among the people of the Parish. I avoided siding with either Side as I Judged the Controversy against the Rule of Holy Scripture to whom I adhere. In July Mr Stuart Came to the Parish Church.

In summer 1843, Donald engaged with Archibald McNiven, Emigration Agent from Mull, apparently to try his luck overseas. He gave him his only cow, potatoes that had been planted in two lots, and household furniture. He sailed with Captain William Baird in Lochindale aboard the *Catherine* of Belfast for Aros Bay, Mull, on 1 July. They then went on to anchor in Tobermory Bay and on 25 July sailed with 275 individuals aboard in the company of another ship, the *Charles Humbertson* of N(orth) B(ritain), also with passengers aboard from the agent. The ship was leaky and infirm, and they had to keep pumping. One child was born and another died aboard. They returned in stormy conditions on 11 August, casting a great quantity of salt overboard, and anchored in Belfast Bay.

As the owner, Mr Herries, and Donald Sinclair differed, and Donald's provisions had run out, 'getting no Government Bread on that unprosperous voyage', he left the ship on 20 August after eight weeks all but one night aboard, leaving £1.6/- as part of his head money, and there was some bread due to him as part of his agreement with McNiven. He and his wife and three children came to Glasgow by the steamer *Aurora*, stayed a week, and having no work there, returned to Islay on 4 September. So much for an abortive attempt to emigrate.

On 23 November, his wife presented him with a daughter, baptised as Marion.

But sickness and death were also part of everyday existence. On 6 May 1846, his oldest daughter, Agnes Sinclair, by his second wife, died. She was born on 6 February 1842. She had been ill with a swelling for 12 days. His son, Donald, died on 13 August 1847, aged 19 years and 3 months. His son Peter died on 6 May 1847, aged 20. The day before, Peter had been sent home in a cart from Alexander Campbell's, where he had been hired. 'His Complaint was head Boiled inside, then Sweating to excess heat & thirst, Rheumatism and Swelling'. He was born on 17 May 1827. Funeral expenses were coffin timber and meal, trimming and joinery, liquor, totalling £3.6/-.

In 1851, his eldest son John came home from the Gartsherrie Ironworks, Old Monklands, Lanarkshire, where he was employed as a carter, with a boil on his left haunch. It was lanced, but continued to suppurate till he died. Funeral expenses were partly paid for from the Iron Works Society.

He now had one son, Alexander, left of his first family. Alexander had worked at Greinack Distillery from 1847 till the beginning of 1852, then went to Liverpool and worked first as fireman and then as cook aboard the Mail Ship *Canada*, plying between Liverpool, Halifax and Boston. In 1854 he engaged as second cook aboard the ship *Lightening*, with Captain Forbes.

In November 1854 he married a lady called Hannah Coats, and in December sailed in the Mail Ship *James Baines*, this time as steward. He sent his father a postal order for £1 in 1855, and said he planned to come to see him.

By 1854, Donald Sinclair's health was beginning to fail. He was now 62 years old. He was under doctor's orders for some weeks in 1857, and had to take castor oil to ease his troubles. In his impoverished state, he had to seek aliment from the Board of Supervision. He recovered, but in 1859 his son Donald by his second wife was dangerously ill of the measles, and had to be blistered with a mustard plaster that opened the windpipe of his throat.

Marion, his daughter, went to stay with Alexander in Liverpool in December 1963. There she got a job under the cook in a house with six servants. Family worship was observed there morning and evening. Another member of the family left the island in 1870. This was Donald, who went to the lowlands and took service at Overton near Strathavon.

Tragedy struck again on 13 April 1874, when his wife Mary Campbell died. She had been ill since July 1873, with a swelling on her neck that grew to the size of a goose egg and kept growing. They had had three daughters and one son. One of the daughters, Mary, was in Glasgow, but she also fell ill and died in March 1876.

Donald himself died on March 13th 1879 at Gartachosin, aged 87.

Donald Sinclair as Schoolteacher

Donald Sinclair's teaching activities took place in the days before the passing of the Education (Scotland) Act of 1872, and reflect the conditions that prevailed in an island in the west of Scotland when the pressures of harvest work kept the children off school, and the master had himself to work in the harvest field. For his teaching, he was paid partly in money and partly in kind, or sometimes with services from the parents. Payments were by the school term or 'quarter', a fourth part of the year. The following list shows the situation in 1840–41:

26 May 1840	John Ogilvie Nariby Do	
	To Teaching 2 Schollars from Nov. 1839 till March 1840 @ 2/- pr. Qr	5
	By a Kitchen Grate	4/-
Winter 1840	To 2 Schollars 4/- By 1 Barrel potato 3/-	
May 1st.	Neil Sinclair Do To 1 Scholr. 1 qr. @ 2	2
	By ½ Barrel Potatoes @ 1/3	
	Donald Cameron Do	
	To 1 Scholar ½ year & 1 Scholar 1 qr.	6
	To making 2 Shirts for the Boys & washing in full	
	Ann Brown Do To 1 Scholr. ½ qr. 1/ Due 2nd 1840. Paid	1/
	Ann Campbell Do To 2 Scholers. 1 qr.	4/4
	Mr John Campbell Mulindra	
	To 3 schollars 1 ½ qr. @ 9/	
	By grass for a Quay & Ram, Grounds for 1 pk Oats, & ¼ pk flax seed, 1 Barrel potatoes	
	George Keith Do 1 Schollar 1 ½ qr.	
	Owing to your kindness when making my wife's Coffin I allow you the time your Son was at School	
	Donald MacLugash Lenanbui	
	To 4 Schollars from Novr. 1839 to May 1840 @ 4	16
April 27th	By leading Dung 8/ grass for a Cow breaking Truffs [turves]	16
	John McCuay Do	
	To 1 Scholar 1 ½ qr. @ 2	3
	By 1 Barrel potatoes @ 3/	
Nov. & May	Charles MacArthur Gartahossin	
	To 2 Schollars from Nov 39/ till May 40/	8
	By Service for your wife	8
	Alexr. Jamieson Do	
	To 2 Schollars winter qr. & part Spring	6
Fby. 14th 1840	By 2 pecks meal @ 3/ Decr. 2nd. 1840 Paid 3/	6
Feby. 27th 1841	To 2 schollars 1 Qr. 4 By 1 Barrel potatoes full paid	3
	Neil McInnish Do	
	To 1 Schollar 2 year 4/ Summer 1/3	
May 26th	By 1 Barrel potatoes @ 3/	
Feby. 27th 1841	To 2 Schollars 4/ By 1 Barrel potatoes 3/	
	John Currie Gartloist Sliabh	
	To 1 Schollar ½ year 4/ Paid	
	John Ramsay Gartloist	
	To 3 Schollars part ½ year	6
Augt. 18th 1840	Paid 1/ Dec. 23rd – Paid 4/	

Mrs McLellan Do
To 1 Schollar 1 Qr. 2/ Paid Cash 2/

Angus Campbell Do
To 2 Schollars 1 Qr. 6/ By 2 barrels potatoes @ 3

Donald Shaw Gartintra
To 1 Scholar 1 Qr. 2/ Nov. 27th 1849 Pd 1/ & meal 1/   2/

Duncan Shaw Do
To 2 Schollars 1 Qr. Aug. 30th By 2   4

Jany 9th 1840   By meal 1 peck @ 1/4 ½

Alexr. Campbell Do
To 1 Scholar 2 Qrs 4 By 2 pks Meal @ 2/9   1/3
1840 Sept.   By 2 pks meal   2/9
in full

Dugald Mc Carge Lenariach
To 1 Schollar 2 Qrs. By   2/

Sumer Qr. 1840   Hugh McCalman Sliabhaka
To 1 Schollar 2/ Feby. 28th 1841 Cash 6d Potatoes 1/

Sumer Qr. 1840   Duncan Stewart Neriby
To 2 Schollars @ 2/   4
Winter 1840/1   To 1 Schollar 2 By Cash 1/1 ½   4/10½

Alexr. MacPherson Tommary
1840/1   To 2 Schollars for 3 Qrs. Each 12/   12
1841 March 2nd   By 2 pecks meal

Stock Dr   To Dr McTavish Spring Bank To 1 barrel potatoes @ 3/6
June 1841   To 1 Barrel potatoes @ 2 By work @ John McNabbs shop 2 ½ days

I continued teaching the School both 1838/1839/1840/1841

November 1838. In Novr. I commenced teaching a little School in my Room No of Schollars in attendance was 40 in Summer 1839 I continued teaching No only 18. In harvest I worked with Dr McTavish and Edward Campbell Rhaw. At Martinmas I opened the School for winter Season Taught 44 Schollars.

Winter 1842/3. I kept open my School during the Winter & Spring.

1845 July 5th. Removed from Garthossen to Avinvogie Schoolhouse. I opened Summer Class here only 17 Schollars attended having in Harvest. Winter Resumed Teaching continued till May 1846 . . . Harvest wrought on Shearing & other work in winter opened a very poor School where I had to give up teaching at Candlemas.

November 23rd 1846. Mr Stuart Minister of this Parish Spoke to me in Sepr. 1845 desiring me to teach a Poor School in view to be opened in Bowmore from that time till Decr. 23rd. I was not engaged with but Doctor McTavish Gave me a room in Gartchossin in Novr. 6 I flitted to it.

Decr. 13th. I commenced Teaching Said school as Mr Stuart Mr Webster Doctr. McTavish & Mr Taylor Schoolmaster fee'd me on the 23 at 5£ Sterling of Wages till May.

Schollars increased to 96 in Spring when I spoke to Mr Stuart for a new engagement he Sent me to the Docr. Who told me if I had either

10 or 12 £ Sterling for a year he thought It might do on the 20th May Mr Stuart Asked me what was said by the Doctor I told him So and Said I would not Stay without getting 20 £ of wages for a year we parted as I understood it displeased him for he Kept Silence till I Said I thought it as well to give up teaching to which he replied he thought so.

Accordingly I dismissed the School that day telling them my time was out As My wages was made up by Subscription Some of Bowmore people who Subscribed disapproved my Conduct & withstood paying their subscription money pretending I was hired for a year of these is McPherson late Supervisor and Some other who paid part of their Subscription on the 29th of Decr. 1845 I left the list of Scholars Starting the term they were at School with Mr Rob. Murray Bowmore who promised to look in to the matter & to return the Slate Safe to me again.

April the 27th. Returned my School List, but no payment except 5/ from Mr Murray.

But Donald Sinclair did not give up teaching. On 15 November 1855, he began teaching the school of Mr John McCrae of Bridgend, during the 20 weeks when McCrae was attending his studies at the College at Glasgow. For this, he was to get £8.10/- sterling, made up of £4.10/- to be paid by McCrae and the rest from fees from the pupils.

> . . . in case I cannot take it from the Schollars Mr. McCrae is to raise it himself and to pay me, also I am to be Supplied by Mr Thos. Scott Blue house in the absence of Mr. McCrae but that to be deducted from my wages when final Settlement shall be made

There follows a list of pupils and of payments, again partly in kind, made by their parents.

Novr. 15	Edward Wilson Carmains	May 19th. Received from Mr
	Son to James Watson	Chisholm Inspector of Parocial
	Donald Wilson Do	Board for these 3 Schollars 11/-
	Wilm. Wilson Do	
	Neil McAffer Do	Dond. McAffer May 17 By Cash in full 2/6
	Mary Currie do	Dr to Edwd. Currie May 17 Cash in full 2/6
	Mary McAulay Carabus	Gr. Dr to Neil McAulay
	Ann Bell do	Dr to Dunn. Bell May 22nd in full 2/
	Jessie Campbell Skerolsa	John Campbell
	Cecil Campbell Bridgend	Alexr. Campbell 1 pk potatoes 1/3
19	Ann Clerk Bluehouse	Geo Clerk April 26 Cash in part 2/6
	Gilbert Clerk	June 14 in full 4/-
	Mary Sinclair Lenanbuie	Dr. to myself
21st.	John Brown Carabus	Jany. 8th By barrel potatoes 5/-
	Catharine Brown do	John Brown Paid in full May 29/56
27	Rodger Brown do	
	Donald Bell do	Widow Bell Cash in full 2/
	Archibald MacDearmid do	Dond. McDearmid April1/6 May 14, 1/6
	John McLellan Carmaine	Peter McLellan April meal in full 3/9
	Hellen MacLellan do	
	Charlote MacAffer do	only two weeks. Don McAffer
	John McArthur Gartlinstra	Dond. McArthur
	Margaret MacNiven Gartloist	Alexr. MacNiven
Decr 5th	Jessie MacNiven do	Jany 19 By 2 barrels Swedish Turnip & May
		25th Cash & Table
		4/6 Bal 1/

Decr. 3rd	Neil Orr Gartintra (?)	Neil Orr June 12th Cash 1/ balance 1/
	John Clark Bluehouse	only a few days Geo Clark
[deleted]		
	Merrion Brown Carabus	John Brown
	Duncan MacDearmid do	Dond. McDearmid
	Donald McDearmid do	
11th	Neil MacEachern do	Neil McEachern
	Malcolm Mac Eachern do	March 2/6 Balance 1/
	Donald Andirson Linanbuie	John Anderson Cash 1/
	Merrion Campbell Rhaw	Jany 9th 1 bottle lamp oil March
8th	1 Cask salt	
	Margaret Campbell do	Edward Campbell
	Edward Campbell Do	
	Catherine MacCuaig Gartehossin	Hugh McCuage
	Hugh MacCuaig Do	April Cash 1/6 May 19th Cash 6d.
Jany 1st.	John Carmichael Scarabus	Hugh Carmichael ½ Qr.
	Jessie Wilson Cornaire	only one month James Wilson no charge
Feby. 25th	Ann Campbell	Dr John Campbell Skirolsa
	Peter McEowin & Ann McEowin	Childn. Archd. McEowin Smith Cornaine
	1 Peat spade in full	
March 5th	Daniel Bell	Grandson to Alexr. Bell, Carabus May 22nd
	in full 2/	
April	Peter MacLiver	Son to Donald McLiver Islayhome
	Margaret MacArthur	for two months 1/

Rural Schoolbuildings in the Eighteenth Century

R T D Glaister

H G Graham[1] presents a dismal picture of the 'wretched discomfort' suffered by the eighteenth century schoolmaster with regard to his accommodation, professional and personal. The tale of misery is repeated in Scotland[2] and leads the historian Ferguson[3] to conclude that 'often the parish school was a miserable hovel with earthen floors on which the pupils scrawled their letters and numbers'. Evidence gleaned from a study of Teviotdale parishes in Roxburghshire[4] does not fit that pattern, but is closer to the situation in Fife: 'it is plain that in Fife we need not take too seriously Grey Graham's description of the usual school'.[5]

Graham makes another characteristic assertion when he notes that in the early eighteenth century 'the traveller passing through the Border country might have asked in vain to see the school at Hawick and learned that there was none nearer than Jedburgh or Selkirk'.[6] Although Graham is referring to a document of the Hawick heritors of 1710, recent research suggests that both Graham and the heritors are wrong and that the source of the confusion is what one means by 'school'. Is it a building, temporary or permanent, purpose-built or rented? Is it where a schoolmaster teaches, with or without regular maintenance, legal or not? Certainly Hawick had a schoolmaster at 1710 and, indeed, since at least 1690.[7] Furthermore it is likely that the heritors had been paying him since at least 1697 so that they should not have been unaware of his presence and they would have known that he taught in the Kirk. Graham misinterpreted the contemporary remark to mean that there was no educational provision in Hawick. The heritors were wrong if they meant the building because there were school buildings in parishes around Hawick. It may be, however, that the heritors were referring to a grammar school. Like many other issues, the historical study of school buildings is clouded by the difficulty of ascertaining firm evidence. No record does not mean no existence,[8] but even when there is a record there can still remain doubts about what the record means. Drawing upon primary sources in Roxburghshire, this paper will identify the existence of school buildings and attempt to examine their quality.

As a background, the 1646 and 1696 Education Acts had required heritors to establish a school in every parish not already provided and to make available a commodious house for the school. Whereas the schoolmaster's appointment and salary were given fairly clear attention, the building was not. A house had to be provided, but the Acts do not specify what is 'commodious', do not indicate if a dwelling house was to be included and do not give guidance about the maintenance of whatever was provided.

Amongst the Teviotdale parishes under study, two, Hawick and Jedburgh, are parishes containing burghs. Although these two burghs have significant differences, they have enough in common to make them markedly different from the rural parishes around them. The existence of a burgh council is the principal distinction, but also these parishes had more than one 'public' school; at least, Jedburgh began the century with two schools, an English and a grammar, and combined them in 1803, while Hawick began with one and ended with two.

At the time of the 1696 Act, Hawick's schoolmaster taught in the Kirk. Hawick's heritors seem to have done nothing, nor were pressed to do anything, as a result of the Act, to provide a commodious house. It was the generosity of Alexander Orrock that stimulated change. He was a former minister of Hawick, who died 1711, leaving 'nine thousand merks for the benefit of the schoolmaster of Hawick'. The first rents and arrears of his bequest were to go to building a school and schoolhouse. The session minutes record the supervision of this fund although the gathering of interest due was not always easy. Interest accumulated until 1731 when, one must assume, it was employed in paying for the grammar school built at the Sandbed. The historian of the Orrock Bequest[9] has traced some receipts dated between 1732 and 1735 for the building of 'ane schooll and house to the schoolmaster of Hawick' although the site was, according to a Heritors' minute of 1766, bought by the Kirk Session in 1728 'for the behoof of the poor'.

Hawick's first purpose-built schoolhouse was, therefore, erected about 1735 and when in 1766 the issue arose of who pays the feuduty on the land (paid every thirty years as it is community and not private property) the session applied to the heritors to cover half the cost, which they did without question. Prior to the new school, the grammar schoolmaster was paid a house rent from the Orrock Bequest.

The grammar school and schoolhouse underwent substantial repairs and improvements in 1763: raising and relaying the garret floor, thatching, plastering, putting in a stair up from the school room, windows, new school seats, etc. A new garden dyke was erected in 1766, and further repairs to the roof were made in 1771.

By 1798 the incoming master, James Kirk, found the state of the schoolhouse to be such that he would not accept the post without the assurance of some change. As a result, it was agreed that a new schoolhouse be hired, the old

one rented out, and any difference in rent to be covered by heritors and council.

When the parish school was ousted from the Kirk in 1710 by the new grammar school, the schoolmaster was paid house rent. It was not until 1739 that the council agreed to build 'a sufficient English school of 30 foot long within walls and 16 foot wide within walls'.[10] In 1756 James Inglis, soon after taking up office, was awarded one half of a sum not exceeding £4 sterling 'towards assisting him in the reparation of his dwelling house'. The other half was perhaps paid by the heritors, and indeed when the great flood of 1767 carried away Inglis' house, he was then given house rent, half of it paid by the heritors.

At the beginning of the nineteenth century there was agitation about the state of the schools. Inglis used a room in the Council House while the schoolhouse was being repaired. Armstrong was granted a similar request two years later in 1806. The council were now adopting the position that it was not their responsibility to contribute anything towards the building or repairing of schools or schoolhouses; they argued this belonged exclusively to the heritors of the parish. They did, however, offer £150 sterling in 1808 to a fund for new schools without future obligation. This attitude, no doubt, prompted the amalgamation of the schools on 1824 and expedited the single new building completed in 1826, financed by the heritors.

Throughout the eighteenth century there were two schools in Jedburgh which gained public support, that is, support from the Burgh Council, heritors or Kirk Session. These were the Grammar School and the English School. About the beginning of the eighteenth century the Grammar School moved into new premises within the Abbey[11] but by 1743 the Abbey accommodation was unsatisfactory because the steeple beside it was likely to collapse. This danger was reported to the Council in January and in March 1744 the council sought the assistance of the heritors, as it was the parish school. The heritors, of course, delayed discussion until the next meeting two weeks later, but the result, after some three and a half years, was to rent a new building. The Council was faced again in 1751 with the need for a 'convenient Grammar School' which would be good for the children and good for the town and they resolved to buy a house which was to be let to the schoolmaster for 30/- per annum. Only two years after purchasing the new accommodation the Council was made aware that the school was 'insufficient' for the needs of the town,[12] but because the burgh finances were in a perilous state it was not until 1758 that a solution was found, namely to pay the schoolmaster house rent – which it had done formerly.

In 1770 the Grammar schoolmaster resigned because no action was taken over his request for a new school and schoolhouse. Five years later his successor, James Brewster, was making a similar petition to the heritors but he was more patient. The heritors ascertained that they had no legal obligation to provide a dwelling house for a schoolmaster and boarders, but gave him £10 to rent a suitable house for a year, without this being a precedent for the future. Their objection did not appear to have been directed towards provision for boarders but rather the legal obligation with regard to a dwelling house.

By 1778 plans for the Grammar School were being considered and detailed accounts of the building requirements were given, for example[13]:

inside measurements	32 feet x 16 feet
height	10 feet
walls	20–22 inches thick
5 windows	2 feet 10 inches x 5 feet 10 inches, with door in proportion
2 vents in gables	
chimney	3½ feet square
master's desk	3 feet square
seating and bookboards	to run from each side wall leaving an aisle 4 feet wide
bookboards	18 inches wide or as master thinks fit

The total cost was estimated at about £82.10.0 which would be paid in three instalments: one-third at the beginning, at the covering of the roof,

and at completion. Its site was to be at the end of the English School within the churchyard. It was eventually completed at the end of 1779.

By 1803, the building was again said to be in disrepair and, when the Act of that year was brought to the attention of the heritors, they claimed that they were not sure that the Act applied to Jedburgh. However, a solution was forthcoming when both Grammar and English schoolmasters resigned and the united school was established. It was accommodated in the old Grammar School, considerably extended, and a new dwelling house, suitable for boarders, was purchased for the schoolmaster.

Information about the existence of the Jedburgh English schoolhouse is less clear. Repairs were being sought in 1698–99. In 1702 a new school was built in the churchyard and it had a loft for the use of the schoolmaster. The Kirk Session was reported to be 'weel pleased and satisfied' with the plan; and gave £3 to 'help settle and encourage the English School'. Furthermore the landward elders gave sixpence a week from their collections for the same purpose.

With its financial support, the session took a special interest in the new start for the English School. Where the session recommended the schoolmasters to the magistrates 'who has built a school and house', the minute is amended with the clause 'which the session likewise approves off'.

Special collections were ordered in 1710 by the session 'for encouragement of a pretty man to be maister' after the session and the magistrates had met about the English School 'to consider what is needful thereanent'. The session's interest thereafter was confined to the money made available by mortifications and the maintenance of the English School was left to the Council, which is recorded as making repairs in 1716 and 1722.

Maintenance of buildings in Hawick seems to have been shared by heritors and council for both English and Grammar schools, although the Orrock fund paid for the Grammar School in 1735 and the council for the English School in 1739. In Jedburgh the heritors had nothing to do with the English School and shared responsibility for the Grammar School with the Council. The English School was built with finance from the session and the council, but was maintained thereafter by the council.

In 1779 the new Jedburgh Grammar School was built. About 1780 Kelso also built a new school.[14] Interestingly it had the English School on the ground floor and the Grammar School above, the scheme suggested in Jedburgh in 1747. The Jedburgh dimensions were 32 feet by 16 feet by 10 feet high while the Kelso ground floor was very similar, 31 feet by 19½ feet by 9¾ feet; the Grammar School above was somewhat smaller. The 1739 English School at Hawick was 30 feet by 16 feet so that there appears to have been something approaching an accepted size for a burgh school in this part of the Borders in the second part of the eighteenth century.

Beyond size, there is little that can be said with regard to the quality of the burgh schools. The principal evidence concerns who should pay, who is responsible, heritors or council, so that existence of a building is established from one of various sets of local records, heritors, council, session or even presbytery when a dispute became serious.

In the rural areas, most of the early references to a school building are in the area of accounts showing repairs. That lets us know who was paying for the maintenance, but it does not indicate whether the school was a rented or a purchased or purpose built property. In addition these references are generally to the school or to the schoolhouse, which may or may not include a dwelling house. Sometimes the reference is clear, 'schoolhouse and dwelling house', but even these could mean separate buildings although there is evidence to show that they can refer to one building. In this study unless there is clear evidence against, it has been understood that the school was one building which could include teaching and residential accommodation and that a reference to repairs meant that there was a maintained building for the school, i.e. the school was not perambulating and it was not in the church.

Attempting to give a date to the first existence of a schoolhouse is impossible. Establishing existence is difficult enough and that is because the evidence is very dependent upon heritors' records. The church records gave clues about schoolmasters because salaries were often matters that required formal settlement and legal procedures and also the schoolmasters had formalities, like signing the Confession, which had to be completed. The schoolhouse was a less regular concern, and if there are no heritors' records there are no accounts of repairs made.

There is no doubt that in the presbytery of Jedburgh the schoolhouse was, and was seen to be, the responsibility of the heritors, but that is not to deny the Kirk Session any role. Clearly the session took an interest and put up finance until the heritors performed their tasks properly. There are several examples of the session's paying for repairs and purchasing furniture in the first half of the century (eg Wilton, 1716 or Ancrum, 1734), and even occasional examples from later (eg Hobkirk, 1767 or Kirkton, 1801). The Roxburghshire sessions were not unusual in this respect because Fife sessions were similarly involved.[15]

The session's function was to set things in motion and thereafter to fill in the gaps, but the principal burden was borne by the heritors, although in some parishes the solution was for the parish meeting, rather than the heritors', to conduct the supervision.

If we discount Abbotrule because it has no local records and was annexed during the century, there were references to a school building in seven out of twelve rural parishes in the period prior to 1740 and the remaining five parishes are mentioned one in each of the following decades. However, that has to be set against the background of the availability of heritor's records; three parishes had none at all, and the remainder all began at a date after 1740. It may, in fact, be that the heritors performed their responsibilities admirably from the beginning of the century, but because there are only church records we give the church a stronger role.

One cannot, therefore, be firm about when a school was first established or who took the initiative. The Bedrule school is an interesting case in this respect. There are full session records for the eighteenth century, but no reference to a building beyond one from the session in 1693 that the money to be recovered in the Commissariot Court, arising from a vacant stipend, should be used by the session to build a house for the schoolmaster. The next mention is in 1795 when the Presbytery report that the teaching room was too small. Oxnam, according to the *Old Statistical Account*, had a school and schoolhouse built from money left by Lady Yester in the 1630s, but there are no heritors' records and no further reference to a school. One can surmise that Bedrule and Oxnam had had buildings since the seventeenth century, that they were founded by the session and by the mortification, but that, since there are session records without a school reference and no heritors' records, the heritors maintained the building from then on, but this cannot be certain.

After a decision of the Commissioners of Supply, in 1720, the local position was that a building costing up to one hundred merks should be provided by the heritors and one would imagine that serious breaches of that guideline would have come before the presbytery. In 1778 there were reports to the synod from the presbytery on the state of the schools and it was noted that the report for Crailing, Hobkirk and Southdean made no mention of buildings. This would appear to have been an oversight for Crailing and Southdean because there is sufficient contemporary evidence of repairs etc. Hobkirk had had a schoolhouse, but in 1777 it was in a ruinous condition and the schoolmaster was complaining. A new school was built three years later.

Very occasional references to buildings come through the presbytery records after visitations, eg on Hownam, 1725 and Hobkirk, 1726, and there was a note in 1765 that Kirkton had no schoolhouse. (The schoolmaster complained in 1787 that the school was too small.) It is likely, therefore, that from 1720 there was a building for a school in each parish most of the time, but that it was not a very substantial building and it could easily fall into disrepair.

The presbytery was invited to intervene in a dispute about the parish school of Eckford. The

heritors' records opened in 1740 with the issue of the site of the parish school which was deemed to have been in an 'inconvenient place of the parish and that there wants a publick school and schoolhouse for teaching of youth'.[16] By a majority vote it was agreed that Eckford should be the place. A piece of ground was to be reserved and the schoolmaster transported the next month. The issue was complicated by the discovery in the session minutes of a note that in 1694 the session and heads of families within the Barony of Eckford were fully agreed to build a house for the schoolmaster with the proviso that it should be for the schoolmaster's use and should not return again to the Duchess of Buccleugh. It was further claimed that having built the school at public expense they had it taken from them and it was then possessed by his Grace's Officer. The Duke of Buccleugh expressed willingness to have his ground appropriated for public use, but the heritors wanted something more definite.

There was no clear conclusion to this dispute, which stretched over four years, apparent in the parish records. In 1752 the presbytery was asked to declare the Eckford school as the parish school, but it concluded that that was the business of the Commissioners of Supply. Whether this was a continuation of the dispute from 1740–44 is unclear, but it looks rather as if, though the parish schoolmaster was settled and agreed, the parish school was not. In 1757 a school was built in Eckford on Buccleugh ground, at a cost of £24.16.2.

This dispute about where to site the parish school arises from the particular nature and history of the parish. The Dukes of Roxburghe and Buccleuch were the major heritors and back in 1700 the Roxburghe estate supported three schoolmasters in the parish. Around the same time the Buccleughs were supporting another. In 1705 Roxburghe paid one master 'according to the Act of Parliament', while Buccleugh paid another. Thereafter the one name came forward and there was a clear parochial schoolmaster. The mystery remains, though it would appear that the estates supported their own schoolmasters, but that there was at some point agreement about the legally settled schoolmaster. There were occasional payments to other teachers during the century and by 1826 there was a side school in the parish and another school supported by fees.[17]

There were, therefore, two or three population centres in the parish, each with traditions of education, and hence the dispute in the 1740s about where to place the parish school. Why the dispute broke out in the 1740s is not known. It could not be because there had been no parochial school before because the presbytery visited the Eckford school in 1722 and there was no comment about the building, though there was about the master. In the light of the representation made later from the Caverton area of the parish, there was probably a new school to be built, or major repairs to be made, a decision time when pressure might bring about change, but the principal heritor, Buccleugh, was unmoved.

One other interesting point from this Eckford case is another reference to a seventeenth century foundation for the school building, pre-1696, along with Bedrule 1693 and Oxnam 1630s.

The difficulty of gleaning precise information about buildings is not confined to Roxburghshire; Bain[18] outlines his conclusions for Stirlingshire and they are very cautious. One fairly common conclusion is that 'repairs and maintenance were a constant problem, especially when the heritors failed in their duty and the Kirk Session had to step in'.[19] Bain[20] supports that view, but in another place[21] he is inclined to describe a more 'laissez-faire' situation where the session just lets things slide and does not complain. Simpson[22] states that presbyteries in Aberdeenshire were also reluctant to take legal steps to enforce the law. The church authorities, therefore, limited themselves to giving a nudge to the heritors and often kept things going themselves in Roxburghshire as elsewhere. Responsibility for the building rested with the heritors and when there was a dispute the arbiter was, in this Eckford case as in another Jedburgh case, not the presbytery, but the Commissioners of Supply.

When one examines the size and conditions of the school buildings, two examples appear in the literature. The first is at Dailly from 1741[23]

and the second is of Aberdour, in Aberdeenshire, in the early nineteenth century.[24] Dailly school was 30 feet long and 14 feet wide, while Aberdour was 34 feet long by 14 feet wide. Boyd[25] also refers to the Loudon school which was 36 feet long by 16 feet wide and Bain[26] quotes the size of the Queensferry school of 1680 as 30 feet by 18 feet. The difficulty for a researcher is that one cannot make meaningful comparisons. Certainly the Dailly building contained 420 square feet while Loudon contained 576 square feet but there is information for these four examples that is not always available; we know that the first pair were single storey, while the second pair were two storey buildings. The differences, therefore, became even greater, for the area of the latter pair is completely devoted to teaching (and a similar area above for the residence) while the single storey building has to have a partition within so that the teaching area is less than the dimensions given. Beale[27] refers to two examples from Fife in the 1720s; one building was to be 30 feet by 15 feet while the other was only 20 feet by 13 feet and he brings forth another factor, obvious but nonetheless confounding, that school size was related to parish size. Unfortunately the Roxburgh evidence cannot confirm that, either with regard to geographical size or to population size.

There are at least a dozen examples from the present study of the dimensions of new buildings, proposed buildings or extensive additions, and nine references to size from the replies to the Sheriff,[28] but there is insufficient clarity as to what the dimensions cover for generalisations to be made. There were two examples from the 1760s, one proposed, one erected, with areas of 700 to 750 square feet, while the Eckford school built in 1757 at 180 square feet was extended in 1780, but to only 250 square feet. One might be able to argue that the area increased throughout the 1750s and 1760s, declined in the 1780s and 1790s and that that followed the way the population had developed, but the premise of comparing like with like cannot be confirmed. Having suffered fifty children taking measles in two days, Minto built a new school in 1792 of 470 square feet, 'the most beautiful and commodious schoolhouse in the south of Scotland', according to the Minto minister in the *Old Statistical Account*. A plan (Fig 1) in the Minto papers reveals that the area mentioned is all teaching area and the building has no residential accommodation. This teaching area is not far below that provided in burgh schools.

An idea of what may have been an acceptable standard can be gained from the presbyterial comments. For example, in 1726 the presbytery deemed the Hobkirk school too small. It was 13 feet by 12 feet and the comment was that it was insufficient for the schoolmaster, far less the scholars. In 1795 the presbytery found the Bedrule school to be too small at 15 feet by 13 feet, and that referred to the teaching room only. Standards have changed during the century, therefore. More space has been given to the teaching area, and accommodation for the schoolmaster was often provided. The new school at Wilton in 1793 had a teaching room of 22 feet by 18 feet and two rooms for the master of 12 feet by 18 feet.

Also there were more buildings with two floors, the house being above the schoolroom, but there is no mention in the records of a local decision about the provision of living quarters. It appears to have remained optional until 1803. One parish, Minto, is recorded as giving house rent and that became unnecessary at some point between 1722 and 1772.

Lastly there is a question of design. The traditional development was from single to double storey with the house on top. An alteration is suggested by the Eckford renovations of 1802 when the improvements were to make the school more comfortable for the children and any repairs were to be made to the schoolmaster's house which would strengthen the building. Within the more detailed specifications it is stated that the gable between school and house was to be rebuilt with a chimney on each side. That would appear to mean an end-to-end arrangement, semi-detached, rather than an internal division in one building.

Although it is difficult to show an increase in the space provided, there is, as one would expect, an increase in cost, but again as the size

of the building is uncertain one cannot make any observations about the scale of the increases beyond that. Looking at the dates of the new schools, proposed or erected, there is a period of activity in the 1750s and early 1760s, and again in the 1780s and 1790s, but why there should have been a lull in the 1770s is impossible to explain.

School building there was, and very little reparation to law, but one must not conclude that the state of affairs was always harmonious or satisfactory. The Crailing petition of 1767 claimed that the school 'needs to be immediately repaired for the preservation of the children's lives' and thirty years later the schoolmaster of the same parish complained that there was so little light in the winter and the room was so small, that he had to send pupils to his house which was a great inconvenience to him and his family. When the Wilton master petitioned for repairs in 1760 the heritors found that the buildings 'may yet stand for some time'.

After reviewing the evidence found on school buildings, the author regretted not taking note of the cost and nature of church and manse repairs and replacements. There is much more information about the ecclesiastical buildings and that could form a useful standard against which to make comparisons. For example, the new Wilton school in 1762 cost £39; the new Wilton Church at the same time cost £288. A more appropriate form of comparison may be with other rural buildings. The details given for the new schools can be compared with the general practices employed in the buildings on the farms and in the countryside. A most valuable survey of rural architecture has been made by Fenton and Walker[29] and it is from that that the following examples will be taken.

The size of a building is dependent upon the kind of materials that are used to build it. Fenton and Walker suggest that stone was not common as a building material prior to the period of agricultural improvement, which, therefore, limited the height of the walls, the width of the building and its 'life'. In Roxburghshire this led to buildings 12 to 13 feet high.[30] The introduction of lime mortar made more solid walls which

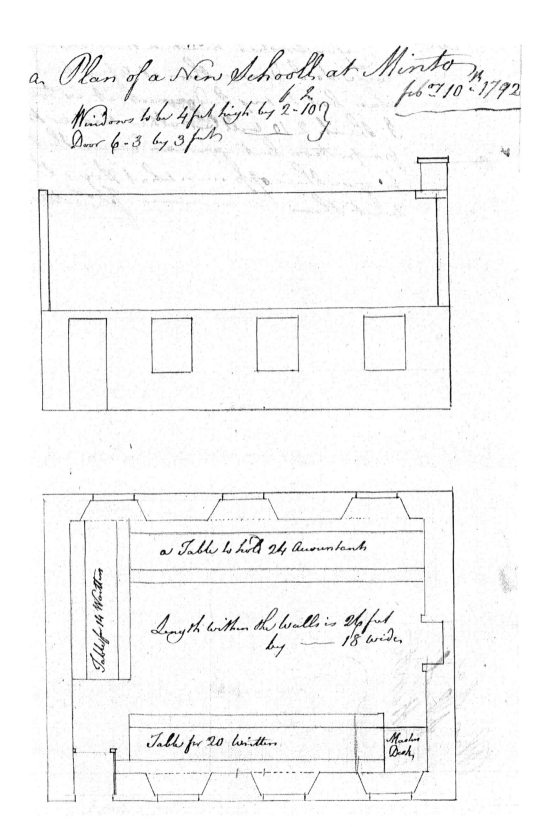

1. Plan of a new school at Minto, Roxburghshire, 10 February 1792. The windows were to be 4 feet high by 2 feet 10 inches wide, the door 6 feet 3 inches high by 3 feet wide.

permitted load bearing and, therefore, upper storeys. Stone and lime walls were used in the buildings of the gentry etc, in the seventeenth century, but by the 1790s even the smaller farmhouses had such walls[31] with the result that the width was of 17 to 21 feet and there were generally two storeys, often with a garret floor.[32]

Looking at the dimensions for the schoolhouses, those of the 1750s and 1760s had a maximum width of 16 feet but in the second period of building, the 1780s and 1790s, the maximum was 21½ feet and the standard was about 18 feet. In the first period the height of the walls was between 6 and 8 feet but in the second, from 8 to 12 feet and most of the planned or actual buildings of the second period were of two storeys.

'One of the consequences of building improvement was that much greater expense went into the house'.[33] We noted earlier that the costs of school building had increased; in the 1750s and 1760s the range was £25 to £40; in the later period, £70 to £88. Part of the increase can be accounted for by the greater capacity of the buildings, and inflation could account for another proportion, but it is reasonable to assume that part of the increase is due to the improved quality of the building itself.

There is, therefore, a clear parallel between the developments that took place in rural buildings generally and in school buildings in particular. The improving movement affected farm buildings and in this rural society the school shared in these broadly contemporary improvements. Indeed the school buildings appeared to be part of the same variety.

Limewashing and harling were known prior to the eighteenth century, but not used on rural buildings until the later eighteenth century.[34] Interestingly, the schoolhouses seem to have been so treated earlier. The presbytery recommended the Hownam school to be limed in 1725 and the Ancrum school was plastered with lime, inside and out, in 1758. The Hobkirk school was 'pinned and harled' in 1760 and in 1788, eight years after the new school was erected, there was a report of 'the present uncomfortable state of the schoolhouse on account of it not being lath'd

and plaistered above stairs and the walls in the Room below'.[35]

Smout[36] describes the tenant's house of the 1760s as having only one glazed window, approximately 1½ feet by 2 feet. Repairs to windows are common features of the records, but one cannot tell if all the windows were glazed. There are sufficient entries from 1750 onwards to suggest that at least from then the schoolhouse windows were glazed. In addition, the school was better served than the tenant's in the number of windows. The Crailing proposal of 1767 had seven windows, three of 1 foot by 1½ feet and four of 3 feet by 2 feet. The Hobkirk school of 1781 had five, two at 5 feet by 5 feet and three at 2½ feet by 2½ feet, the Ancrum proposal of 1787 had five also, each 3 feet by 4½ feet, and the Minto plan of 1792 has six of 3 feet by 4½ feet. In addition, it can be seen that the size of the windows is increasing and so was the cost of repair which led the Hobkirk heritors in 1780 to cover the windows with 'Wier tirlace', wire mesh.

Another important consideration was the roofing material and re-thatching was a common repair. Fenton and Walker describe various forms of thatching, some more advanced than others, but it is impossible from the records to identify developments with regard to thatch. There was, however, the change from thatch to slate at the end of the century although Somerville[37] noted that the first slated building in Hawick was about 1757. Eckford had a thatch repair in 1791, but in a major renovation in 1802 changed to slate. Of course the picture is less clear-cut than that one example would suggest. Southdean thatched a new school, and a new manse, in 1786 and repaired the thatch in 1800–02. Kirkton made a thatch repair in 1802, while Hobkirk's new school of 1781 and the Ancrum proposal of 1787 both had slate roofs. Even more surprising is Cavers parish which thatched its manse in 1779, but slated the new school two years later. In general these developments follow the findings of Fenton and Walker that 'in the last decade of the eighteenth century in the South-East all new buildings of two storeys or more were slated with blue or . . . grey slates'.[38]

Fenton and Walker suggest that the introduction of slate was most prevalent where slate was available locally, but the Roxburgh parishes were using Welsh slate. In addition, the building specifications often make reference to foreign timber so that the buildings were not then formed from those materials close at hand. The references to foreign timber, and often Russian logs in particular, seemed to follow from a general shortage of wood in this part of the country. This, however, is perhaps only partially correct because Fenton and Walker point out[39] that the use of slates often necessitated the use of foreign timber because native timber was not normally level enough.

Somerville[40] observed that in the middle of the eighteenth century the few two storey buildings had outside stairs and the Crailing plan of 1767 and the Wilton school of 1792 had outside stairs, but the Cavers schoolmaster of 1782 was fortunate in having an inside stair to his quarters.

Flooring too was given attention latterly. As late as 1792 the Wilton school was deemed to be in need of flooring, but in the 1780s Ancrum had laid flagstones and Eckford had laid a composition of lime, sand and clay. Of course, the increasing number of two storey buildings meant that the schoolmaster's house was floored with wood.

With regard to furniture and fittings, the Minto plan shows the desks round the walls with the Master's desk beside the fire and these seem to be the principal components. There are frequent references to replacement desks and benches, but whether there was a real distinction between readers' and accountants' tables is not known. It is likely that the fire was stocked by the fuel brought by the pupils though there is no mention from the records of the time. Thomson[41] observed that it was the practice in his father's time about 1790. Fenton[42] notes that the burning of coal required a different hearth from that of peat which is confirmed by a reference from Kirkton in January 1807: 'from want of peats the schoolhouse must necessarily be warmed with a coal fire which requires a grate'.[43]

The building of a new school was undertaken

with some thoroughness. In 1787 the Ancrum heritors called for estimates and had that advertised on two market days at Jedburgh. The previous year at Southdean they were even more enthusiastic and the minister had 'to advertise at the market crosses of Jedburgh, Hawick and at the Kirk doors of Jedburgh, Ancrum, Minto, Cavers and Hawick, Hobkirk and Bedrule'. The workmen were to be obliged 'to uphold the work for three years'.[44] The manse was extended at the same time and when an error was discovered payment was, in fact, withheld from the tradesmen.

There is a serious danger in writing an account such as this that one overrates specific and isolated examples because they are interesting or unusual or because they do not fit with the more traditional view. In Roxburgh, conditions in the rural parishes did improve throughout the century. It is almost certain that from the 1720s there was a schoolhouse in every parish and that by the 1780s most schoolmasters were also provided with a dwelling house. These buildings were not substantial, in that they needed frequent repairs, or had to be rebuilt, and often material from the old building was used in the new. However, in the context of the times and the community, few buildings were substantial, so that major repairs had to be conducted, eg rethatching, and the re-use of the longer lasting materials, such as stone and timber, was common and prudent. It should not be surprising to see the Kirkton heritors pay seven shillings in 1788 to the widow of the schoolmaster for the two doors which she left in the schoolhouse.

In the context of the times and the community, the school buildings were in line with best practice in terms of methods, materials and size. The schoolhouse was probably comparable to the buildings of a tenant or small heritor. The schoolroom was equipped with basic teaching furniture and had more windows than the normal house. The general improvements in rural housing that took place in the later part of the eighteenth century are reflected in the school buildings.

It cannot be argued that this positive perspective was uniform for all parishes or all occasions. The presbytery could find fault. Schoolmasters did complain. Heritors did decide to 'make do' with old buildings when the advice was to rebuild. The Ancrum heritors drew up specifications for a new building in 1787, but cancelled the project at the next meeting because the existing school, which lay alongside the church, 'must be kept up as a necessary apartment upon sacramental occasions'. Elsewhere the church was used as a school, but here the school was needed as a church.

There is an account in Tancred[45] of the parish school of Hobkirk in the early 1840s. From the present research Hobkirk had a new school in 1780, 33 feet long, 15 feet wide with walls 12 feet high. It had five windows, was slated and was two storied. It also had the mesh over the windows. Eight years later it was lathed and plastered. In 1826 the Hobkirk school was given as 43 feet by 15¼ feet by 12¼ feet. From that evidence the Hobkirk school was a good example of its kind, well built in the 1780s and probably extended before 1826. The Tancred account is:

the schoolmaster's house was little better than an ordinary cottage. It consisted of two rooms, with a trap door and a ladder to the loft above. It had a room thrown out on one side for the scholars. At one end of this room stood the bookcases of the Hobkirk Library. The floor was composed of a mixture of clay, the benches were without backs and very narrow, and the room was badly lit … There was no need of ventilation as badly fitting doors and windows supplied all that was required.

There was no real discrepancy in detail between the clinical descriptions of the formal records and Tancred's personal recollection of childhood experience, but to some extent they represent two different perspectives and reality must lie somewhere in between.

Tancred also observed that there were no sanitary arrangements and indeed that an open ditch, 'the Lousey drain', flowed through the playground with all the unpleasant results. Other schools must have suffered similar discomfort. Southdean school was beside the common stable and in 1801, though perhaps away by Tancred's time, Hobkirk schoolhouse had the common stable built at its back.

Schoolbuildings in Roxburghshire, therefore, were not ideal, but they may not have been as bad as elsewhere and certainly they were suited to the communities they served.

Notes and References

1 Graham, 1901, 424–7.
2 Scotland, 1969, 62–5.
3 Ferguson, 1978, 200.
4 Glaister, 1983.
5 Beale, 1983, 136.
6 Graham, 1901, 421.
7 Withrington, 1965.
8 Withrington, 1970.
9 Walters, 1954.
10 Borders Regional Council, Hawick Burgh Council Records 1/1, 3 February 1739.
11 Watson, 1909
12 *Ibid*.
13 Scottish Records Office (hereafter National Archives of Scotland – NAS), HR 172/2, December 1778.
14 Smith, 1909.
15 Beale, 1983, 135.
16 NAS, HR 530/1, 4 September, 1740.
17 *British Parliamentary Papers* (1826), xviii, 95.
18 Bain, 1965, 105–7.
19 Scotland, 1969, 64.
20 Bain, (no date), 26.
21 *Ibid*., 86.
22 Simpson, 1947, 140.
23 Wright, 1898, 144; Boyd, 1961, 46.
24 Kerr, 1910, 204; Scotland, 1969, 189; Ferguson, 1978, 200; Simpson, 1947, 144, 215.
25 Boyd, 1961, 46.
26 Bain, (no date), 27.
27 Beale, 1983, 135.
28 *British Parliamentary Papers*, xviii, 95.
29 Fenton and Walker, 1981.
30 *Ibid*., 53.
31 *Ibid*., 91.
32 *Ibid*., 105.
33 *Ibid*., 56.
34 *Ibid*., 99.
35 NAS, HR 312/1, 20 June 1788.
36 Smout, 1972, 283.
37 Somerville, 1861, 340.

38 Fenton and Walker, 1981, 69.
39 *Ibid.*, 56.
40 Somerville, 1861, 340.
41 Thomson, 1875.

42 Fenton, 1976, 198–9.
43 NAS, HR 277/2.
44 NAS, HR 191/1 February 1786.
45 Tancred, 1907, 300–1.

Bibliography

Bain, A. *Education in Stirlingshire*, London, 1965.

Bain, A. *Education Act of 1696 in West Lothian* (Department of Educational Studies Publication No 1), Callendar Park College of Education, 1974, 86

Bain, A, *Life and Times of the Schoolmaster in Central Scotland in the 17th and 18th Centuries* (Department of Educational Studies Publication No 3), Callendar Park College of Education, (no date), 26.

Beale, J M. In Withrington, D J, ed, *History of the Burgh and Parochial Schools of Fife*, London, 1983.

Boyd, W. Education in Ayrshire Through Seven Centuries, London, 1961.

Fenton, A. *Scottish Country Life*, Edinburgh, 1976.

Fenton, A and Walker, B. *Rural Architecture of Scotland*, Edinburgh, 1981.

Ferguson, W. *Scotland 1689 to the Present*, paperback edn, Edinburgh, 1978.

Glaister, R T D, 'Education in the Presbytery of Jedburgh in the 18th Century', PhD, Open University, 1983.

Graham, H G. *The Social Life of Scotland in the 18th Century*, vol 1, 3rd edn, London, 1969.

Kerr, J. *Scottish Education*, Cambridge, 1910.

Scotland, J. *The History of Scottish Education*, vol 1, London, 1969.

Simpson, I J. *Education in Aberdeenshire before 1872*, London, 1947.

Smith, J. *History of Kelso Grammar School*, Kelso, 1909.

Smout, T C. *A History of the Scottish People*, paperback edn, Glasgow, 1972.

Somerville, T. *My Own Life and Times*, Edinburgh, 1861.

Tancred, G. *Rulewater and Its People*, Edinburgh, 1907.

Thomson, J. *The Life and Times of William Thomson*, Kelso, 1875.

Walters, A M, History of the Orrock Bequest and Two Hundred Years of Secondary Education in Hawick, *Transactions of the Hawick Archaeological Society*, 1954.

Watson, G, History of Jedburgh Grammar School, reprinted from Jedburgh Gazette, 1909.

Withrington, D J, Lists of Schoolmasters teaching Latin, 1690, *Miscellany of the Scottish History Society*, 10, 1965.

Withrington, D J, What is and What might be: Some Reflections on the Writing of Scottish Educational History, *Scottish Educational Studies*, 2 (2), 1970.

Wright, A. *History of Education and of the Old Parish Schools of Scotland*, Edinburgh, 1898.

SERVANTS OF THE OLD COLLEGE, UNIVERSITY OF GLASGOW: MISDEMEANOURS AND DISCIPLINARY METHODS

A D Boney

There were two categories of servant in the University of Glasgow in the seventeenth, eighteenth and nineteenth centuries, those of 'regular' employment with an annual salary and 'casuals', employed temporarily and paid by the day. There was no guarantee of permanency with those employed over the longer terms. The posts were annually renewable and continuity of employment depended on satisfactory service and behaviour. The following were the annually renewable posts:

Bedellus
Janitor (also called Porter)
Under-Janitor (also called Janitor's Man)
Chamberlain (also called Chamber Keeper)
Scavenger
Gardener

Either the Under-Janitor or Scavenger could also serve as Bell Ringer, for which duty there was extra payment.

The basic salaries paid tend to give a misleading impression of relative status [1]:

Salaries paid in 1703, all in Scots money

Bedellus £52 (Thomas Young)
Janitor £120 (Claud Hamilton)
Under-Janitor £20 (James Taylor)
Chamberlain £33.6.8d (David Holms)
Scavenger £13.6.8d (Walter Langmuir)

The Bedellus was the oldest established of them all dating back to the incorporation on 23 September 1451 of the Arts Faculty, the founding alumni.[2] The office of Janitor or Porter is of later foundation dating back to the Nova Erectio of 1577, the 'new foundation' charter ensuring the collegiate organisation of the University.[3] Whilst the basic salary of the Bedellus, was lower than that of the Janitor the former took precedence over all the others in the proportions of the extra earnings which came from a wide range of perquisites, including payments from students on matriculation, at examinations and on graduation. There were other sources of such income open to all servants, and it is difficult to assess the actual income for any of them.

The Bedellus in the seventeenth and eighteenth centuries was the appointee of the Rector, and on ceremonial occasions preceded the Rector whilst suitably robed and bearing the mace. From the seventeenth to the nineteenth century he officiated at the Blackstone examinations, viva voce examinations during which the student sat on a slab of black marble incorporated into a chair. At these examinations the Bedellus kept the time. In many ways, with his several other duties, he was the Rector's 'maid of all work' (as described by one historian of the University).

The Janitor resided in the College and was the guardian of the main gate, responsible for preventing unauthorised persons from entering the grounds or buildings. As the title implies, the Under-Janitor was the Janitor's assistant and factotum, assisting in the several other duties, especially the supply of candles and fires in the lecture halls. The Chamberlain was the bed-maker, linen supplier and general cleaner for the students in residence. The Scavenger was responsible for cleaning the courts and paths. From 1704, a Gardener was employed primarily for the Physic Garden, with an annual salary of £72 Scots. Prior to this the gardens were maintained more on a casual basis. Decisions on conditions of employment and any disciplinary measures were made by the Faculty, which was the governing body, consisting of the Rector, Principal, Professors and Regents in the seventeenth century. In the eighteenth century, the title of Regent was abandoned and all became Professors. Any suspension of a servant due to a misdemeanour could lead to loss of pay and loss of rented accommodation supplied by the University.

Misdemeanours and Judgements

1. Adam Wilson, Gardener

Adam Wilson was employed on occasions in the 'Great Yard' (also 'Great Orchard') at the rear of the College Building in the High Street. The sums he earned were variable; £14 Scots in 1684, £85 Scots in 1686 'for work about the Colledge Yeard', and £13.6.8d Scots in 1691. On 4 September 1692, the Faculty met to consider 'the complaint against one Adam Wilson, one of the gardiners of the Colledge'.[4] Wilson was then 'compeared' and admitted that '… he cutt three elm trees and one ash tree of the planting belonging to the Colledge in the Great Orchyeard', offences committed 'without knowledge or allowance of the Masters thereof'. It was decided that he should pay the University £20 Scots for each of the four trees cut down, and the Faculty '… ordain him to be sent and lye in the Tolbooth till he repay the same'. The Tolbooth, the Town House or Prison, had been built in 1626 at the junction of the High Street

and the Trongate, about 300 metres down the High Street from the College.[5] No further reference is made to Wilson. Presumably he sold the trees to a merchant or merchants in the town. The Faculty's valuation of each tree was based on an Act of Parliament. The valuations suggest well-developed trees, so Wilson may not have been the only person engaged in the felling process. The timing of the Faculty meeting also suggests that the offences were committed in the summer vacation period. The Faculty was determined that any money made from the sale was to come back to them.

2. William Craig, Gardener

William Craig was appointed Gardener for the Physic Garden from Candlemas 1719, under the 'Bottanist' and Overseer of the Garden, John Marshall. Marshall died in September of the same year. Meanwhile a joint Chair of Botany and Anatomy had been founded by King George I in 1718, and the first occupant, Thomas Brisbane, took up his post in March 1720. Brisbane taught Botany and supervised the running of the Physic Garden but refused to teach Anatomy. He was said to be sickened by cadaver dissection and further claimed that such a requirement was not stated in his Royal Commission. The teaching of Anatomy was carried on by surgeons in the town, who were paid out of class fees. Brisbane continued to receive his professorial salary of £360 Scots and remained in office until 1742.

Craig seems to have worked competently for the first couple of years after his appointment, ordering plants from local nurserymen with the order forms countersigned by Brisbane. However, changes were in the air which suggest that he was not working altogether satisfactorily. At the Faculty meeting on 29 June 1722 there was discussion on the future improvements in the working of both the Physic Garden and the Great Garden [6]:

> … And considering that it may be necessary in order to the prosecuting of the said proposal which the ffaculty approved of that there may be for some time two Gardiners and William Galbraith Gardiner being named as a person

well qualified for taking care of the Physick Garden and other parts of Gardinery and James Loudon being named as one skilled in training hedges and evergreens. The ffaculty appoint Dr Brisbane to agree with the said William Galbraith to enter Gardiner to the College at Martinmas next and they appoint Mr. Jo. Loudon to agree with James Lowdon to enter likewise at the same time and the Faculty considering likewise that after Martinmas they will not have occasion for William Craig do yt order him to be warned away from their service.

John Loudon, at that time a Regent, was to be the first Professor of Logic in 1725, and was assuming some responsibility for running the Great Garden.

Six days later the Faculty met again to consider a serious case of misbehaviour.[7] Brisbane and Loudon had informed Craig that he was to leave the service of the College at the following Martinmas, whereupon Craig had 'rooted out and destroyed some valuable plants in the Garden upon Monday last & att the same time behaved himself very rudely and indecently to the sd Masters'. John Stirling, the Principal, on being informed of this had consulted some colleagues on the Tuesday, with the result that Craig had to surrender his keys to the Garden to Stirling, who also discharged him from '. . . all further attendance upon & to do with the sd Garden'. All tools and utensils belonging to the Garden were to be handed over to the Bedellus, Thomas Young. The Faculty meeting of 5 July was to receive Stirling's report and agree to his actions. Craig's behaviour had resulted in an instant sacking. This not only deprived him of a job but also his home. The resident Gardener was entitled to a rented cottage in the Blackfriars Wynd, a short street at right angles to the High Street and which bordered the Physic Garden. James Loudon, one of the two due to start work at Martinmas, was to be asked to start immediately in place of Graig. The other Gardener, William Galbraith, could not take up an earlier appointment.

There were still some echoes of the affair in the following year. A precept dated 13 February 1723 addressed to the College Factor, Andrew Carmichael, authorised him to pay £1.13.4d 'for the extracts of Mrs Craig's assignays their discharge to the University of the whole rent and due by it to the sd. Mrs Craig and this without receipt shall be your warrant'.[8] Mrs Craig was owed some money for rent paid in advance to the College, but seemingly she owed money to her assignees. On 23 July 1723, another precept was issued by the Principal authorising the Factor to pay 'two pounds seventeen Shill and eight pennies Sterlin' to Willian Craig. No reason is given but there is a proviso, 'Of the above sum there is seven shill Sterlin to be paid to William Galbraith to the Physick Garden in the acct of Rob Dick Gardiner at Castlemilk, to whom Wm Craig owes'.[9] The sum owed was probably for the purchase of plants.

3. John McAulay, Bedellus

John McAulay is first listed in the annual accounts for 1730. His predecessor in office, Thomas Young, had served the University for 35 years. By contrast, McAulay's period of service is the shortest known for a Bedellus, as seen in the Faculty minutes for the meeting on 22 March 1732.[10]

> The Rector having acquainted the meeting that he had thought fit to dismiss John McAula from being the Bedal to the University for refusing to officiate. He appointed Dugald Weir to be Bedell in his room, who was called in and promised to be faithful to his office.

The Rector was John Orr of Barrowfield.

McAulay's refusal to officiate left the University without a leading figure for its ceremonials. Just how protracted this refusal was is not known, but a substitute had to be found. The servant chosen as the stand-in was Archibald Campbell, the Under-Janitor. In due course Campbell sought recompense for his extra duties:[11]

> To the Revd Principle and rest of Honrble Faculty The Humble Petition of Archibald Campbell Humbly Sheweth that whereas I have done the office of Bedellus for Six Months

I humbly entreat that you would take it to Consideration And do as You shall see Meet and keep it off the first end of his Fee as you and the rest of the Faculty shall see Meet.

Coll. Glasg. 27 June 1732

Campbell's claim was based on six months of extra duty. The Faculty decided that he be paid 'ten merks Scots' (£6.13.4d). Despite being dismissed out of hand McAulay received £33.6.8d Scots – 80 per cent of his annual salary. Notably, his annual salary was £40 Scots, less than the £52 paid to Thomas Young. However, Young also served as an unofficial Master of Works, which may explain the difference.

4. Dugald Weir, Bedellus

Dugald Weir's appointment as Bedellus was announced to the Faculty on the same day as John McAulay's dismissal was announced, as already described. At some time during his service Weir was also deprived of office for an unknown offence, but neither the offence nor when it was committed is mentioned in the Faculty minutes. The only reference is to be found in a letter from Weir begging for reinstatement, but this missive is undated [12]:

Unto the Honble and Reverend the Rector Principal Dean of Faculty and Remanent Members and Professors of the University and College of Glasgow The Petition of Dougald Weir Bedellus humbly Sheweth That your Petitioner having by his own fault given Ground of Offence to your Lordship and the Remanent Members, for wi I stand justly Suspended from My Office and being most Sensible of the Offence I have given I do Most humbly beg pardon for the same and do hereby solemnly promise that I shall never in time coming be guilty of any Like offence and shall endeavour to behave my Self becomingly for the Future. May it Therefore please your Lordships and Remanent members of the University Meeting to Repone me to My sd Office and your Petitioner shall ever pray &c.

Dugal Weir

The Rector and Faculty accepted Weir's letter of apology and he was restored to office. He died at some time either in late November or December 1739. A minute of the Faculty meeting of 25 April 1740, records the payment to his widow of half a year's salary from Whitsunday to Martinmas 1739, '... after which he died'.[13]

5. Robert Crosse, Chamber Keeper

The Faculty meeting of 4 May 1758 gave consideration to a request from John Donaldson, Chamber Keeper since 1738. Donaldson's submission was '... that he is unable thro' age and infirmities to Discharge the duties of said office by himself, and has earnestly desired the meeting to appoint a proper person to assist him'.[14] A prior arrangement had been made, since the minute continues '...The University meeting do hereby unanimously constitute and appoint his nephew, Robert Crosse to be his Assistant in the said office'. There was an additional clause; it was agreed that Crosse should succeed Donaldson '... at the expiration of five years reckoning from Whitsunday next. Provided always that the said John Donaldson die or resign before the end of the said five years that the said Robert Crosse shall ipso facto be his successor in said office'.

Donaldson's annual salary was £33.6.8d Scots. As his Assistant, Crosse was paid £9.12.0d Scots. At the Faculty meeting of 29 January 1760 Crosse's behaviour came under examination:[15]

Sundry complaints of gross faults having been made to the meeting against Robert Crosse, Assistant to John Donaldson Chamber-Keeper and being duly summoned he confessed to the truth of the said facts laid to his charge. And the meeting annul the minute of 4 May 1758 in his favour unless upon his future good behaviour they shall see cause to restore him the Reversion of his Uncle's office which is to be during the pleasure of the University meeting.

The nature of the complaints against Crosse are not known but they were of sufficient magnitude to lose him his guaranteed succession to his Uncle's job. His behaviour subsequently must have been satisfactory. In the College Accounts for 1763, five years after his appointment as Assistant, he is named and paid as Chamber Keeper with the salary of £33.6.8d Scots. John Donaldson meanwhile received a pension of £12 Scots, but he died in 1764.

Crosse's tenure of office came under scrutiny in 1772, as reported in the Faculty minutes for the 26 November meeting.[16] A Mr Jaques, an M.A. in Law, complained that Crosse '. . . had behaved in a violent and unwarranted manner' in pretending by force to remove the lock from the door of Mr Jaques's room. The Meeting ordered Crosse 'to ask pardon in the most humble manner from Mr. Jaques which was done'. Some further complaints had been received regarding one source of perquisite which came to Crosse, namely, '... He demands more than one shilling from students in the Mathematical class for fires. He shall not pressure to ask more than one shilling from each student and the like in every private class with Certification to him. If any complaint shall be repeated and verified he shall instantly be deprived of his office in College'. One is left wondering just for how long these attempts at extra charging had gone on.

A milder rebuke came in April 1776, as reported in the Faculty minutes. This time Crosse was not alone but joined by John Alexander (Under Janitor) and Alexander Gowan (Scavenger). They were ordered to '... collect their dues from the students themselves and not to bother the Professors'.[17] Crosse died at some time in late 1792, and his successor was Donald Cameron.[18] Crosse had some 34 years total in service, despite some slips in behaviour on the way.

6. John Fisher, Scavenger

John Fisher was appointed Scavenger in 1761. His sacking in 1766 remains a mystery. On 4 June 1766 the Faculty decided to hold a meeting on the next day at 3 o'clock '...to determine in the affairs of John Fisher, Scavenger and any other affairs of the University that shall be ready and the said John Fisher and John Bryce Janitor are ordered to be summoned to attend at that hour with such witnesses as they shall have chance to adduce'.[19] No record of the next day's

meeting is available, and the reason for this omission is to be found in the minutes of the meeting held on 6 June:

> A vacancy having been made in yesterday's meeting (the minutes of which are kept in retentis) of the office of Scavenger by the dismission of John Fisher for misdemeanour the meeting proceeded to choose another into that office and accordingly did make choice of William Hunter to perform the office of Scavenger during the pleasure of the University which office he is to execute under the direction of John Bryce the Bedal.

One is left wondering at the nature of Fisher's misdemeanour that prevented it from being placed on record. The other notable feature is that the Janitor and Bedellus were of the same names. That two individuals were involved is verified in the University's records. John Bryce, the Janitor, died in 1772; John Bryce the Bedellus died in 1775. Fisher's dismissal may have had some implications for John Bryce the Janitor in that the new Scavenger was to work under the direction of John Bryce the Bedellus. Perhaps the Janitor was held to be at fault for not properly controlling Fisher's behaviour.

7. Alexander Duncan, Janitor

Alexander Duncan was appointed in 1772 in succession to John Bryce. He was to receive a sharp reminder of his responsibilities in December 1775, as recorded in the Faculty's minutes.[20]

> Complaints having been received that the classes are by improper persons disturbed at the hours of teaching the Janitor whose Business it was to hinder such persons to give disturbance was rebuked for his negligence, with certification that if he continues to neglect his duty he will be dismissed from his office by the meeting.

On 17 January 1776, 17 days after the above reprimand, Duncan was again in trouble. John Anderson, Professor of Natural Philosophy informed the meeting of Faculty, that 'on Friday last his class was disturbed by an improper person coming in'. A meeting of the *Jurisdictio-*

Ordinaria having been called it had decreed that the Janitor be fined half-a-crown, which the Faculty ordered to be paid immediately.[21] The *Jurisdictio-Ordinaria* was the University's own court exercising judicial authority. It was doubly unfortunate for Duncan that Anderson's class had been disturbed. Anderson was by nature argumentative, delighting in stirring up trouble, and frequently at odds with his fellow Professors. In all probability he himself dealt effectively with the intruder. Somewhat to the annoyance of his colleagues he was inclined to call meetings of the judicial body for sometimes trivial offences, although there may have been some justification in this instance. Anderson's quarrelsome nature resulted in him being suspended from the *Jurisdictio-Ordinaria* in 1784. We can assume that Duncan learned his lesson. He continued in service until his death in 1787, with no further adverse report.

8. Peter Forrest, Janitor

Peter Forrest was appointed Janitor in 1787 in succession to Alexander Duncan. His misbehaviour first comes to notice after some 8 years in service. The Faculty meeting on 18 May 1795 discussed complaints against Forrest.[22] He had, for a long time, been remiss in his duties in not properly attending to his responsibilities regarding the Main Gate to the College, for which he had been frequently admonished in the past. The Principal was to charge him '… to be more attentive in future to preventing disorderly persons from entering the College, and from entertaining improper persons in his house'. If he did not comply and there were any further complaints he would be suspended from office. Finally, he was only to show the library to 'decent and respectable people'. Since the Janitor's residence was beside the Main Gate it was not surprising that there would be strong objections to him using it as a meeting place for friends. It was a tradition in the University that the Janitor could stock and supply wines for professorial entertainments and to make a small profit on the proceedings. Forrest's daughter, May, on occasions cooked the food for small professorial dinners. Whilst the town's licensing authorities

disapproved of this wine supplying practice, the University allowed its continuation as a demonstration of its independence of town rulings. Whilst the Faculty introduced their own rulings to more strictly control the practice in the late 1780s, it was not until 1829 that the Principal, Duncan MacFarlan, made a proposal which met with the unanimous approval of the Faculty, namely, '… the practice of selling liquors in the Janitor's house be discontinued'.[23] Perhaps Forrest and his friends had been making too liberal a use of the wine stocks. The nature of the admonition given on 18 May 1795 rather suggests that this was due to a culmination of numerous previous offences.

The ruling made in May 1795 that only decent and respectable people should be shown the library was in advance of the coming summer vacation. In the eighteenth century, the College buildings and its grounds were tourist attractions. Forrest's next contretemps was in August 1795. On 27 August a meeting was hurriedly called of those Professors still in residence.[24] A strong complaint had been received from Isaac Milner, Dean of Carlisle Cathedral, who, on a recent visit to Glasgow, 'coming to view the College, met with insolent and abusive behaviour from the College Porter'. Forrest may well have met his match.[25] Milner, then 45 years of age, was an eminent divine, mathematician and natural philosopher. From humble beginnings he had entered Queens' College, Oxford as a Sizar in 1770, had come first in the Mathematical Tripos of 1774, and was elected a Fellow of Queens' in 1776. He was renowned for his prowess in academic disputations and his standing in the University brought him the Presidency of Queens' College in 1788. He was appointed Dean of Carlisle in 1791, spending 3 to 4 months of the year there, and always ensuring that he chaired any Chapter meetings. He evidently managed both his appointments with success, running 'tight ships' in each case. The nature of the confrontation between Forrest and Milner at the College Gate can be imagined. With his combined academic and ecclesiastical standing Milner would no doubt have expected some deferential response to his request for entry.

Forrest thought otherwise. Just how well Milner interpreted replies in a loud broad Lowland Scots accent is not known. But Forrest had the last word – the Main Gate stayed shut.

The Professors meeting on 27 August called Forrest before them and stated the nature of the complaint made by Milner. Forrest's behaviour regarding the Dean's request was deemed 'improper and insolent'. The outcome was deferred until the following October when all members of the Faculty would be in residence. No further mention of the affair is to be found in the minutes of the October meeting or later. For reasons unknown the matter seems to have been dropped. In addition to the Principal, the Faculty contained Professors who were also Ministers of the Church of Scotland, and others were Elders. Perhaps the affair brought back memories of past differences between presbyterians and episcopalians. Forrest continued in employment.

In March 1802, a serious complaint against Forrest was lodged by James Balloch, a medical student, in a letter addressed to the Principal and read out at a Faculty meeting:[26]

Reverend Sir

I am sorry to address you on such a disagreeable subject, but it is of a nature that calls for your intervention and that of the Faculty. Peter Forrest, the Porter, and his family have long been in the habit of insulting friends when they come to visit me: unwilling to trouble the Faculty I bore this with patience but their behaviour last Monday night in particular was so intolerable that I am compelled to apply for redress. Whilst standing within the Gate of the College, and wishing some friends (who had just left my room) a good-night, I was driven into the street by the violence with which the Porter's daughter shut the gate. I knocked repeatedly for re-admission and received the greatest abuse in reply. I was let in by the Porter himself who, after locking the gates (thereby preventing my friends coming to my assistance) seized me by the throat with both hands, and in this manner, dragged me, almost suffocated, up and down the court, till he, falling in the

struggle, I made my escape, not without bruises and having my clothes very much torn. These circumstances I can prove by testimony of several of my friends, and one of the College Servants. Trusting that such improper conduct will not be overlooked, I remain

                          Reverend Sir

Glasgow College   Your Most
                Obedient Servant

24 Febr. 1802   James Balloch.

The meeting then went on to hear evidence of Balloch's complaint, and called in Forrest to hear his defence. The Faculty decided that Forrest's conduct had been highly unjustifiable, 'and in respect of his conduct, both in this instance and for several years past, they adjourn this meeting until Thursday next at 3 o'clock to determine what Measures it may be proper for the Faculty to take, with regard to the office of Porter to the College'. In fact this next meeting was involved with a discussion on what at first sight seems a separate issue, namely, 'That it would be in many respects highly beneficial that the right of appointing the Porter, now belonging to the Principal and his successors in Office, were possessed by the Faculty'.[27] Whilst the Rector could appoint and dismiss the Bedellus the same responsibility for the Porter (Janitor) lay with the Principal. At the time the Principal was Archibald Davidson, Dean of the Thistle. With Forrest's record of unpredictable and sometimes violent behaviour the Faculty's decision at this meeting was a direct outcome of his several misdemeanours.

Further discussion of Forrest's conduct followed at the Faculty meeting on 17 May 1802.[28] Davidson informed the meeting that since 5 May he had received various complaints from several Professors of 'gross improprieties in the conduct of Peter Forrest' with the result that he had come to the conclusion that Forrest 'was an unfit person to hold office', a conclusion which seems to have been a long time coming. Yet whilst recommending Forrest's dismissal Davidson proposed that he should receive 'a small alimentary annuity' to save him from absolute want. This provision would be £7 Sterling annually for life, to commence at next Lammas (1 August). Forrest would be dismissed as from 10 June. In addition to the £7 (to be paid out of College funds), Davidson also proposed that an additional alimentary provision of £5 Sterling should be paid to Forrest on 1 January in each year, this to be paid by the Janitor who succeeds him.

After some deliberation the Faculty eventually agreed with Davidson's proposals. Forrest was called into the room and dismissed in their presence, and he agreed to go away on the terms described above on 10 June. A committee of Davidson and three others was elected to ensure that the whole business was brought to a conclusion, and to take any legal steps necessary to enforce the removal if this became necessary. Where Forrest was concerned no chances were to be taken. Why it took so long to remove a servant who had been a thorn in the flesh to members of the society for so long remains a mystery. Perhaps Davidson, who had appointed Forrest, could not bring himself to remove him, or could not admit to himself that he had been wrong to appoint the man in the first place. Davidson was by now well advanced in years – he died on 3 July 1803. A replacement Janitor was required as from 19 June 1802. The Faculty decided that Archibald Cameron, currently the Chamber Keeper, should be appointed as interim Janitor until 10 January 1803, '… in order that they may have full time to find a proper person to be recommended to the Principal by them to be appointed by him College Porter'. Note the implication: the Faculty would choose the man whom the Principal could appoint. Their experiences with Forrest evidently left them with distrust in Davidson's judgement. Forrest had been 15 years in post. The affair with Balloch was not the sole cause of his dismissal but effectively brought matters to a head as far as the Faculty was concerned. However, he came away with a regular payment of £12 per annum. From 1789–1801 he and his daughter regularly received payments from the College funds for supplying food and drink for small dinner parties on various celebratory occasions. There is a curious dichotomy in that whilst his general conduct obviously left much to be desired he was still to be trusted with such entertainment responsibilities.

In January 1803 Archibald Cameron has his appointment renewed for another twelve months on the understanding that he could be dismissed at a month's notice if he proved unsatisfactory in any way.[29] At the same time it was decided that Cameron should pay Forrest the £7 at Lammas as well as the £5 on 1 January. Faculty was here back-tracking on their original agreement that the Lammas £7 should come from College funds. The basic annual salary of the Janitor was till £10 Sterling (equal to £120 Scots). However, he lived in college accommodation rent free, with free coal and candles, and with his overall salary much larger due to a number of perquisites. Cameron was to continue in office as Janitor until 1817. In this same year the name Peter Forrest again surfaces in the Faculty's records. It was now decided that he be paid 5 shillings per week by the newly appointed Janitor Walter McNair.[30] For how long he continued to receive this annual £13 'alimentary allowance' is not known.

9. James Walker, Scavenger and Bellringer

The Faculty meeting on 7 December 1827, discussed a complaint made against James Walker. He had been irregular at ringing the bell at six o'clock in the morning.[31] As with similar academic institutions bells governed the life of the University. At six o'clock in the morning, the 'Small Bell' was rung, followed by the 'Great Bell' in the Steeple one hour later. The 'Small Bell' was then rung throughout the day 'at the hour of meeting of the classes' (the 'Hurry Bell', a reminder which is still rung throughout the day in term time in the present-day University). The 'Small Bell' was then rung at six o'clock in the evening, and finally the 'Great Bell' at seven o'clock. It would be a bad start to the day if the first ringing did not take place. Walker's irregularity resulted in a ruling that the morning bell at six would henceforth be rung by John Blythe, the Night Watchman, for which he would be paid one shilling per week, to be deducted out of Walker's salary.

Walker's conduct came under review in November 1831 by a Committee set up by Faculty to determine the duties and offices of the College servants.[32] The Committee decided that Walker was altogether unfit for the duties of his office, and that he be dismissed. However, since Walker had a young family, and because it would probably be some time before he found suitable employment elsewhere, he should be allowed the rent of his dwelling and five shillings weekly to be paid directly to his wife until the following Whitsunday (15 May). Hence he could live on in the accommodation rent free and his family receive some financial support for another six months.

10. Thomas Yuille, Scavenger and Bellringer

Thomas Yuille was appointed in succession to Walker. Within a year or so he was complaining to the Faculty that some students were not paying him the one shilling he was entitled to from all students in the University, with the medical students being the worst offenders. He made similar complaints in 1835, 1836 and 1840. However, in December 1847, the Faculty gave consideration to complaints of Yuille's neglect of his duties and drunkenness.[33] He was to be reminded of his duties and warned that he might not be re-engaged on May next.

The Faculty instructed the Committee on the duties and offices of servants and to pass on these resolutions to Yuille. This committee, chaired by A A W Maconochie, Professor of Civil Law, reported back to the Faculty through its Chairman on 27 December 1847.[34] This report was of some length. Yuille had been ordered to appear before this Committee in the Fore Hall at midday on the previous Saturday, together with the other servants. The principal, Duncan MacFarlan, then referred Yuille to his own copy of his duties and responsibilities, and then pointed out the numerous complaints made since the summer, both of neglecting his duties and 'gross and frequent intoxication', for which he had already been severely reprimanded. The Committee then informed Yuille that they would recommend to Faculty that he be given notice of termination of his employment on

1 May next, and that there would be only the slightest chance of any re-engagement, depending on conduct. The Committee then reported that after this meeting on the Saturday, Yuille had walked out of the College without informing his colleagues, and before he could hand over to the Night Watchman. Hence his duties had been 'utterly neglected'. The Committee had reason 'to suppose that in the state of recklessness and half intoxication in which he had habitually been during the winter he has again resorted to the Bottle' – this despite being warned at the Saturday meeting that any further inebriety would result in instant dismissal. When summoned by the Committee on the following Monday, Yuille explained that he had suffered from an attack of influenza. This was not believed. In consequence, the Committee recommended to Faculty that Yuille be immediately dismissed, such a move 'having become essential for the future efficiency of the other servants, the safety of public property committed to them, and it may well be added the respectability of the College'. Whilst his instant dismissal was recommended, out of consideration for his wife, and to give him time to reform if that is possible, he should receive all the Class fees yet remaining to be collected on his behalf. It was also ordered that he give up his keys, leave the College, and that the other servants be told he was not to enter the College again.

The Faculty approved and endorsed the Committee's report. And resolved to dismiss Yuille, with allowance for the outstanding Class fees. He was to hand over his keys and utensils to the Chamberlain and not to enter the precincts of the College in future. On 7 January 1848, the Committee reported to Faculty that its instructions had been carried out. Yuille had submitted a petition asking for his case to be reconsidered, but no such allowance was to be made.[35] This lengthy and formal dealing with Yuille's affair was intended to send a clear warning to the other servants. Habitual drunkenness was not to be tolerated, and if neglect of duty was also involved, judgement would be swift and sure – instant dismissal.

Lachlan McPherson, Bedellus – a Mild Reproof

Lachlan McPherson was appointed Janitor in 1853. After the death of the Bedellus, John Calder, in 1862, the post was held in abeyance as a separate appointee and combined with that of Janitor. McPherson assumed the dual role with the result he is referred to under both titles. His family background is not without interest, as reported in the local press in September 1899 after his death at the age of 82 years.[36] His grandfather, a farmer at Laggan, served under his chieftain Cluny in the 45 Rebellion. His father, an NCO in the 42nd Foot (The Black Watch), had served in both the Peninsular Wars and at Waterloo. Prior to his appointment as Janitor, McPherson had been butler to Mr Walter Crum of Thornliebank who was father-in-law to Sir William Thomson (Lord Kelvin) on the latter's first marriage. It was this previous experience as a butler that landed McPherson in trouble.

A Senate minute of the meeting on 3 November 1870, mentioned that McPherson was earning extra money by waiting at table at dinner parties given by leading citizens in the town. The Senate passed a resolution prohibiting him from such evening work 'except at Professors' houses'. At the same time a remit was passed to the Committee on the duties and services of College servants to enquire into the duties of the Janitor as the Principal's servant, and to consider his remuneration.[37] McPherson promptly sent in an application for an increase in salary as compensation for being prohibited from the extra work outside the College. The above Committee reported back to the Senate on 24 November.[38] It failed to see how any compensation could be granted for a source of income which was a 'systematic violation' of an order of Senate and the contract entered into by the Janitor. However the Committee recognised that his responsibilities and duties had been 'largely added to', and whilst no immediate increase in salary was recommended, such a recommendation might be made 'before long' subject to his continuing in his duties to the satisfaction of the Senate. Such an increase would be made on the

grounds of the 'special duties imposed on him'. This would seem to be a belated recognition of the dual role played by McPherson since 1862 as Janitor and Bedellus. Another result of the Committee's deliberations was to decide that the Janitor was not the personal servant of the Principal, Thomas Barclay, other than his being of service to the Principal as Head of the University, as with all the other servants. Whilst McPherson received a mild 'rap over the knuckles' over his extra earnings, his salary was to be increased. In April 1871, the Senate decreed that his annual salary would be raised from £105 to £120 as from the following May.[39]

The £105 per annum had dated from 1 May 1862, as decided at a Senate meeting earlier on 29 April.[40] This arrangement followed an earlier decision to pay all of the servants from College funds, and not to rely on piecemeal contributions from perquisites. The increases in such payments were in compensation for loss of the many extra earnings, mainly from students. For the Janitor this income was accompanied by a rent-free house and free coal and gas. In the 1880s McPherson's salary was raised to £130 per annum. On his death in September 1899 the following entry was made in the records of the Senate meeting of 13 October[41]:

> The Senate resolved to record in their minutes their deep regret at the death of the late Bedellus, Mr. Lachlan McPherson, who had served the University faithfully and well for the space of forty-six years, and instructed the Clerk to convey to his widow and family an expression of the Senate's sympathy with them in their bereavement.

As mentioned earlier, McPherson died when 82 years of age. From 1883 a Sub-Janitor had been appointed, paid £65 per annum, to assist him.

The 1870 complaint about his working outside of the University was made at a time of major changes in the University. On 7 November of that year the inaugural meeting was held in the new buildings on Gilmorehill, the buildings and grounds of the 'Old College' on the medieval site in the High Street having been sold to the City of Glasgow Union Railway Company. On

1. The Senate of the University of Glasgow standing in order of seniority on the Lion and Unicorn Stair in the Old College, 29 July 1870, on leaving the building for the last time. Lachlan McPherson, Bedellus, stands on the left of the picture bearing the 15th-century mace. Principal Thomas Barclay stands at the foot of the stair by the pillar on the left, with Professor John Caird, Divinity and Primarius, at his side. John Caird was to become Principal in 1873. Sir William Thomson, Professor of Natural Philosophy, stands behind Principal Barclay. (From the University Archives.)

29 July 1870 the Principal and the twenty-five Professors making up the Senate posed on the 1690 Lion and Unicorn Stair for a group photograph, the official record of their leaving the 'Old College' (Fig 1). Lachlan McPherson was included in the photograph, carrying the fifteenth-century mace in his role as Bedellus.

Summing up

The eleven cases of misdemeanours, of varying degrees of improper behaviour described should be seen in perspective. Between 1669 and 1899 some 80 servants of all grades were employed by the University, and the great majority served their masters without serious complaint. Indeed there are some striking examples of longevity of service:

John Alexander, Under-Janitor
51 years, 1733–1784

Alexander Gowan, Scavenger
then Under-Janitor
49 years, 1770–1819

*John McLachlan, Bedellus
47 years, 1775–1822

David Holms, Under-Janitor then
Chamber Keeper
46 years, 1692–1738

Lachlan McPherson, Janitor/Bedellus
46 years, 1853–1899

John Donaldson, Scavenger then
Chamber Keeper
39 years, 1724–1763

Thomas Young, Bedellus,
35 years, 1694–1729

John Bryce, Bedellus
35 years, 1740–1775

Robert Crosse, Assistant, then
Chamber Keeper
34 years, 1758–1792

John Calder, Bedellus
30 years, 1832–1862

Walter Langmuir, Scavenger,
28 years, 1696–1724

William Galbraith, Gardener
28 years, 1722–1750

(* Known as 'Honest John' to the students)

Of the above, one only, David Holms, retired with a pension; the others died in service.

The relatively small number of misdemeanours dealt with is perhaps not surprising. In the social climate of the time working for the University offered a much prized job security, with a regular income, rented accommodation and a small pension if one survived to advanced years in service. The latter event was a rarity, but with death in service some allowance was usually made to the dependents and whilst this payment might be over a limited period, in cases of subsequent severe hardship some charitable relief was invariably given. The other feature which gave some insurance to the University against lack of application or bad behaviour was that all posts were annually renewable on 1 May.

On reflection we may question the naivety of Adam Wilson who thought that he could get away with chopping down four trees in the Great Garden in the summer of 1692. We may also wonder how Peter Forrest, as Janitor, one of the two senior positions in the servant body and clearly a person of uncertain temper and application to his work, could have survived for 15 years in office despite regular complaints about him from Professors. The violent assaults by him and his daughter on the student James Balloch gave the opportunity for the Faculty to bring matters to a head. However, Dean Milner would not have been pleased to find that his complaint had resulted in no more action than a reprimand. Whilst violent behaviour towards a student almost cost Robert Crosse his job as Chamber Keeper, in another instance a violent confrontation between a student and a servant brought a very different result.[42] In November 1835, William Harris, a medical student, complained to the Faculty that the Chamber Keeper, William Taylor, had insulted and assaulted him in not allowing him entry into the class of Dr Charles

Badham, Professor of Practice of Medicine. The Faculty called for verbal accounts from the two involved and from student witnesses. The subsequent decision was in Taylor's favour. The Faculty ruled that he had been in 'strict discharge of his duty' in refusing Harris entry into the classroom without producing his class ticket. Had he succeeded he would have suffered academic penalties. The Faculty merely regretted that some violence had taken place on that occasion.

Drunkenness on duty, which led to the sacking of Thomas Yuille for his chronic failure to reform, was a misdemeanour closely watched. There was no ruling against the consumption of alcohol on the premises either for servants or for tradesmen from the town working in the College. The practice of supplying the latter with 'morning drinks' and afternoon 'four hourses', or alternatively adding 'drink money' to their wages, were customs of long standing. In the eighteenth century, whenever there were occasions of 'publick joy', such as Coronations, Royal birthdays or births, the servants shared a gallon of ale, it being remembered that one gallon Scots was equivalent to about three gallons in Imperial measure. Spirits of any kind were not allowed for the servants. Tradesmen doing an unpleasant job, such as cleaning out a well, were usually rewarded with either brandy or whisky. One instance of generous treatment by the Senate is worthy of mention. In September 1862 it was decided that each servant should be given £5 'To allow them to visit the International Exhibition in London'.[43]

The several histories of the University published over the years have rightfully given most attention to the academics and administrators who have controlled and guided its role as a seat of learning. The servants, the lower stratum of the society, have received only occasional mentions as individuals. Those tending to receive the most attention in the University's records were those achieving some notoriety through bad behaviour. However, in the histories of the 'Old College', examples of notorious behaviour have been described for some Professors.

Abbreviations

CA   College Accounts, plus reference number and year

GUA   Glasgow University Archives, plus reference number.

FM   Minutes of Faculty Meetings, plus. reference number of volume, page number and date

SM   Minutes of Senate Meetings, plus reference number of volume, page number and date

Notes and References

1 CA 266502, 1703
2 Durkan, J and Kirk, J. *The University of Glasgow, 1451–1577*, University of Glasgow Press, 1977, 10.
3 *Ibid.*, 283.
4 Innes, C and Robertson, J, eds, *Munimenta Alme Universitas Glasguensis*, 3, Maitland Club, 1854, 510.
5 Gibb, A. *Glasgow: The Making of a City*, London, 1983, 51.
6 FM 26634, 29 June 1722, 65.
7 FM 26634, 5 July 1722, 69
8 GUA 42652.
9 GUA 42664
10 FM 26639, 22 March 1732, 14.
11 GUA 40379
12 GUA 31123
13 FM 26648, 25 April 1740, 79.
14 FM 26650, 4 May 1758, 260.
15 FM 26651, 29 January 1760, 11.
16 FM 26690, 26 November 1772, 91.
17 FM 26691, 29 April 1776, 15.
18 FM 26694, 11 February 1783, 278.
19 FM 26653, 4 & 6 June 1766, 121–124.
20 FM 26690, 27 December 1775, 355.
21 FM 26690, 13 January 1776, 367.
22 FM 26695, 18 May 1795, 30.
23 FM 26699, 11 June 1829, 157.

24 FM 26695, 27 August 1795, 45.
25 Personal communication from the Very Rev Henry Stapleton FSA, Dean of Carlisle, 17 September 1991. Also data from *Dictionary of National Biography*.
26 FM 26696, 2 March 1802, 90–91.
27 FM 26696, 5 March 1802, 92.
28 FM 26696, 17 May 1802, 105.
29 FM 26696, 8 December 1802, 151.
30 FM 26698, 8 August 1817, 134.
31 FM 26699, 7 December 1827, 96.
32 FM 26699, 2 November 1831, 194.
33 FM 26700, 14 December 1847, 379.
34 FM 26700, 27 December 1847, 382–383.
35 FM 26700, 7 January 1848, 385.
36 *Evening News*, 25 September, 1899.
37 SM 26707, 3 November 1870, 81.
38 SM 26707, 24 November 1870, 91.
39 SM 26708, 13 April 1871, 138.
40 SM 26706, 19 April 1862, 187.
41 SM 26717, 13 October 1899, 167.
42 FM 26699, 6 November 1835, 296–7.
43 SM 26706, 17 September 1862, 196.

A Wartime Threshing Machine

Jane Durham and Helen M Kemp

Wartime conditions created problems for farmers, as shown by the following letters, covering the period from June 1940 till October 1943. The correspondence, kindly made available by the late Mrs Jane Durham of Scotsburn, Kildary, Easter Ross, was from the threshing machine supplier, Allan Brothers, Engineers, Ashgrove Engineering Works, Ashgrove, Aberdeen (Fig 1), and concerned the ordering, making and installation of a threshing mill on the farm of W G Paterson, The Ord, Invergordon, Ross-shire. These now old-fashioned looking blue carbon copies give a vivid portrayal of wartime difficulties. They also illustrate a form of business which, to a certain extent, was run on personal contacts and a system of favours, and which clearly did not fit in entirely with the methods of operation required by the Ministry of Agriculture and the Emergency Powers brought into play during World War II. As mentioned in the letter of 25 March 1943, an order placed by 'your esteemed Senior', Mr Paterson's father thirty-six years previously 'at Perth Highland Show in 1904 and the good turns he did us afterwards', obviously still carried some weight within the company of Allan Bros, ensuring, as much as may have been possible at the time, a manipulation of, or 'wriggling' under the 'restrictive orders' and form filling of the Ministry of Agriculture.

There were not only difficulties presented by the restrictions placed upon the transporting of goods during the war time period, but also, as this reference in Allan Bros' letter of 27 June 1940 which raised the problem of getting the same 'prime pre-war quality of all kinds of wood'

illustrates, in obtaining goods and materials. Their letter of 10 October 1941 tells that, 'Costs of production have … gone all to pieces since we quoted you' and from 28 October 1941, 'Makers insist on charging the price current at delivery'. These increases led to the cost of the threshing machine rising from the initial first estimate on the 27 June 1940 of £554, to the eventual price on completion in October 1943 of £658.

As the letters only afford us one side of the correspondence, we are left with some questions that we can only surmise the answers to, as for example why Mr Paterson was unable to take delivery of the completed plant at the beginning of February 1943, which resulted in an additional delay of six months to the receipt of his threshing machine. They do however illustrate the in-depth knowledge of farmers' working practices that Allan Bros. held, and their appreciation of the farmers' problems and dependence, as always, on the vagaries of the weather and the turning of the seasons.

27th June 1940

Dear Sir,

We now enclose estimate for proposed thrashing plant and also print showing lay out and trust you will find all details quite clear and easily understood. Owing to the Byres and covered Courts being alongside the whole length of the barn we do not see that a better straw arrangement can be got than the one discussed and incorporated in our print. The mill itself is rather far from the sheaf door and we have quoted for a Self feeding sheaf carrier which would cut down the number required to feed the mill to <u>one</u> and he would only have to cut the strings and spread out the sheaves on the Carrier as the sheaves would be forked direct from carts to Carrier which item would accordingly be a very labour saving one. We quite understand that you may not go on this season but if you have decided on a new plant you should place your order in time to get it made as long as properly matured and good quality timber is available. We ourselves have a good stock of prime pre-war quality of all kinds of wood sufficient to keep us going until the month of May next but after that we do not know what sort of stuff will be available but we do know that it will not be from pre-war sources. We will be very pleased to send you any further particulars or information which you may care to have.

Yours faithfully,

Allan Bros.

27th June 1940

SPECIFICATION OF TENDER

Dear Sir,

Referring further to our recent correspondence and visit of our Representative. We have now pleasure in quoting for proposed plant and specifying the various details as follows –

THRASHING MACHINE One 48 inches wide 'B' Type 'Allan' Semi-Portable Full Finishing Thrashing Machine with all details according to our latest standardised model per enclosed catalogue and detailed specification with the following additions

1. Drumshaft to be extended through barn wall and fitted with outer ball bearing plummer block with bolts for stone fast and loose pulleys and beltsetter.

2. Chaff and caving [short, broken straw from threshed grain] deliveries to be combined for entry into blower provision being made for taking off clean chaff when required by itself.

CHAFF AND CAVING BLOWER One Chaff and Caving Blower having steel centre with steel shaft running in ball bearings and having all internal surfaces of steel. Complete with all driving connections and the following galvanised steel piping 8 inches diameter. One offset, one square and, one bend, one half bend and 24 feet piping.

STRAW CARRIER One Straw Carrier 50 feet centres working at right angles with intake hopper and bevel gear drive. The carrier to be of the solid welded chain and rake type with three intermediate sliding door deliveries and end delivery and the outer end to be fitted with tension gear for keeping chains at proper working tension. All bearings to be fitted with grease lubrication. Complete with all driving connections etc. [This was marked 'Cancel']

GRAIN ELEVATOR One Grain Elevator 19 feet centres with connecting chute to mill. The elevators to have inside belt fitted with stamped steel cups 5 inches wide. Elevator to deliver into Hopper and provision made for bagging the grain or delivering into truck as desired. Complete with all driving connections.

SHEAF CONVEYOR One Self Feeding Sheaf Conveyor about 20 feet centres by 4 feet wide inside from sheaf door to drum. Canvas type on three belts and complete with all details include driving connections. [This was marked 'Cancel']

BRUISER One steel countershaft 6'0" long x 2 ¼" diameter with two ball

CONNECTIONS bearing plummer blocks one with bolts for stone and other mounted on W.I. standard, one pulley about 18" dia. (drive from motor) one do. About 16" dia. (drive to Bruiser) one belt 34 feet long x 4" wide x 4 ply.

GENERALLY All materials to be of the best quality and the workmanship of the highest class.

TELEPHONE No. 1361.

TELEGRAM AND CABLE ADDRESS:
"ASH," ABERDEEN.

A B C (5TH EDITION)
AND
PRIVATE CODES USED.

One Minute's Walk from
Kittybrewster Station,
L. & N. E. R.,
and
Woodside Electric Car

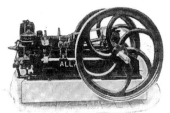

ALLAN BROTHERS,
(RICHARD S. ALLAN)

ENGINEERS,

ASHGROVE ENGINEERING WORKS,

ASHGROVE, ABERDEEN.

SPECIALITIES:
OIL ENGINES.
THRASHING MACHINES.

11th July 1940.

Letterhead of Allan brothers, Aberdeen. See the letter of 11 July 1940.

DELIVERY & ERECTION The whole of the above to be delivered per motor and fitted up by us. It is understand that we will supply all necessary installation plans, that you will do Mason and Joiner work and give our men help with any heavy lifts during erection. Our men will provide their own board and lodging.

PRICES

One 48 inches wide "B" Type Full Finishing Thrashing Machine with all additional details specified – £375 0 0

Chaff and Caving Blower and Piping £29 0 0

Strawcarrier with all details
[Marked 'Cancel'] £72 10 0

Grain Elevator do do £31 0 0

Sheaf Carrier do do
[Marked 'Cancel'] £35 0 0

Bruiser Connections   £11 10 0

£554 0 0

(Five hundred and fifty four pounds less 2 ½% Discount).

Guarantee In addition to our standard guarantee of performance as given on page 4 of our catalogue we undertake to finish off the above plant in the most approved manner and to leave all details to your complete satisfaction.

Yours faithfully,

Allan Bros.

11th July 1940.

Dear Sir,

We have to acknowledge your favour of the 9th inst. and note what you say about lay out of proposed barn out-fit and think the most has been made of the buildings as they are and that the plant would be a good and convenient one.

If you decide to go for next season the matter should be fixed up in good time.

We may say it is just 36 years since we got the first order from your Father and you can rely on us if History repeats itself doing our best for you.

Yours faithfully,

Allan Bros.

10th October 1941

Dear Sir,

We have a letter from Messrs A Mackenzie & Son, Achnagarron saying that you have again been considering the installation of a new mill and that if you cannot get the whole plant we specified you might be prepared to go in for a Portable and then take it off the wheels and incorporate it in the whole outfit when times settle up a bit.

The position here is that we have 58 Portable mills besides a few fixed ones on order. Thirty of these machines are Portables for next years Government programme and are ordered so far in advance to give time to get the raw materials forward as it is now taking much longer to get everything than formerly. We expect to finish up this seasons Government orders and a few of the most urgent private ones about the middle of January and as there is little chance of our managing a Portable sooner, we could put your whole proposed new plant through after that and should be able to install it about the end of January of early March and we hope this may suit you. We enclose illustration of Portable and price list the corresponding machine to the fixed one quoted you being the 48" B.P. type (Medium) priced at £540 (Five hundred and forty pounds). Costs of production have however gone all to pieces since we quoted you and the present price of the outfit as specified to you on 27th June 1940 would now be £695 (Six hundred and ninety five pounds) less 2 ½% and there is nothing surer than that prices will have to be very considerably increased for next season which means the rise comes into operation the first week of March.

Our advice to you would be to put in the fixed plant and be done with it all at the same time.

We trust you have had a good crop and a good harvest.

Yours faithfully,

Allan Bros.

28th October 1941

Dear Sir,

We have another letter from Messrs Mackenzie & Son regarding proposed 48" wide Portable mill on pneumatics and also a stacking elevator of medium length but we are not greatly enamoured with the elevator proposal as they are an item we do not like when fixed on the end of a mill. The following are the various types of elevators that have been made.

1. Portable elevator about 20 feet centres. This type is of course on its own wheels (iron) but possibly could be fitted with Pneumatics and can be hauled behind the mill.

2. Swinging type Elevator – turns round a half circle and can deliver at either side or behind mill. Is fixed to the mill.

3. Fixed Elevator attached to mill but can only deliver straight behind. We enclose print of this type which is our own make and one of which we are making for a 36 inches wide Portable machine for one of our Clients who uses lorries and is to cart the straw direct home from the fields during thrashing. This elevator is made so that it can be taken off when not required. This type of elevator can work between two rows of stacks or alongside one row but the straw has to be built either between where the stacks were or alongside where the one row was. The fashion in some districts is meantime to Bale the straw but this is only a passing phase for paper making and what we would recommend to you is a <u>Double String Trusser</u> which allows the straw being easily handled both when thrashing and also when moving the straw again to where it is to be used. The Trusser would be handy when you put the mill inside or if you had no need for any trussing it is an item that would be quite easily sold. All the elevators stack the straw loose so that subsequent handling is slow. If you decide on a Portable machine for fitting up inside afterwards you would need to fit the Chaff and Caving Blower on the machine as it would suit the inside layout which needs the special

bottom riddle case for the blower. The Chaff and Caving Blower is we think a good thing on a Portable as it saves time shifting the refuse and keeps the mill and immediate surroundings clear of all rubbish. If you must have an elevator No. 1 would we think suit your purpose best but we do not make this type and think it would be difficult to get one. The cost of the various items would be as follows –

(No.1). Portable Elevator about 20 feet on iron wheels about £170 (One hundred and seventy pounds) and Pneumatic wheels about £25 (Twenty five pounds extra). The above prices are approximate only and Makers insist on charging the price current at delivery.

48 inches wide B.P. type Portable on Pneumatics and with all details ready for the road £540 (Five hundred and forty pounds).

Chaff and Caving Blower with shaft running in ball bearings with driving connections and all galvanised piping to deliver about 20 feet from thrasher £35 (Thirty five pounds).

Double String Hornsby Trusser (fixed pattern) fitted complete on end of thrasher. Space between top of mill and trusser to be completely covered in with release door £87–15/- (Eighty seven pounds, fifteen shillings). Prices for thrasher, C. & Caving Blower and Trusser are less 2 ½% one month and include delivery at your nearest station or per road as found most convenient and our man sent to start machine.

We do not see that we can promise delivery sooner than about the time given in our previous letter but if you decide to go on you may be sure we will do our best for you.

Yours faithfully,

Allan Bros.

3rd December 1941

Dear Sir,

We duly received your favour of the 24th ult. ordering 48 inches wide mill for which we

thank you and will give all details our most careful attention. We got the print returned by Messrs Mackenzie yesterday and their letter has come in today. The arrangement is now as you will remember much the same as we proposed originally and will we think be a much straighter out job and a better working one with much less space wasted. Before we make out a new and final print we will give the arrangement a rough sketch out and send it to Messrs Mackenzie for your discussion and approval so as to be sure of having all details right.

We hear rumours of a considerable amount of crop being still out in Ross-shire and hope you are not one of the unfortunates.

Yours faithfully,

Allan Bros.

3rd August 1942

Dear Sir,

We are in receipt of your favour of the 30th ult. regarding new thrashing outfit on order. We have been keeping you in mind right along and have put through the accessories such as Straw Carrier etc. and as a matter of fact these are all finished, the intention being to slip through the mill at the first opportunity.

The Ministry of Agriculture who have sixty 48" portable machines on order with us, however, queered the pitch by ordering us to complete twenty machines for them before all others but we think we will be able to get your machine through about the month of October.

This is rather disappointing and we will be pleased to hear if you can carry on with the old mill until shortly before the new one is ready.

Yours faithfully,

Allan Bros.

18th September 1942

Dear Sir,

We are sorry there is to be some considerable delay in getting your esteemed order for 48 inches mill completed as the Ministry of Agriculture has ordered us to finish all government machines first and these instructions have of course to be obeyed. Copy of Ministry's letter enclosed.

This order is very disappointing as we have all details of your job completed except the mill itself.

Yours faithfully,

Allan Bros.

5th October 1942

Dear Sir,

We duly received your letter and delayed replying until we were sure what we could do about delivery of your mill.

We may say that we have all the iron work of the machine ready but we cannot get the wood work put through. The position at the moment is that we have still sixteen 48" Portable machines to put through for the Ministry and this will take us to the end of December.

As far as we can see we should have your machine ready to go out about the middle of January next and the job completed about a fortnight later. As already advised you we have all the rest of the work ready and it is certainly most disappointing to be held up for completion of the job after we had so much of it done.

We will however do the best we can for you under the circumstances.

Yours faithfully,

Allan Bros.

4th February 1943

Dear Sir,

We are pleased to be able to advise you that at last we have got your mill etc. at the finishing stages and should be able to forward the whole outfit in the course of a fortnight and will be pleased to hear this will suit you. Motor transport is now barred so that we will have to mount the machine on temporary wheels and suppose you will be able to haul the mill and cart the small stuff from Invergordon Station.

The only snag we are now up against is getting a suitable Railway waggon but will start agitating for one in good time.

Yours faithfully,

Allan Bros.

9th March 1943

Dear Sir,

We duly received your letter of the 10th ult. and were intensely disappointed that you were unable to take delivery of the mill etc. as we had great difficulty in getting the machine and so many attachments made. There was no room here to store so much stuff and as the mill is fitted with a special screen and blower which rendered it quite unsuitable for converting into a Portable there was no option left us but to send the machine and most of the other details to another Customer who had a very similar plant on order and who could take immediate delivery and so cleared our place. We understand that an order is coming from the Ministry of Agriculture at an early date taking over our total out-put as they did last year so that we are unable to say whether it will be possible to get another outfit put through for some time.

Yours faithfully,

Allan Bros.

17th March 1943

Dear Sir,

We are in receipt of your letter of the 15th inst. and note what you say. As we already advised you we were very much disappointed that you could not take delivery of the mill, when it was finished and your letter of the 10th ult. was so decided against delivery that we had to get the mill out of this because we really put your job through against Ministry instructions and if we had been caught the results might have been very serious. The same thing is going to happen this year unless we are mistaken as about the beginning of last month we had to send full particulars of all machines on order and <u>missed out your one</u> and we understand further restrictive orders are to be issued soon but we should know very soon now. We want to get your job done if at all possible and later when we know what is actually to happen we will write you to send us a letter saying that your present mill is absolutely useless and we will then specially approach the Ministry regarding the matter.

Yours faithfully,

Allan Bros.

25th March 1943

Dear Sir,

We are in receipt of your letter of the 23rd inst. For which we are obliged. We are afraid we have little to add to our letter of the 17th inst. except that we have heard from the Ministry that some sort of control is going on thrashing machines and orders are coming to us about the end of this month what we have to do but we will write you as soon as we have definite information. One thing is certain that we will do our level best to get your machine etc. put through again and after we hear definitely from the Ministry we will know better how to go about the matter as we never forgot the order we got from your esteemed Senior at Perth

Highland Show in 1904 and the good turns he did us afterwards.

Yours faithfully,

Allan Bros.

19th April 1943

Dear Sir,

Referring to your esteemed order for Thrashing Machine. We have today got instructions from the Ministry of Agriculture that all orders on our books as at and after the 31st March 1943 are to be disregarded and the machines re-ordered under approval of your local War Agricultural Executive and the approval confirmed by the Ministry.

Form AM/HRM/No.1 is necessary and we have written for a supply of these forms and on receipt of them we will send you one and write you further.

Yours faithfully,

Allan Bros.

In this month, the Department of Agriculture for Scotland issued an instruction that as from 31 March 1943, the supply of tractor ploughs, binders and threshing machines had to be approved by the appropriate Agricultural Executive. Subsequent letters are coloured by this fact.

23rd April 1943

Dear Sir,

We are in receipt of you favour of the 22nd inst. and note what you say. We have had during the last month or so to make five returns of all orders on our books unless is was attempts to trip us up if we had any variations but so far we have managed to wriggle through.

The whole thing now depends on the decisions of the Agricultural Committees so that you will need to impress your one of how urgently you need a machine. We had instructions a long time ago to disregard any fixed machine orders and that was the reason we had to get the one originally made for you out of the way at once.

We hope you will be able to get your Form passed.

Yours faithfully,

Allan Bros.

7th May 1943

Dear Sir,

We beg to advise you that your order for 48" B. type thrashing machine has been approved and that Official notice to that effect has just come in from the Department of Agriculture for Scotland so that the matter is now definitely all in order.

Yours faithfully,

Allan Bros.

12th May 1943

Dear Sir,

We are in receipt of your letter of the 10th inst. We were recently ordered to finish off 17 Portable machines for Northern Ireland the balance of a large order we had from that Government on December 22nd 1941 and these machines are meantime going through and as your machine was ordered on November 24th 1941 it holds the record for longevity.

It will be the first one of the first group to be put through after the above machines and we are pretty sure this time we will have your machine and all details through in time to start threshing this year's crop.

Yours faithfully,

Allan Bros.

9th June 1943

Dear Sir,

We are in receipt of your favour of the 8th inst. and note that Messrs McKenzie are anxious to get a start on the alterations to your buildings and we think you should let them go ahead as soon as you can do so without inconvenience as you will most likely find that some delays with materials etc. are almost sure to take place. We have all the attachments for your job made and stored away and as already advised your machine will be the first private one to go through and we will be able to get it started somewhere about the middle of next month (July) so should be able to dispatch about the end of August and to have your job completed about the middle of August. As we previously mentioned to you we do not think we will be allowed to send your outfit by road so will have to mount the machine on temporary wheels for transport from the Station.

Yours faithfully,

Allan Bros.

17th August 1943

Dear Sir,

We have now got your mill finished and being painted so that it will be ready for dispatch next week and you might kindly let us know if everything is ready for it coming on.

We had intended to send the whole thing per motor but that is now banned so we will have to send per rail and we wrote Mr McKenzie Achnagarron recently to see if a motor could be picked up to take the machine from the Station to Ord.

The mill will be over twenty feet long and stripped of the bottom riddlecases etc. will weigh something about three tons and there will be a second load of attachments and parts.

Yours faithfully,

Allan Bros.

17th August 1943

Dear Sir,

We beg to advise you that the thrasher and all other parts have been loaded today and are being forwarded per L.N.E. rail carriage paid to Invergordon Station. The Railway Co. are not sure when they will arrive but you can let us know and Millwrights will be along as early as possible.

Yours faithfully,

Allan Bros.

1st October 1943

Dear Sir,

We beg to acknowledge your favour of the 29th ult. with cheque value £658 which we have placed to credit of your account and enclose receipt with thanks.

We hope the new plant will give you the most complete satisfaction in every way and being rather a complete one it should certainly save labour. We are pleased to hear your harvest is completed and hope you have got everything secured in good condition.

Weather has been very unsettled here and we are afraid a good deal of the crop especially in later spots is a good deal damaged.

Yours faithfully,

Allan Bros.

So after three years of effort, Mr Paterson got his Mill.

Footnote: Allan Brothers were also active during World War I. In 1919, they published a list of the names and addresses of 3000 uses of the 'Allan' Oil Engine, mainly in Scotland, but also in England and Ireland.

Shorter Notes

Repairing an Easter Ross Mill in 1789
Alexander Fenton

The following letter, transcribed from an original document lent by F Munro, Portmahomack, Ross-shire, provides an interesting background to the repair of a water mill at Edderton. The getting of timber is described, and the tenants thirled to the mill clearly had to be encouraged in performing repair services. Patronage and favours also played a role. The roof was evidently covered with grass sods.

Ja⁵. MacKay, 27 Feby 1789

Sir,

I am ordered by Sir John Ross to Write you this to Acquaint you that as he has the Miln of Eddertⁿ. to Repair and the Timber to Carry from the Saw Miln here, he expects that you & the other Tenants on his Estate in that Parish will give him all the Assistance in your Power in Carrying this Timbers and the Rest of the materials he says he will Carry the Timbers with the Cattle of This Town as far as they can go. which I suppose will be to Munros house in the Lairg. and that you & the Tenants will Carry it from thence. If you grant him this favour. He says he will order a Guinea for the Poor of your Parish & told me that he desir'd to Acquaint James Simson of this. You therefore Intimate this to the whole Tenants thirld to that Miln as Sir John Ross's Request. and tho they are not Bound to perfom any Services in Repairing it. yet that he hopes they'll not Refuse him this his Request and I am sure you will Show them a Good Example.

Now In my own Candid opinion that Considering all the Indulgence they met with & the deductions &c. given by Sir John, they should with heart & hand go to Work. & give him all the Assistance possible. It may be a mean to merit his Countenance & favour which they shᵈ. very much study. And if they do not at this time show themselves as men of Gratitude in Acknowledging past favours, I will not take it upon me to say what the Consequence may be or where it will land, ere three years be at an end. youl therefore take the matter to your Consideration & act the proper part. – Youl please be Dunᶜ Craig measure the Miln & acquaint you how many thousand Divots it will Require & get them Cast. I am yours &c. Excuse haste.

James Brown Gibson, 5 July 1892 – 12 July 1914 Montrose Photographer

This article on James Brown Gibson was written by his nephew, James BM Gibson, formerly of Montrose and now resident in Ontario, Canada. Mr Gibson had come into possession of the Tuckwell Press publication *Glenesk. The History and Culture of an Angus Community*, edited by Alexander Fenton and John Beech. He noticed that the book contained unprovenanced photographs which he recognised as his uncle's work, taken from a long-lost photograph album. Curious to know where the photographs had been found, Mr Gibson contacted the EERC. Some of the photographs are held in the Glenesk Museum, Angus, as they contain scenes of early twentieth century life in Glenesk. Mr Brown plans to publish a volume of his uncle's photographs, which, hopefully, will give this very talented photographer the recognition that his work deserves [John Beech, EERC].

Born in Montrose, Angus, Scotland, James Brown Gibson left Montrose Academy at 14 to become a butcher's delivery boy in his father's shop. Lack of formal education, however, was bolstered by an agile, curious mind that took him far beyond the comparatively restricted world of boys his own age. In the short 22 years that this remarkable young man had at his disposal, he created a series of award winning photographs which act as a local time capsule of the years 1910 to 1912, when he was most active as an amateur photographer.

While still at school he began studying the weather – not by merely looking out of the window to see whether it was raining, – but by designing, building, and erecting a weather station in the garden. He consulted it twice a day so that he could note the high and low temperatures, the atmospheric pressure, and the wind speed and direction. To those readings, he added a synopsis of the prevailing weather conditions and, as the day progressed, he would note significant changes. His weather station was equipped with a wet-cell battery so that he could read its settings at night, and it had a frost-warning bell wired into an electric panel in his workshop.

James made numerous references to the position of stars and planets in the night sky. When Haley's Comet appeared in 1910, James viewed it through a telescope inherited from his sea-faring great grandfather, and carefully noted every observation made over the several nights it was visible. He corrected the local newspaper editors who were calling it Drake's Comet.

In 1909, Marconi arrived in Scotland to demonstrate wireless transmission by sending a signal over the River Tay. James was ready for him. He already had a special receiving aerial set up in the garden and had purchased a rudimentary wireless receiver with which to listen for Marconi's broadcast.

It was photography, however, that became James' main interest. Photographs of him as a young adult in one of his own albums show a delicate, finely chiselled face with an expression of inquisitiveness, which seems to have captured his personality exactly. By the age of 18, he was cutting, coating, exposing, and hand colouring his own glass negatives, and had designed and built several styles of camera. One, a pinhole camera that he used to capture a

lightning strike, brought him his first public recognition in the form of a medal from a local photographic club. Other cameras were used to take scenery and portraits. His subjects ranged from family snapshots, which included rigging up a mechanical triggering device so that he could be in the picture, to serious competition studies. Express trains at full speed on the Perth to Aberdeen run; stills of steam engines and waterwheels at Craigo Mill; scenery in Glen Esk and around Montrose; all came in front of his lens in a historical record of the period. The photograph that won him another silver medal for 'Harvest at Wilson's Farm' depicts the old labour-intensive methods used when agriculture, in all its phases, depended on the horse.

The entries in his only surviving diary, which covers the six-month period Monday, December 6, 1909, to Sunday, July 3, 1910, give a day-to-day, almost minute-to-minute, account of James' life. He was meticulous and intensely interested in all that was going on around him. During this period he mentions his attempts to persuade his father to give up the ubiquitous horse and buggy in favour of a motorcar. Possibly the diary ends there because James became too busy to maintain the disciplined detail he had set as a goal for himself. His advocacy on behalf of modernisation was successful, and soon he was learning to drive – first a hired Model T Ford which came complete with liveried chauffeur – and later, by February 1914, SR 707 the family Sunbeam. It was James who designed the new garage complete with workshop, chauffeur's quarters, oil and petrol stores and central heating. Unfortunately he did not live long enough to enjoy his dream, but the legacy of his photographs lives on for all to see.

James BM Gibson.

Footnote: James BM Gibson has published three volumes of his autobiography. Three copies of volume one, *Sook Th'm Fur a While, Wullie!*, which charts his life from 1925–1950 (the year he emigrated to Canada), can be found in Montrose Public Library, Angus. Volume two, *The Final Move* and volume three, *Being Tenth is Not So Bad*, have also been published and relates to his life in Canada. These volumes have been circulated to members of his family, and can now also be found in the European Ethnological Research Centre.

Captain Gustav Ekeberg's Sojourn in Shetland of 1745
Translated and edited by Kristina Söderpalm and Brian Smith

Introduction.

Carl Gustav Ekeberg (1716–1784) is one of the best-remembered of Swedish East India Company captains. He was a good navigator – he made the voyage to China nine times as captain – and a good example of the scientific mind characteristic of many men engaged in the Company. Ekeberg began his career with studies in pharmacy and medicine, and on his first voyages for the Company with Spain as destination he was ship's doctor. On these voyages he got the opportunity to train himself in navigation, and in 1742 we meet him as fourth mate on the *Drottningen af Sverige*. In 1745 he signed on as third mate on the *Stockholm*, which in January left Gothenburg together with his former ship for a joint expedition to Canton. Both ships, however, were wrecked on Shetland on the outward route. The crews of both ships were rescued; Ekeberg and the others sojourned in the islands for several months.

25 years later, when Ekeberg was in command of the East Indiaman *Finland*, he was delayed off Shetland during a snowstorm. He took the opportunity to write an account of his enforced stay in Shetland, and subsequently included it in his work *Capitaine Carl Gustav Ekebergs Ostindiska Resa åren 1770 och 1771*, published in Stockholm in 1773. This gives a unique account of Shetland society at an early date, written by someone interested in the mode of life of his 'simple-hearted and good-natured' hosts.

Having the opportunity, between snow and hail showers, to see the southern cape of Hitland, with its hills all covered with snow, which gave it a frightful look, I was reminded of my three months' stay here, after a disastrous shipwreck on its south-east coast, on 12/23 January 1745, when I, together with others, was rescued. I am going to insert here, if the reader does not mind, a short narrative about it, while the ship *Finland*, delayed by adverse weather, and filled up with snow and hail, is struggling in these waters.

This little archipelago, consisting of one large and numerous small islands and holms, is situated between the latitudes of 60 and 61 degrees. The length of the big island, from Sombrough Head to Rona Hill in Nort Maven, which is a big peninsula, is 54 miles or 18 leagues; it has many tongues and wicks, and is subdivided into 17 parishes. On its western side lies Fula, 20 miles from the mainland, which is a fishing place only in the summer season; it measures nearly 5 miles around. Its soil is said to drive rats away. House, Burra Vestra, Waley and Papa are fairly big islands, and are situated closer to the mainland, north of Fula on Hitland's west side. Veskeris is the name of some rocks which are situated ten miles from the mainland, opposite a large wick called Magnus Bay. Yell is so big that it comprises two parishes. Between two big islands is a sound called Blome Sund. The most northerly one is Unst; next to Unst is Fetlar. Outscheries are three small rocks 15 miles from the mainland on the eastern side. Noss has a rock leaning to the east which is called Hanglip. Whalsey is to be found above the former. Brassey forms together with the mainland a splendid harbour, big enough for a fleet of a hundred sails; the Hollanders call it Buysbay. There is also an island Musay. These are the bigger islands; there are also countless holms and skerries, which together comprise four parishes.

Larwik, the only town in the whole island, situated in Gullbervik parish at Brassay harbour, has not very many inhabitants; here resides the governor, who has the title Admiral, as well as the vice governor, and their secretaries. In the entrance of this harbour the ship *Drottningen af Sverige* was stranded on 12/23 January 1745. Opposite, on the western side of the mainland, in the parish of Tingvall, lies Scallovay, a big village; in both places, as well as in many others throughout the islands, there are remains of fortifications, which are said to have been built by the Picts.

Several Scots families and other gentry have their estates here, the tenants of which mostly pay their rents by fishing. The country is very

Kay Holm and Hascosay, in Yell, Shetland. The snowy conditions are reminiscent of the weather when Captain Ekeberg was held up there. Courtesy of the Shetland Museum. Photo: Jack Peterson, 1940s.

mountainous and elevated. The valleys in between are overgrown by high heather, which gives the cattle their feeding, and the lower valleys contain enough peat to give the inhabitants their heating. The more accessible parts are transformed into fields by digging, as there are no other implements. And the soil consists of mould from the decomposed seaweed mixed with sand and some clay, which is quite fertile for oats and barley; of these crops, however, there is a shortage, although they consume them with great restraint. They build their houses from flat slabs, which there are plenty of – the joins are pointed with clay – but materials for the roofs they have to get from Norway, or from stranded wrecks, as there is not a single tree on the whole island. The houses of the more well-off have more partitions and floors, are paneled with boards, and have large windows and fire-places – the latter, however, are without dampers; but those who are worse off have to be content with a single house, in which the

fire-place is placed opposite the doorway, and with a hole in the ceiling for evacuation of the smoke. On one side of the fire-place the people have their home, on the other the cattle. The horses and sheep must in summer as well as in winter look for their feeding out on the pasture. They do not use barns or other outhouses. The cut corn is stacked. Threshing is done when required, and grinding on some stream on a smooth slab with another stone above, like a so-called *fotviska* [small water-mill]. Each time they eat, they knead the meal with water in a bowl, and from this they make small round cakes, which they bake by raising them in front of the burning peat. They call this bread 'Banex'[bannocks]. The ground malt they pour into a raised barrel, then hot water is poured upon it. After a couple of days they draw it off and drink, and thereafter again pour hot water until there is no flavour in it to be perceived. The muddy dregs left at the bottom, after being rinsed from the bran, they mix with oatmeal and cook as porridge and then eat it with mutton grease – a dish called 'Suun'[sowens]. Besides, their food in general is made up from kale, fish, mutton, eggs, seals and game birds.

The Shetland horses are of a special kind, small and low, and besides their mane they have something like a beard hanging from the mouth down to the breast. They are only used for transporting seaweed, which is thrown upon the fields and used as manure, in baskets, and for bringing home the sheaves of cut corn. They are especially convenient for journeys on their mountainous roads, and it is a thrill to see people ride on roads of two or at the most three feet wide, around the mountains, with a bold cliff hanging over their heads and a precipice downwards to the sea. Used to the swift-footed horses as they are, they usually carry out such rides without any accidents heard of.

Their sheep seem to be of a special kind in comparison with those I have seen in Scotland and England – smaller and rich of wool. They, like the horses, seem to be well fitted for the climate and region. Every *bonde* [farmer] has enough of them. They provide them with most of their food and all their clothing. The country has besides eagles no predatory animals, so they [the sheep] can be easily looked after. Everyone has them marked with his own mark; when grazing they go in flocks of hundreds, but when they are going to be clipped each owner clips only those of his own. They can even endure much hunger. In several places, on account of blizzards, walls are erected forming small yards: within these the sheep gather, lying closely together to get protection. They get covered with snow and might have to endure three to four days of starvation, until the snow has melted, which does not take long because of the varying winds. It happens now and then however, that the hungry ones eat the wool of their neighbours, which forms balls in their stomachs, causing their death. The women spin the wool with distaffs, and make clothes and even underwear from it for themselves and the males. They also knit stockings that can stand comparison with the same made from silk.

The sea provides them with many kinds of fish, and even oysters, lobsters, and shrimps. The many holms and skerries are sure refuges for many kinds of birds, from which they get both eggs and feathers. In the steep cliffs uncountable flocks of wild doves have their nests, which can be caught without bother; to make no mention of a multitude of snipes, curlews and starlings, who continuously follow the shores. In the spring swans and wild geese make their visits and always have to leave some of their company in the lurch. Where the waves have made cavities otters have made their dwellings. The dogs bred to hunt them don't fail to get hold of them, and drive them out to be caught or shot. There is no shortage of seals. Of these the Shetlanders have great benefit for food and oil, and from their skins for clothing. A special method of preparing the hides for shoes has been developed. A round piece is cut out from the raw hide, three times the length of the foot, then holes are pricked all around, through which a strap cut from the same hide is passed. The foot is placed in the centre of the leather piece, and the strap is drawn together and fastened round the shin. Thus the worse off wear shoes without any seam. From their imprints in the snow it is difficult to judge which creature has been treading there. In several places, especially in the parish of Dunrossnes, the most southern part of the island, where the soil is sandy, rabbits are to be found, which are caught with nets in great numbers. A great part of these products, which they with ships of their own export to Hamburg, they exchange for salt and other necessities. On their return the ships call at Norway, and from there they bring boats, which they beforehand have disassembled in order to save space onboard.

Thus I have briefly given an account of what seemed remarkable to me on this island, by a people who are simple-hearted and good-natured and whom nature has taught to be pleased with only a little.

Noticeboard

The Launch of Scottish Life and Society: A Compendium of Scottish Ethnology

On 23 November 2000, the Trustees of the National Museums of Scotland and the Trustees of the European Ethnological Research Centre launched the first volume to be got ready in the 13 volume series, *Scottish Life and Society: A Compendium of Scottish Ethnology*. This was volume 11, entitled *Institutions of Scotland: Education*. The launch of this volume, and a presentation of the European Ethnological Research Centre and its activities, was spearheaded by Sir William Fraser GCB, FRSE, Chairman of the Scotland Inheritance Fund. It took place in the Museum of Scotland, Chambers Street, Edinburgh, and was very kindly hosted by the Director, Mr Mark Jones.

Sir William outlined the history and aims of the EERC. It is a Charitable Trust (Reg. No SC0241.992), founded in 1989 to promote research into Scottish life and to publish the results for wide educational and general purposes. Its Trustees are chaired by Professor Tom Devine, Director of the Research Institute of Irish and Scottish Studies, University of Aberdeen. The Director of the EERC is Professor Alexander Fenton, and the staff consists of a part time Administrator, one full time Deputy Director and two part time Research Assistants, two part time freelance Research Assistants, and six volunteer Editors of specific volumes.

The publications of the EERC, which are produced in five groups, reflect its purposes, which combine local, regional, national and international emphases. They try to feed back to the people of Scotland in analysed form some of the tremendous body of material that has been gathered from them, and at the same time to provide comparative information about Scotland for researchers in other countries:

Flashbacks

These are based on oral history, the personal stories of people from different areas and from different walks of life, who speak for themselves. So far they have dealt with an Edinburgh family, farmworkers male and female, tattie howkers, a shepherd, fisherfolk, miners, gunpowder mill and bomb factory workers, a church minister's family, a journalist, midwives, and the Scottish Women's Timber Corps. All these allow the authentic voice of the people to be heard. The EERC collaborates with relevant bodies in this activity, for example the Scottish Working People's History Trust, the Royal College of Nursing and the School of Scottish Studies of the University of Edinburgh, as well as with various individuals. A *Guide to the Recording of Oral History and Folklore* can be supplied by the EERC on request.

Part of the inspiration for the series came from Norway. There, the National Association for Folk Health organised a 'memory competition' in 1964 for people over 70 years old, with the aim of providing the elderly with useful tasks. They were asked to write down everything they could remember about working life and holiday times during their childhood and adolescence. The outcome has been a large number of books, under the heading 'Daily life in XX within human memory'. The Scottish Flashbacks have in part a similar welfare purpose.

Sources in Local History

Whereas Flashbacks deal with oral history, the Sources in Local History are especially concerned with manuscript sources, especially the diaries and account books of farm folk and tradesmen. Though these were never intended for anything other than private purposes, nevertheless they provide invaluable information about their place and time, and about the work and ways of thinking of the writers. Along with the Flashbacks, they put on record the history of 'the people below'.

The Review of Scottish Culture

The fourteen issues now in print provide fresh information on aspects of Scottish life and culture at all social levels.

Occasional Books and Papers

Of the eleven items published, four are examples of international collaboration, with the Department of Irish Folklore, University College, Dublin, with the Alimentarium (Food Museum) at Vevey, Switzerland, with Professor Nils-Arvid Bringéus, Sweden, and with the International Commission for Research into European Food History. A recent volume is a local history of the parish of Glenesk in Angus.

Scottish Life and Society: A Compendium of Scottish Ethnology

This is a major thirteen volume project, which will be an indispensable resource for 'life-long learning', setting an educational base-line for examining the interlocking strands of history and traditional and contemporary culture, at the turn of the millennium, that make up 'national identity'. The headings are: *An Introduction to Scottish Ethnology; Farming and the Landscape; Scotland's Buildings; Boats, Fishing and the Coastal Environment; The Food of the Scots; The Culture of the Dwelling; Crafts, Trades and Professions; Transport and Communications; The Individual and Community Life in Scotland; Oral Literature and Performance Culture; Institutions of Scotland: Education* [published in November 2001; *Institutions of Scotland: the Church and Religious Expression; Institutions of Scotland: the Law.*

The Education volume contains articles by 27 contributors, on the traditions of Scottish education, forms of administration and provision, types of institutions, and specific aspects that look at the teachers as well as the taught. It is readable, and will be a required text-book in educational circles.

All of this work could not be carried through without a considerable level of support. The Trustees of the National Museums of Scotland kindly provide premises and a core grant for essential purposes. The Scotland Inheritance Fund is very supportive, providing funding for a salary and as a contribution to publication costs. Grateful thanks are due to a number of benefactors - the late Dr Ronald Cant and Mrs Evelyn Macpherson supported many research and publication projects; Miss Greta Michie left the residue of her estate so that books on Glenesk could be produced, and in pursuance of her wishes, her book, *Glenesk. The History and Culture of an Angus Glen,* was published just in time for this launch too. A major bequest from the late Miss Kathleen Dickie was what led to the founding of the Scotland Inheritance Fund. The Russell Trust has always been generous with assistance, and the Scottish Executive has also given support.

Following Sir William's address, Professor Fenton said a few words on the genesis of the Compendium project. In the 1950s, he had worked for four years as Senior Assistant Editor of the *Scottish National Dictionary.* He then learned to appreciate the meaning of the things that lay behind the words, and from the Editor, the late David Murison, he learned the value of systematically organising data from sources of all possible kinds. In 1959, he moved to the museum world, turning literally from words to things, and was responsible for setting up the Country Life Section of the National Museum of Antiquities of Scotland. Out of this flowed the founding of the Scottish Agricultural Museum in the Royal Highland Showground at Ingliston, and the setting up of what is now known as the Scottish Life Archive. Data of all kinds went into the Archive, organised by theme and by locality, and this is now a major archival resource for all aspects of Scottish ethnology.

Here, the systematisation of the data was undoubtedly inspired by the experience of lexicography, and led to the concept of an alphabetical Lexicon of Scottish Ethnology. It soon became evident, however, that it would be much more practical and generally useful to work in a thematic way, and so the EERC has adopted this approach. The project, in its format, is almost unique in Europe, though a close parallel is provided by the eight volume series, *Magyar Néprajz* (Hungarian Ethnology) being produced by the Institute of Ethnology of the Hungarian Academy of Sciences in Budapest.

The first of the mainly multi-author volumes has now appeared, on *Education*. It happens to be volume 11, because that was the first to be completed by its editor, Dr Heather Holmes. Next to come is *Scotland's Buildings*, and publication will continue at the rate of at least two volumes a year. The publisher is Tuckwell Press, East Linton.

A full list of EERC publications follows.

Publications from the European Ethnological Research Centre

Personal *Flashbacks* (oral) stories of people from different localities and backgrounds.

1. Slee, Dorothy. Two *Generations of Edinburgh Folk*, Edinburgh, 1993, 64pp, £7.99. Out of print.
2. MacDougall, Ian, ed. *'Hard Work ye Ken': Midlothian farmworkers*, Edinburgh, 1993, 97pp, £7.99. Out of print.
3. MacDougall, Ian, ed. *Hoggie's Angels: Tattie howkers remember*, East Linton, Edinburgh and Midlothian, 1995, 130pp, £7.99.
4. MacDougall, Ian, ed. *Mungo Mackay and the Green Table: Newtongrange miners remember*, East Linton, 1995, 165pp, £7.99.
5. MacKenzie, John Alexander. *A Mallaig Boyhood*, East Linton, 1996, 165pp, £7.99.
6. MacLean, Isabella G, ed Colin MacLean, *Your Father and I*, East Linton, 1998, 158pp, £7.99.
7. Roberston, Uiga, Robertson, John, eds. *Timber: Memories of life in the Scottish Women's Timber Corps, 1942-46*, East Linton, 1998, 188pp, £7.99.
8. McVeigh, Patrick. *'Look After the Bairns': A childhood in East Lothian*, East Linton, 1999, 146pp, £7.99.
9. MacDougall, Ian, ed. *'Oh! Ye had to be Careful': Personal recollections by Roslin gunpowder mill factory workers*, East Linton, 2000, 192pp, £9.99.
10. MacDougall, Ian, ed. *Bondagers: Eight Scots women farm workers*, East Linton, 2000, 210pp, £9.99.
11. MacLean, Colin. *Monkeys, Bears and Gutta Percha: Memories of manse, hospital and war*, East Linton 2001, 98pp, £7.99.
12. Reid, Lindsay, ed. *Scottish Midwives: Twentieth-century voices*, East Linton, 2000, 193pp, £8.99.
13. Purves, Andrew. *A Shepherd Remembers*, East Linton, 2001, 160pp, £9.99.
14. Holmes, Heather and Finkelstein, David. *Thomas Nelson and Sons. Memoirs of an Edinburgh Publishing House*, East Linton, 2001, 130pp, £7.99.

Sources in Local History

Largely manuscript sources, especially the diaries and account books of farmers and tradesmen.

1. Pearson, Mowbray, ed. *Flitting the flakes: The diary of J Badenach, a Stonehaven farmer, 1789-1797*, 1992, 321pp, special offer £9.99 (published price £25).
2. Pearson, Mowbray, ed. *More Frost and Snow: The diary of Janet Burnet, 1758–1759*, 1994, 127pp, £14.99.
3. Fenton, Alexander, ed. *At Brechin with Stirks: A farm cash book from Buskhead, Glenesk, Angus, 1885-1898*, 1994, 95pp, £14.99.
4. Love, John, McMullen, Brenda, eds. *A Salmon for the Schoolhouse: A Nairnshire parish in the nineteenth century. From the diaries of Robert and Elsie Thompson*, 1994, 160pp, £8.99.
5. Whatley, Christopher, ed. *The Diary of John Sturrock, Millwright, Dundee, 1864–65*, 1996, 126pp, £8.99.

6. Hewison, William S, ed. *The Diary of Patrick Fea of Stove, Orkney, 1766-96*, 1996, 400pp, £20 hardback. Out of print.
7. Dunbar, John G, ed. *Sir William Burrell's Northern Tour, 1758*, 1997, 143pp, £14.99.

Scottish Life and Society: A compendium of Scottish Ethnology

The EERC's major project, which, when completed in thirteen volumes, will set an educational base-line for examining the interlocking strands of history and traditional and contemporary culture that make up 'national identity'.

1. An Introduction to Scottish Ethnology
2. Farming and Landscape
3. Scotland's Buildings
4. Boats, Fishing and the Coastal Environment
5. The Food of the Scots
6. The Culture of the Dwelling
7. Crafts, Trades and Professions
8. Transport and Communications
9. The Individual and Community Life in Scotland
10. Oral Literature and Performance Culture
11. Institutions of Scotland: Education (published East Linton, 2000, 535pp, £25)
12. Institutions of Scotland: The Church and religious experience
13. Institutions of Scotland: The Law

Review of Scottish Culture

Fourteen volumes are in print. *ROSC* is a journal published jointly by the EERC and by NMS. It provides information on aspects of Scottish life and culture at all social levels, and is the only journal of its kind in Britain. It was launched in 1984 and taken over by the EERC in 1989.

Some sample articles are:

Marshall, Rosalind K. The wearing of wedding rings in Scotland, *ROSC*, 2 (1986), 1–13.

Smart, Robert. 'Famous throughout the world': Valentine & Sons Ltd, Dundee, *ROSC*, 4 (1988), 75-89.

Turnbull, Michael. Joseph Hislop (1884-1977): A cultural ambassador, *ROSC*, 8 (1990), 21-26.

Batey, Colleen E. A Norse horizontal mill in Orkney, ROSC, 8 (1993), 20-28.

Robertson, Mary E. Black Africans at the court of James IV, *ROSC*, 12 (1999-2000), 34-45.

Gemmill, Elizabeth. Signs and symbols in medieval Scottish trade, *ROSC*, 13 (2000–2001), 7-17.

Occasional Books and Papers

These are intended as guides to further research, or as contributions to international ethnological research.

1. Fenton, Alexander. *On Your Bike: Thirteen years of travelling curators for the Scottish Country Life Museum Trust*, Edinburgh, 1990, 28pp, £2.50.
2. Morrison, Andrew 1. *Small-Scale Shopkeeping in Scotland: A guide to Investigation*, Edinburgh, 1993, 12pp, £1.
3. Fenton, Alexander. *Craiters . . . or Twenty Buchan Tales* (in the Northeast Dialect), East Linton, 1995, 109pp, £5.99.
4. Holmes, Heather. 300 *Years of Scottish Education: A handlist of the Education Acts in Scotland, 1696-1996*, 1996, Edinburgh, 46pp, £3.50.
5. Lysaght, Patricia, ed. *Milk and Milk Products from Medieval to Modern Times*, Edinburgh, 1994 (with the Department of Irish Folklore, University College, Dublin), 229pp, £25.
6. Fenton, Alexander. *The Northern Isles: Orkney and Shetland*, 1997 (first published 1978), 736pp, £20.
7. Schärer, Martin, Fenton, Alexander, eds. *Food and Material Culture*, Proceedings of the Fourth Symposium of the International Commission for Research into European Food History, East Linton, 1998, 358pp, £25.
8. Fenton, Alexander, *Scottish Country Life*, East Linton, 1999 (new revised edition, first published 1976), 249pp, £14.99.
9. Storrier, Susan. A Guide to the Recording of Oral History and Folklore, Edinburgh, 2000, 1 1pp, free.
10. Fenton, Alexander, ed. *Order and Disorder: The health implications of eating and drinking*

in the nineteenth and twentieth centuries, Proceedings of the Fifth Symposium of the International Commission for Research into European Food History, East Linton, 2000, 338pp, £30.

11. Michie, Margaret Fairweather, comp and ed Alexander Fenton, John Beech. *Glenesk: The history and culture of an Angus glen,* East Linton, 2000, 272pp, £20.

12. Bringéus, Nils-Arvid. *Man, Food and Milieu: A Swedish approach to Swedish ethnology,* East Linton, 2001, 203pp, £16.99.

Alexander Fenton

Dr Alan Gailey

Congratulations are in order to Dr Alan Gailey, whose Festschrift was published at the end of 2000. The book, edited by the former Curator of the Welsh Folk Museum, Trefor M Owen, is entitled *From Corrib to Cultra. Folklife Essays in Honour of Alan Gailey* (Institute of Irish Studies in association with the Ulster Folk and Transport Museum), and contains 17 studies by colleagues in Ireland and further afield. These reflect Alan's wide range of interests, with an emphasis on Irish and on Scottish subject matter.

The process of establishing the Ulster Folk Museum was begun in 1958. Its first director, George B Thompson, was appointed in 1959, and the present fine site at Cultra Manor was acquired in 1961. Alan Gailey joined the staff almost at the outset, in 1960, as Research Officer, and became a Keeper of Non-material Culture in 1975. In 1986 he became second Director of the Ulster Folk and Transport Museum, and retired from that post in 1996.

Alan was trained as a geographer and lectured in the subject at the University of Glasgow. His early writings reflect his training and interests, in Scottish islands, crofting, estate tenants, rural settlement, and traditional forms of buildings. These interests were transferred to Ulster when he joined the Museum staff, and to them were added topics such as Irish folk drama, chapbook literature, theoretical aspects of the nature of tradition and the concept of cultural identity, as

well as a considerable number of contributions on aspects of material culture. It was a pleasure to work with him in editing, in 1970, the conference papers which were published as *The Spade in Northern and Atlantic Europe*, this including an all-night sitting in his house to complete the proof-reading of the volume against a tight deadline. His published items number 133 (not 103, the figure erroneously given on page 1), and no doubt the list will continue to be extended in the future.

The Festschrift volume is available from The Institute of Irish Studies, Queen's University Belfast, 8 Fitzwilliam Street, Belfast BT9 6AW; www.qub.ac.uk/iis/publications.html, in paperback and in hardback.

Alexander Fenton

Centre for Research on Families and Relationships (CRFR)

The first public meeting of the Centre for Research on Families and Relationships was held on 8 May 2001 in the University of Edinburgh. It was attended by a substantial number of people from varied academic and professional backgrounds. Members of the staff of the Centre briefly outlined the structure and objectives of what promises to be a particularly important organisation.

The CRFR, set up in January 2001, is funded by a three-year SHEFC Research Development Grant. Its co-directors, Sarah Cunningham-Burley, Lynn Jamieson, Kathryn Backett-Milburn, and Fran Wasoff, are supported in the Edinburgh University headquarters by a Senior Research Fellow and a Research Liaison and Information Officer, amongst others, and also by Associate Directors based in three other Scottish Universities (Glasgow Caledonian, Glasgow, Aberdeen), plus a Research Fellow at Glasgow Caledonian.

The Centre aims to stimulate, support and conduct high quality inter-disciplinary, multidisciplinary and cross-institutional research on families and relationships in and of relevance to Scotland, at the same time provoking debate, and creating new vehicles for research commentary and dissemination. It also hopes to act as a focal point for a network of research users, including representatives from policy-making organisations, voluntary sector groups and agencies and educational institutions, while at the same time strengthening links between these entities and with practice, the private sector and the general public.

CRFR findings and relevant policy and statistical information will be circulated by a number of means including a web site, e-mail networks, publications and by a programme of face-to-face events, these undertaken in collaboration with other bodies where appropriate.

Contact:
Centre for Research on Families and
    Relationships
23 Buccleuch Place, Edinburgh, EH8 9LN
Tel 0131 651 1832   Fax 0131 651 1833
crfr@ed.ac.uk
www.crfr.ac.uk

Susan Storrier

Strictly Mundial World Music Festival – Zaragoza, Aragon, Spain, 15–18 November, 2000

Second generation to the annual *WOMAX* world music festival, *Strictly Mundial* proved to be a chaotic but often marvellous meeting of artists, music promoters and academics from many parts of the globe. The three and a half days of the event were devoted to an extensive programme of concerts, a trade fair and a set of lectures and conferences. The latter generally occupied morning slots – a demanding piece of scheduling given that performances could continue until near dawn – but despite the fragile state of many delegates both talks and round table sessions were animated and incisive. Four topic areas were examined in turn: the musical variety of the Iberian peninsula; North Africa past and present; Latin American and Caribbean musical traditions; and aspects of world music promotion. The presentations as a whole were extremely informative and stimulating and revealed recurring themes, most notably the flexible and heterogeneous nature of musical tradition and the need to embrace modernity.

The trade fair consisted of numerous stalls manned by musicians, promoters and vendors of recorded music and instruments, festival organisers, research associations and cultural institutions (notable among these was the European Network of Traditional Music and Dance, an organisation formed in 1999 to promote traditional music in its heritage, social and artistic aspects throughout Europe). Information and ideas were readily exchanged in a pleasant and helpful atmosphere, and it was also possible to accumulate generous quantities of written and recorded material from many parts of the world.

Undoubtedly the heart of the festival was the fifty or so showcase concerts performed at various venues in the city. The artists represented the best of their respective musical styles and traditions and on occasion shared the stage with each other to produce unique and very exciting sounds. As access to concerts by local people was hindered by an insistence on the purchase of expensive day or three day passes – one of the most loudly voiced criticisms of the festival, especially given the amount of municipal funding involved – performers had to deal skilfully with scant audiences to produce vibrant or intimate atmospheres. Particularly memorable performances included those of Ala dos Namorados (Portugal), the Basque group Alboka performing with Márta Sebestyén (Hungary), followed by fellow countrymen Oskorri, and the superlative Cesaria Evora (Cape Verde). It is a pity that in the midst of such a gathering Scotland was not represented in any way. Aragon itself however produced one of the finest concerts in the form of Norte Flamenco, a mixture rather than fusion of Aragonese music with gypsy traditions.

At the end of the festival each delegate was presented with a compilation recording. Lavishly designed and generously annotated, the CDs (of which there was one for each topic area) were arbitrarily distributed. I got the North African CD – interesting but not what I would have chosen. There were problems too with the catalogue. This, although extremely glossy, became available only on the last day (the appendix to it appeared two days earlier). As the catalogue contained the sole description of performers, choosing a concert had often been a hit or miss affair. In addition some of the information translated into English was quite unintelligible and one had to rely on the original Castilian texts. Nevertheless there is much merit in the publication, its 23 articles looking at diverse aspects of all four topic areas. Not surprisingly the Iberian peninsula, apparently considered as overwhelmingly Spanish, receives most attention with contributions on pop and electronic music 'with roots', black Spanish music, new Flamenco, the music of the plateau, the Mediterranean regions, the Pyrenees, the Basque Country and the Celtic legacy. Portugal has to make do with just two pieces – the music of the region of Miranda de Duoro, and Portugese music as seen from Madrid.

The days immediately before *Strictly Mundial* and small interstices during the programme presented the opportunity to undertake some research – collecting data on Celtic music sales in Zaragoza, interviewing performers of Celtic and Aragonese music and conducting a questionnaire with the general public on attitudes towards Celtic music in the region. Funding was very kindly provided by The Russell Trust and The Scotland Inheritance Fund.

The European Network of Traditional Music and Dance is interested in establishing links with Scotland and can be contacted via:

Gwenael Quiviger, Co-ordinator,
90, rue Jean-Jaurès – BP 136 – F–79204
Parthenay, France.

mdeuropnet@district-parthenay.fr

Susan Storrier

Understanding Tradition: A Multidisciplinary Exploration, University College Cork 22-23 June 2001

This is a generous title. How far did the event meet it? The conference was most certainly multidisciplinary, with representatives of numerous arts and social science disciplines, plus a good number of individuals whose main interests lie beyond the academic, such as dancers and musicians. Many delegates had travelled from other parts of Europe or from North America, so it was very much an international gathering also.

There was no lack of exploration – very far from it. The topic of tradition was examined in many contexts and always with fervour and profundity of knowledge. Understandably enough there was considerable emphasis on current Irish matters (Riverdance and the effects of the upturn in the Irish economy having an especially high profile), but many offerings drew in comparisons from beyond Ireland or had general relevance. As with all parallel sessions, it was frustrating having to choose between concurrent items of interest. Nevertheless, the compact scheduling (some 65 talks were offered in one-and-a-half days) ensured maximum attendance and high energy levels throughout.

But did we understand tradition? Well, only to a limited extent – certainly that is the conclusion I drew from the majority of contributions I heard. Within the theoretical or synthetic papers, attempts at getting to the heart of the concept were angled towards defining tradition, demarcating its boundaries and describing its relation with concepts such as modernity, individualism, globalisation and science. These attempts proved at best inconclusive, the albeit excellently constructed display of thought often going round in circles and manifestly not being able to deal with such a slippery, vast and fundamental phenomenon. A more amenable and potentially very fruitful area of initial analysis might have been that of attitudes towards tradition – who considers it in a positive or negative light and why? –, but this was scarcely touched upon. In contrast, specific studies, of which there were many (dance, music and the material culture of the home were the areas I witnessed most discussion of), were extremely informative with the processes in action in disparate contexts showing remarkable similarities. These included shifting backgrounds and accelerated rates of incorporation of new ideas within traditions, coupled with the redundancy of existing ideas, and increasing worry about the latter in particular.

Susan Storrier

The Michaelis-Jena Ratcliff Prize

The Michaelis-Jena Ratcliff Prize is the most prestigious award in ethnological studies, worth in the region of £4000 per annum. It is awarded annually between March and June, and submissions are required by the previous December. Applications may be from individuals or from book publishers, but any published work should have appeared within the previous two years. It is not, however, essential for the submission to have been published first, and theses are welcomed. It is expected that the length of the work should not be less than 80,000 words.

For an Application Form and Guidelines, apply to Miss Carole Hope, WS, Drummond Miller, WS, 31/32 Moray Place, Edinburgh EH3 6BZ.

The Prize for the year 2000-2001 was won by Dr Gary West, for his thesis on *Working the Heartland. Farm, Family and Neighbourhood in Post-Improvement Perthshire: an Historical ethnography.* In this highly original work, Dr West uses as a basis the experience of his own family, supported by documentary research and the recording of oral traditions. He outlines the local background of agricultural improvement and then goes on to discuss family labour, the bothy system, neighbourhood activities, exchange labour, charity labour and communal labour. The background of material culture, for example in grain threshing and sheep clipping, forms a base for the development of theory. Particular attention is paid to concepts of belonging and identity.

The runner-up was Dr Roger Leitch for his thesis on *Seasonal Workers, their Dwellings and Living Conditions in Scotland, 1770-1970,* University of Dundee, 1999. The strength of the book lies in its descriptions of work undertaken by fishermen and fisher girls, by salmon netsmen, by migrant agricultural workers, by hillmen, herds and shepherds and several other craftsmen. Of especial note is the presentation of crafts practised by the travelling folk – metal-working, basket-making and the like.

Alexander Fenton

Reviews

THE MAKING OF THE MUSEUM OF SCOTLAND
Charles McKean

NMS Publishing Limited, 2000
160pp. Illus. £20.00. ISBN 1 901663 11 6

The National Heritage (Scotland) Act, 1985, brought together two national museums. The National Museum of Antiquities of Scotland had existed (at first as the museum of the Society of Antiquaries of Scotland) since 1780, and the Royal Scottish Museum, founded in 1854. The amalgamation marked a government solution to the long years of effort that the NMAS had put into seeking funding and a site for a new national museum of Scotland, and tied in also with the Royal Scottish Museum's plans for expansion. The Trustees of the new organisation, the 'National Museums of Scotland', under the inspiring chairmanship of the late sixth Marquess of Bute, finally succeeded in January 1990 in getting Scottish Office agreement to funding for a new building, sited at the west end of Chambers Street in Edinburgh, to be the 'Museum of Scotland'. On the basis of a competition, the architects Benson and Forsyth were chosen and the Museum was opened in November 1998.

The building was intended to be 'a benchmark for the quality of Scottish cultural endeavour at the end of the twentieth century', and its interesting outer form, clad in Clashach stone from Morayshire, draws much attention. From its top there is a wonderful view of Edinburgh and its surroundings, which in itself instils a sense of the living presence of past history, enhancing the impression gained from a viewing of the collections, starting with archaeology at the bottom and ending with the twentieth century gallery at the top.

Lord Bute made an important comment in 1984: 'The new Museum of Scotland is neither a title nor a building, but rather a concept to be developed'. This present book, written by an architect, has an obvious sympathy for the building, and the stages of its erection and fitting out are closely documented and illustrated by a splendid range of photographs, diagrams and cartoons. It is a eulogy of a considerable architectural achievement. Two chapters deal with the displays and with the planning that went into the telling of Scotland's story, in conjunction with the architects whose exhibition brief states that their aim 'is to ensure that the exhibition relates to the environment outside, both to the immediate environment of Edinburgh, and to Scotland as a whole . . . literally through windows, visually through photographs and graphics, and metaphorically through context and information' (34). The brief imposed constraints on architects and design and curatorial staff alike, but the outcome is well-balanced and visitors become aware of the interplay between displays, architecture and the outer world as they move around. This is quite an achievement, in line with John Bute's thinking, and it is capable of making a strong educational impact over a wide spectrum of ages. It is in relation to these factors that the book makes its prevailing impact and deserves all praise for doing so. It is a matter of supreme congratulation that the Museum of Scotland now exists in such a fine and functional form.

What is lacking in the same level of detail, however, is the earlier story that, to a greater or lesser degree, had been pointing forward to a museum that would be specifically dedicated to telling Scotland's story from early times to the present. Although in the early stages the Society of Antiquaries of Scotland's Museum had mixed content, it had begun to hive off material that was non-Scottish or that concerned natural history already in the 1820s. In 1851, it was transferred to Government care though still managed by the Society, and in the following decades it played a prominent role in the development of Scottish archaeology and of Roman studies in Scotland as professional academic subjects. Though always inhibited by a serious lack of space and staff, outstanding collections relating to the historical periods of Scottish history were steadily built up. Already in the 1870s, a small but important group of ethnological items had been gathered by Sir Arthur Mitchell, whose book, *The Past in the Present; and What is Civilization?* Edinburgh 1880, is one of the earliest pieces of ethnological writing in Scotland. My own role when I joined the staff of the National Museum of Antiquities in 1959 was to build up the 'Scottish Country Life' collections, and to establish an archive of information, the 'Scottish Country Life Archive' (now much expanded to include all aspects of Scottish ethnology and known simply as the 'Scottish Life Archive'), in line with best practice in the great folk museums of other European countries. Displays on important rural ethnological themes, mounted in a first floor gallery at 18 Shandwick Place, Edinburgh (the use of this building marked the beginning of the NMAS's quest for display and storage space beyond what was available in Queen Street). became very popular and led to an invitation from the Directors of The Royal Highland and Agricultural Society of Scotland to exhibit in the Royal Highland Showground at Ingliston. Four-day Showground exhibitions began in 1965 and served as an outstanding focal point for making contact with people throughout Scotland and for pinpointing objects to be collected and background information on many aspects of rural life, as well as great quantities of photographic material. It seemed desirable to have a permanent building in which to show the country life collections. After investigation of the possibilities at the Bush Estate just south of Edinburgh, in conjunction with the University, the Showground was settled on as the better option. To help with fund raising,

a limited company, the Scottish Country Life Museums Trust, was established in December 1970, and in 1977, the first exhibition was held inside the Scottish Agricultural Museum as a built structure. SAM closed in 2000, to be reincarnated in a much greater entity, the Museum of Scottish Country Life at Wester Kittochside near East Kilbride, which opened in July 2001. Without the background collecting and organisational work carried out by the NMAS, this development would scarcely have been possible.

On other fronts, the NMAS achieved some success in expanding its facilities, though this tended to be behind the scenes, largely relating to storage-huts at Drem in East Lothian, later at Port Edgar on the Firth of Forth, and at Granton, for the country life collections and the Conservation Laboratory; and the old Leith Custom House for 'medieval to modern' material. There was also the acquisition of York Buildings in Queen Street, across the road from the main museum, which gave the Scottish Life Archive its first proper home, provided much needed office space, and included galleries in which a series of small but thematically important and publicly attractive exhibitions were held. Though on a small scale, these were in many ways the precursors of the kinds of displays and display techniques now to be seen in the Museum of Scotland.

As Director of the NMAS from 1978 to 1984, I was heavily involved in these matters, which were largely bringing to fruition the thinking of Dr Robert Stevenson, head of the NMAS from 1946–78. They helped to give shape and substance to the concept and creation of the Museum of Scotland, and the Museum of Scottish Country Life, and their story, as an essential part of the background, deserves to have been at least outlined in Charles McKean's book.

Nevertheless, *The Making of the Museum of Scotland* is a handsome volume, packed with information and extremely well illustrated, and at the same time the text is very readable.

Alexander Fenton

HERITAGE AND MUSEUMS. SHAPING NATIONAL IDENTITY
Ed J M Fladmark

Donhead Publishing Ltd, Shaftesbury 2000
xvi + 393pp. £38.50. ISBN 1 873394 41 1

This volume consists of papers presented at 'The Robert Gordon University Heritage Convention 1999'. There are 30 chapters, divided into three parts: on the Museum of Scotland, subtitled 'Capturing the Spirit of a Nation'; on the Scottish Partners, 'Towards a National Iconography'; and on International Exchange, 'Learning from Others'. These are ambitious targets, standing, as the First Minister, the late Donald Dewar says in his Foreword, 'as a milestone at the crossroads of two momentous happenings. One was the opening of the Museum of Scotland, and the other was the reinstatement of the Scottish Parliament'. He sees these events as complementary markers of national identity, thereby giving each a high level of responsibility for the future. This book assesses the part played by the makers of the Museum of Scotland, and looks more widely at the question, who are the makers and keepers of national identity? It should be read in conjunction with Charles McKean, *The Making of the Museum of Scotland*, also reviewed in this issue of *ROSC*.

The first 12 chapters are mainly on the Museum of Scotland, and are written to a large extent by members of staff of the museum. They outline the thinking behind the Museum of Scotland. The curators and the architects discuss the vision that shaped the building and its contents, the strategy that directed display and interpretation, and the marketing of the idea, with the museum being seen, in Mary Bryden's words, as a 'gateway' to discovery of the past. Objects are interpreted as three-dimensional records, and selections are made that illuminate crucial periods in Scottish history – for example, the Jacobite relics that signify the time when the Catholic Stewarts were threatening the Protestant establishment, and have become a focal point for a particular modern, popular, romantic vision of Scottish history.

Although the Museum has aimed at telling Scotland's story, it is not certain that it has succeeded for everyone. Charles McKean, for example, wonders if it is a 'national shrine or distorting mirror', and an investigation by academics from the Department of Marketing at Stirling University found that 'research has highlighted how many of the visitors articulated ambivalence, both in the ability of the Museum to tell the story of Scotland, and the desirability of actually being told. In other words, for many of the visitors, the link between the Museum and construction of their own sense of a Scottish national identity is not readily apparent'(156–7). Such comments should not be taken as negative, but should serve as pointers to further thought about what the concept of national identity is, and indeed about whether or not there is or can be a single concept, valid for everyman.

The second part consists of contributions by members of staff in related cultural bodies: the Scottish National Portrait Gallery, Historic Scotland, the National Trust for Scotland, the Scottish Tourist Board (as it was then called), the Scottish Museums Council, and Scotland the Brand. Tartan plays a prominent role as a 'national patriotic symbol', as evidenced in portraiture, and inevitably, Sir Walter Scott and his stage-management of the visit of George IV to Edinburgh in 1822 are used as a key to the 'creation of Scotland'. Sir David Wilkie is given honourable mention as a history painter turned genre painter, who was able to convey in his art something of 'Scott's complicated views and feelings about Highlanders', though the book otherwise pays little attention to the Highland/Lowland division which is such a strong element in Scottish identity, nor to the subsuming of Scottish identity under Highland identity. It is also worth remembering that British identity can form part of the broad Scottish concept, and indeed Wilkie, who was appointed Principal Painter to the Crown when Victoria came to the throne in 1837, conveyed this aspect in his painting, *Chelsea Pensioners Reading the Gazette of the Battle of Waterloo*, unveiled in London in 1822. In it, Scot and English mingle.

Another subject area is opened up by the holdings of objects as well as of monuments and buildings, of Historic Scotland and the National Trust for Scotland, which may be centralised or local, spreading throughout Scotland. All are elements in the historical, cultural identity of Scotland, and it is perhaps surprising that so little is said about the science of site-interpretation. A monument and its setting, well and truly interpreted, with account being taken of environmental factors as well as the record of historical changes and of its symbolism (like Culloden), can create powerful feelings of identity at local and wider levels. It is much less easy to recreate such feelings in a strictly museum context, into which objects have to be imported, but messages of a broader kind can be promulgated through thematic assemblages of objects that have local, regional and national significance. Close collaboration between the national museums, the Scottish Museums Council, whose membership includes 322 non-national museums, and the other cultural bodies contributing to this section of the book is an obvious desideratum. This is, in fact, being done in part by electronic means. The Scottish Cultural Resources Network (SCRAN) is a computer service that integrates information from both national and local museums, which in its continuing growth is presenting an ever more holistic overview of the nation's collections and monuments.

Professors Griggs and Fladmark consider the commercial value of a 'collective national image', and Scottish Enterprise launched 'Scotland the Brand' in 1997 as part of its drive for economic development. This somewhat oddly named unit is trying to establish, for marketing purposes, 'a more cohesive attitude and approach', including a 'national logo' that 'companies and organisations could use throughout the world to establish a more coherent national image'. This is aimed at commerce and tourism, but it will require very careful interpretation of the elements of the national heritage, singly and together and including the oral and musical aspects, if the image is to be representative for all the country, varied as it is. And informed control will be needed to prevent the re-invention of 'tradition' or quite simply the creation of 'fakelore'.

The third part of the book explores the experience of Sweden, Norway, Denmark, Russia, and of America in setting up the Museum of the American Indian. The Scottish museum world should undoubtedly take note of the Swedish government report of 1995 which states that 'One aim designed for the museums is that they should encourage national, regional and local identity' (280). This must be balanced against the statement by Stuart Hannabuss that 'Even the history itself can be manipulated and unreliable, and this we associate with the heritage industry and its styles of interpretation'. People readily believe what they are told, whether as a passing 'cultural tourist', or as a native of a district or country. Interpretation at a heritage centre, or explanation in a museum display, may be misleading, but it will become the canon if presented with an air of authority. We therefore have to ensure that those who seek to instil a sense of identity do so with real knowledge, and this should be not only a matter for the staffs of cultural institutions and bodies, but also something that sits high on the list of educational priorities in schools and universities.

This book covers a lot of ground. It has gaps that remain to be filled, such as an assessment of the impact of politics at local authority or central government level, on the individual, for this shapes identity almost to a greater extent than anything else nowadays, and is continually adapting and re-creating community and broader national forms of culture. But even if reading of this book leaves the reader wondering what on earth 'national identity' is, or whether it exists in itself or through the eyes of outsiders, still it raises questions over a wide range of issues, and stimulates thought about them.

A Fenton

INSTITUTIONS OF
SCOTLAND: EDUCATION
(Scottish Life And Society: A compendium of Scottish ethnology. Vol 11)
Heather Holmes, ed

East Linton, Tuckwell Press in
association with the European
Ethnological Research Centre, 2000
xvii+558pp.illus. £25.00. ISBN 1 86232 1868

This book, *Institutions of Scotland: Education* launches the European Ethnological Research Centre's series Scottish Life and Society: A Compendium of Scottish Ethnology whose aim is 'to examine the interlocking strands of history, language and traditional culture of Scotland within an international context, and their contribution to the making of a national identity.' Contributors recognise education as one of the main sources of Scottish national identity and an important element in Scotland's cultural independence from England.

This volume examines and celebrates Scottish educational institutions and their historical traditions to the present day. It is divided into four parts: part one provides an overview of the traditions of Scottish education; part two deals with its administration and provision; part three is concerned with the types of institutions and the education they provide; and part four focuses on developing some of the themes and issues of the other sections. Each chapter has its own bibliography that enables quick access for further research and investigation within the themes. The writers, not all educationalists, are distinguished within their fields, and their perspective sometimes focused, sometimes broad, gives a rhythm and a cadence to the essays which stimulate and provoke and keep the reader onside.

Lindsay Paterson writes that 'Scottish educational traditions have been central to imaging the Scottish nation for many centuries'. He examines the myths as well as the traditions which make Scottish education distinctive and concludes that these traditions hold a power which 'sets the terms of debate and provide a framework for argument and language'.

There are challenges to the traditional view of democracy within the Scottish education system. Questions are raised about the early partnership between the church and state; the nineteenth century influence of philanthropy in educational provision which helped only those who were deserving of help; and the prevailing philosophy of early twentieth century schooling which created a leadership class based on intellect and social conformity and provided limited educational opportunities to those who were not recruited to that élite.

Part 2 deals with the administration of the educational institutions and the education they provide. It is comprehensive in approach and will serve as an excellent guide and source of reference for all who need a quick revision of where we have come from and how we got here. It takes us from the 'first positive intervention by the state in Scottish education' in 1496 and the First Book of Discipline in 1560 through the changing roles and influence of church, state and individuals in education to the establishment of successive government education departments and bodies such as the Scottish Examination Board, the Scottish Consultative Council on the Curriculum and the General Teaching Council. The significance of many education acts are highlighted and not just the well known few, the difference in provision across the whole of Scotland is examined, and the contribution of significant figures such as Henry Craik, Secretary of the Scotch Education Department from 1885–1904, is examined and analysed in context.

Authors illustrate the strong association between the values of the educational system and the needs of society at a particular time. This gives the reader insights into the roots of difficulties which remain with us still – the problems of the relevance of the curriculum and the motivation of pupils in secondary schools, the challenge of providing equal educational opportunities for all in a system that has been intellectually élitist and slow to respond; and the relationship between educational theorists and the responsibility to provide education for a mass audience.

The third section examines the type and nature of Scottish educational institutions and ranges from elementary institutions, through secondary education, the university and further education sectors to special education, technical schools, independent institutions and residential schools. The inclusion of archive photographs enlivens the text and gives further evidence of the variety of these institutions, their curriculum and their constituency. Oral evidence from pupils and teachers serves as a reminder that problems such as class size, feelings of exclusion due to social or financial inadequacy, lack of appropriate career guidance, troubled and troublesome pupils persist as current problems for which there is no quick solution.

The quotation at the end of the chapter on special education 'There has been little evidence of concern about pupils' views and perceptions' reminds us of the essentially bureaucratic nature of Scottish education. While Alison Closs is enthusiastic about the reforms in special education she concludes that how education is experienced by children 'depends more on the prevailing policies and practice of their local authorities and on the effectiveness of their parents and concerned professionals as advocates, than on any national consensus or format.'

The chapter on the universities and on further education institutions is hopeful that the traditions of the past can still influence the shape of the present and of the future. It is interesting to note the assertion that 'while the four ancient universities have been drawing closer to the British pattern, the newer universities with their numerous part time courses, mature students and links with local communities have revived older Scottish traditions.'

Two essays on the teaching profession, Willis B Marker on Scottish Teachers, and Women in Education by Lindy Moore, illustrate the unequal nature of opportunity for men and women – the different career structure, the unequal salary scales and, until the mid-twentieth century, a marriage bar for women. It is difficult not to subscribe to the view that the history of Scottish education is the history of men in Scottish education.

The origins of many contemporary educational issues are further developed in the various contributions to the fourth part of this book – discipline, curriculum and assessment, literacy, the Gaelic language, catholic education, and adult and continuing education. The final contribution Society and Schooling by Richard Johnstone and Steve Waterhouse concentrates on the last decades of the twentieth century and outlines the major changes in the relationship between school and society that have taken place in the last 15 years. They examine in particular the relationship between school and work, the increasing professionalism of teachers, their opportunities for research into teaching and learning and the place of Scottish education within Europe. The latter was a welcome signpost into the future as educationalists tackle not only the legacy of the past but wrestle with the challenges of an increasingly complex and culturally diverse society. Within this they will try to use the best traditions of Scottish education to create a new Scottish cultural identity within a European space.

Institutions of Scotland: Education makes a major contribution to our ability to reflect on the past, to be informed about the present and to have a glimpse of the challenges that we face in the future in Europe in the next millennium.

Jem Fraser

SCOTTISH MIDWIVES: TWENTIETH-CENTURY VOICES
Lindsay Reid
East Linton, Tuckwell Press in association with The European Ethnological Research Centre, Flashbacks no 12, 2000
193pp. £8.99. ISBN 1 86232 160 4

The author of this splendid Flashbacks volume is Lindsay Reid, a doctoral student at the Wellcome Unit for the History of Medicine, University of Glasgow. While undertaking research into the background to changes in midwifery practice in the 1990s she found her investigations hampered by a lack of written evidence and thus came to track down, through letters to the press and by word of mouth, a large number of retired and working midwives whose varied and memorable views of the profession are recorded here.

Fortunately for those without a detailed knowledge of the medical world, the testimonies are preceded by an explanation of specialist terms. There are also nine pages of introduction which form a quite excellent overview of midwifery in Scotland. Until the end of the nineteenth century childbirth in this country took place largely at home, under the supervision of the respected figure of the midwife, also known – amongst other terms – as the 'skilful woman', *bean-ghluine*, or most commonly the 'howdie'. Such individuals' knowledge was gained from experience and practice, and generally served very well, requiring the presence of a male medical practitioner only in emergency. From the mid-eighteenth century, however, it became the norm for the doctor to attend even routine births, though this in no way implies a reduction in the howdie's role which remained of extreme importance, especially in terms of post-natal care and in household management during the mother's confinement. Annie Kerr explains:

> That's what I was there to dae – to work and save her till she gathered her own strength again. I gave her a basin to wash herself. I never took nowt tae dae wi the washin. I looked after the baby and everything for her and did aa the housework. (42)

Twentieth-century legislation gradually made formal training compulsory, but, in part owing to resistance on behalf of some mothers and medical practitioners, it was not until the 1950s that the midwife without formal qualifications disappeared entirely from the scene. The latter half of the century presented further challenge and change. In the '70s the full hospitalisation and indeed over-medicalisation of maternity care was imposed, only to be followed by a swing back in recent years to greater autonomy for midwives and more choice for mothers, including, in some instances, a return to home births.

The accounts look at the whole gamut of twentieth-century midwifery experience. Twenty-four women and one man talk about the highs and lows of a job that demands the highest possible levels of skill and dedication. The informants come from all over Scotland, from both rural and urban areas, the oldest born in 1902 and the youngest beginning their working lives at the turn of the millennium. Both informally and formally trained midwives speak. The latter place emphasis on their often arduous, ill-fed training days, some, such as Ann Lamb, being introduced brusquely to the business of childbirth in Edinburgh's poverty-stricken Grassmarket:

> We went to lots of classes because you never learned if you didn't go, and out on the district as well. It was a hard training . . . Sometimes you would be going down the street to see a woman and a head would pop out of a window. 'Oh nurse come and help me.' You had never seen her before, you didn't know her name, and up the stairs you went and delivered the baby. She would know who *you* were.
>
> There was no antenatal care and poverty was very bad. It was terrible, they had no clothes, no nothing . . . (12)

Such awareness of, and tolerance towards, lives briefly encountered is typical of the testimonies. Anne Bayne, working in Glasgow, has this to say of a new father:

> In the early fifties there were the razor gangs. I delivered one of their babies . . . They lived in a prefab, a lovely little house, and he was an awful nice laddie. I said, 'Why do you do it?'. He said, 'Oh well, we dinnae need the police force. We just sort things out amongst oorsels' . . . Well, we got to the bus that night and he shook hands with me, thanked me, handed me my bag and put me on the bus. (99)

At times it must be a struggle to maintain morale, especially against a backdrop of demanding collective and personal standards and the constant possibility of things going wrong, though fortunately this seems to have been remarkably rare:

The next woman I wis gaan tae be wi, her baby wis due in three wiks . . . She says, 'I've proved them aa wrang. I've aye been telt I couldnae hae a family and here's me three wiks fae haein the baby'. An she took a brain haemorrhage and died at wik . . . She nivver had her baby. She would maybe ha been aboot twenty-eight. We were jist devastated . . . There wis sad things bit a lot a happy things tae. (Doddie Davidson, 50)

Humour helps, and wit and a sense of fun are manifested repeatedly in this book. One of the tamer anecdotes is recounted by Anne Chapman:

This big dog came out barking and yowling. I was frightened and just stood stock still. This man came out. 'Come on, nurse, come on.' I still stood and he said, 'It micht bite ye but it'll no hurt ye'. When I went back I told one of the others about that and said, 'Don't be frightened to go in there because the dog might bite ye but it'll no hurt ye'. (67)

Of course there are many rewards in midwifery and the accounts consistently reveal an enormous, readily expressed sense of happiness:

One of the joys I had of delivering babies at home was this lovely feeling of warmth and a great atmosphere. It was a great joy once we had got the baby and I used to wrap it up all nice and cosy and give everybody a wee quick look. I'd have lovely warm sheets and a warm nightie and bath towels just ready – things for the mother and things for the baby. (Ella Clelland, 123)

. . . I think, 'Well it was a privilege' . . . the privilege of being committed to serving and caring for people who needed and trusted you, makes me feel now that it was such an honour. (Anonymous midwife from the Outer Hebrides, 62)

We hear from only one mother, Nikki Morton, who later became a midwife. Her feelings regarding the maternity care she received are surely not entirely unique:

I had my son here six years ago, before I was a midwife. I was admitted about 11pm and somebody brought in a reclining chair and there was a wee lamp on in the corner. They moved the bed out of the way and I had all my tapes with me with soft music and that was my first experience of childbirth. My memory of my labour in that room is really happy. (193)

This book presents the reader with a profound sense of care and ability. The people who speak in it seem the sort of boundlessly capable, compassionate and up-beat people one would want by one's side at any troubled time. For many readers their combined story will primarily constitute an insight into a largely hidden tradition. For others it will first and foremost give a heightened sense of confidence in the Scottish medical services. It will certainly be extremely encouraging reading for anyone who is expecting a child and thinking of using the services of a midwife.

Susan Storrier

A SHEPHERD REMEMBERS. REMINISCENCES OF A BORDER SHEPHERD
Andrew Purves
East Linton, Tuckwell Press in association with the European Ethnological Research Centre, Flashbacks no 13, 2001
280pp. 1 photograph. £9.99. ISBN 1 86232 157 4

Undoubtedly this is the best of the Flashbacks to date. It is the autobiography of Andrew Purves, born in 1912, the son of a Border shepherd. As a young lad Andrew was fascinated by his dad's profession and his long career as an inbye shepherd is further testament to a strong sense of vocation (perhaps infatuation would be a better word). It is clear, however, that had his career interests and opportunities lain elsewhere, he would have made an equally successful popular or academic writer. In fact his book puts the work of some seasoned professional authors squarely in the shade and verifies his own statement that 'There is no reason why a person should not work happily with his hands, and at the same time retain an interest in the things of the mind' [73].

The text shows enormous artistry, with an uncluttered yet evocative written style and a highly effective structure. There are two sections. The first deals with the first 32 years of Purves' life in various rural border parishes. These comprise Linton (Roxburghshire), the parish of Roxburgh itself, Fogo (Berwickshire), Glendale (Northumberland) – for which a separate chapter on war conditions is furnished – and Gala Water (Midlothian). Different localities, but little difference in farm folks' way of life.

The second section of the book examines salient themes in rural Border life in the first half of the twentieth century, and describes many phenomena not dealt with explicitly or in detail in other sources. Lairds and craftsmen, farmers and farm workers, housing and leisure, droving, and of course shepherding, including sheep sales, are all presented, the studies analytical as well as descriptive. Points of particular importance or interest are judiciously mentioned in both sections of the volume, but without repetition as such. There are some surprises for those not familiar with rural life of the area and period, especially in terms of attitudes:

Most of the relatives of farm workers who had emigrated were engaged in farming in Canada or Australia. What a sense of freedom they must have felt, those emigrants of the nineteenth and early twentieth centuries, having their own land, doing their own thing and working for themselves, free from the tyranny of farmer employers and in the case of small farmers who had emigrated to better themselves, free from the petty restrictions imposed by lairds. The privations, the heartache and homesickness, that many of them suffered ere they got their feet in the new land, seem eminently worthwhile. [225]

When the draft ewes were sold I always experienced a feeling of parting with old friends. At the sale itself one felt sorry for the poor beasts standing in the pens looking so bewildered, far removed from the familiar surroundings they had known for the past four or five years. I often pondered on what sort of home they would go to and whether they would be as well looked after as they had been by me. I was deeply moved at the draft ewes sale at St Boswells in September 1978, just a few months after I had retired from herding at Ladyrig. On approaching the pen where the ewes from Ladyrig were I recognised many of their faces, and when I spoke to them I could have sworn they knew my voice, even though we had been parted since the month of May. [206]

Precious and excellently-written store of often unique information which this volume is, I would have to say, however, that the biggest motivation behind reading until imprudent hours was getting to know the man himself. Intelligent, able, hardworking, unselfconscious, outward-looking, reasonable, tolerant, perceptive, reflective, analytical, critical, unsentimental, sensitive, independent, somewhat aloof, this is no ordinary character. The book ends in 1944 when Purves' father (and partner) retires and before, an epilogue tells us, he strikes out on his own as both an inbye and hill shepherd and briefly as a seasonal worker undertaking other types of agricultural work. Eventually he weds and settles in Roxburgh parish once more. Given Purves's now very advanced years, it is doubtful that the second half of his life story will appear in print, which is a tremendous pity. Not only would I relish more of this excellent writer's style while finishing the plot, so to speak, of his life, but I would also welcome the opportunity to learn of the Borders during the 'Second Agricultural Revolution', from World War II onwards, and above all discover how Andrew Purves manages to fit the responsibilities of wife (to whom he dedicates *A Shepherd Remembers*) and offspring around all that sheep husbandry.

Susan Storrier

ORDER AND DISORDER: THE HEALTH IMPLICATIONS OF EATING AND DRINKING IN THE NINETEENTH AND TWENTIETH CENTURIES
Alexander Fenton, ed.

East Linton, Tuckwell Press, 2000
342pp. £30.00. ISBN 1 86232 117 5

This excellent book brings together nineteen papers delivered at the Fifth Symposium of the International Commission for Research into European Food History in 1997. The contributors are all authorities in their various but related fields and their essays presented here must be essential reading for everyone interested in the history of the complex relationships between eating and drinking and the health of both managed populations and the private citizen.

In a prelude to the main business of the symposium, Professor Hugh Pennington reminds us that danger, even catastrophe, from our food has not yet been consigned to history. He presents an authoritative insider's account of the contemporary battles to contain BSE in cattle and the threat from new and virulent strains of E Coli. Readers secure in the belief that we are no longer at any risk of death from our food will be briskly disillusioned.

The symposium itself relates to what was essentially a period of a hundred years of recovery. By the middle of the nineteenth century it had become all too evident that the rapid industrialisation and urbanisation of the greater part of the working population of Western Europe had created a new but already debilitated proletariat. Poverty and poor food, very often combined with appalling housing conditions, had damaged the physical, and perhaps even the moral, health of a large and vital section of the population. As the century continued there were real fears in Europe's industrialised countries that the collective strength of the state had been seriously undermined. Public health measures were introduced to halt this process of degeneration. In Britain the full extent of the disease and disability that still existed among the industrial poor at the end of the century was revealed for the first time by medical inspections of the large numbers of men from Manchester and the other great centres of industry who had to be rejected as recruits for the army during the Boer War. This revelation gave rise to a sudden loss of confidence in the physical capacity of the industrial working class to sustain the Empire and Britain's place in the world and new limited medical services were introduced.

The essays presented here all relate to those years of the late nineteenth and early twentieth centuries during which the medical history of Europe was essentially one of slow recovery, interrupted by a severe relapse in the great economic Depression after the First World War. While the major problem for health authorities over this whole period was the plight of the great mass of the poor, there were those among the more prosperous sections of society who were eager to enhance their personal sense of physical well being. Since the medical profession had little to offer in promoting positive health, vegetarianism and other dietary regimes seemed to promise the best route to improved spiritual and physical well being. The essays presented here refer both to the protection of the mass of the poor and to the ambitions of those who looked for personal improvement.

Four essays relate to the work of Sir John Boyd Orr between the two World Wars. Derek Oddy provides an excellent review of the inter-related changes in diet, income and health that followed from the rapid urbanisation and industrialisation as it affected Britain in the nineteenth century. John E Burnett sets the scene as it had become in Scotland in the 1920s and 1930s, making very effective use of the extensive records of the diligent and pro-active health authorities in Glasgow, which as one of the world's largest industrial cities, had its full share of badly housed poor subjected to the further hazards of insufficient and often dangerous food. David Smith's essay relates to the years of unemployment, poverty and subnutrition during the Depression between the wars, focusing particularly on the background to John Boyd Orr's publication of *Food, Health and Income* in 1936 and the Carnegie Survey that he set up in 1937.

Together these three essays make a very important contribution to the continuing controversy that was provoked in the late 1980s by revisionist historians who disputed the extent of the deprivation caused by the Depression in the 1930s. These three essays provide new and intriguing insights, not only into the true extent of the problem, but also into the reluctance of the National Government to acknowledge that such a problem existed.

The fourth in this group of essays, by David Gunnell, is a preliminary report on a follow up study now being carried out on Boyd Orr's Carnegie Survey. Its aim is to relate the social circumstance and diet of the children assessed in 1937 to their present stature and health as adults. This is an ambitious and potentially very important investigation and the findings presented in this preliminary report are already of great interest. When the study is completed it is bound to command attention, not only by medical scientists. A study of such importance will inevitably provoke much public discussion and controversy and its interpretation will require careful scrutiny well beyond the scope of this review.

It is a little disappointing that, in Dr Oddy's essay, Noel Paton is again denigrated for his resistance to the idea that rickets was caused wholly by a deficiency in the diet and for his insistence that lack of understanding and inertia were major contributors to the inadequacy of the diet of the poor. As Hans-J Teuteberg notes in his informative history of the discovery of vitamins, the essential cause of rickets was eventually discovered to be a lack of exposure to sunlight and not to faulty diet. Katarzyya Cwiertka lends further support for Paton's position. In her essay on the 'Propagation of Nutritional Knowledge in Poland', she discusses the interaction of poverty and lack of understanding in creating the nutritional problems of the industrial poor at the beginning of the twentieth century and makes it clear that it was the lack of understanding that became the predominant factor. Inger Lyngø also observes that, certainly by the thirties, 'the important message was that knowledge was more important than money'.

Although industrialisation and urbanisation came at slightly different times and at different speeds to the countries of Europe, all experienced the same nutritional problems affecting their new industrial poor. The essays by Teuteberg, Cwiertka and Lyngø together with others by Godina-Golija, van Eekelen and Thoms give a good account of how the knowledge necessary to overcome these problems was disseminated in Germany, Poland, Norway, Slovenia and Holland.

By the middle of the twentieth century relative prosperity had almost eliminated subnutrition as a mass problem in Europe. Now the issue was the creation of a sufficient understanding of nutrition to allow individual informed choice, either to prevent disease or to promote the fullest possible enjoyment of life both physically and mentally. Van Eekelen gives a commendably balanced summary of the controversy over the relationship between diet and coronary heart disease and Jakob Tanner ventures with equal care into the vexed questions of 'Food, Fibres and Health.' These may be regarded as well considered situation reports on issues that seem set to run and run.

Two contributions, from Arouna Ouédraogo and Sabine Merta, on vegetarianism take us away from the relationship between nutrition and physical health as it concerns the public and the state. Initially promoted by voluntary agencies in the late nineteenth century as a contribution to the moral and social regeneration of a degenerate urban poor and the reform of society as a whole, vegetarianism later came to share with other cults – such as the whole wheat movement, the nutrient salt movement, the fasting movement and Fletcherism (the 'Chew Chew Fad') – an aim to promote spiritual and moral enhancement of the individual. These two fascinating essays on somewhat metaphysical practices will be of great interest to the social historian and to the general reader. The food scientist would also be unwise to lose sight of the possibilities of serendipity from the experience of cults that attracted such a degree of enthusiasm.

This collection of essays provides good

evidence that since the mid-nineteenth century the great advances in the science of nutrition have not been translated directly to improvements in eating and drinking. John Burnett and Adel den Hartog in their essays on the promotion of soft drinks (Coca Cola) and the manufacture of health biscuits illustrate very well the influence of the food and drinks industries. All reasonable people will be aware of the commercial interests in the promotion of proprietary food and drink and be duly cautious of advertising. However, many people will be much less aware of the possibility of inadequacies, bias and political motivation in the advice given by governments.

Peter Scholliers describes the efforts of the Belgian government to manipulate the use of alcohol. Early in the nineteenth century the production, and therefore the consumption, of alcohol was encouraged for economic reasons; by the middle of the century the consumption of alcohol was seen to contribute to the debility of the workforce and was discouraged; later in the century it was feared that alcohol fired violence and civil disturbance and consumption was further discouraged; in 1918 it was assumed that the use of alcohol would inhibit the reconstruction of the country after the war and it was banned completely. Scholliers presents his thesis as a discourse between government and the medical profession. It detracts from the excellence of his thesis that he has been tempted to treat the medical profession as a corporate body with an agreed view on alcohol consumption to be contrasted with that of the government. There were of course doctors who took a stand on public affairs and made their views known. For the most part, however, doctors were individuals with a professional duty to care for individuals. It was therefore inevitable that the silent majority should regard the consumption of alcohol as a matter for individual discretion rather than collective decision.

Christoph Merki gives a unique account of the manipulation of the use of tobacco in Germany by its National Socialist government. This is an aspect of that government's eugenic policies that has not featured even in the most respected and comprehensive histories of the Third Reich. The restrictions imposed on the use of tobacco were not simply a reflection of Hitler's personal distaste for smoking but were part of considered state policy directed at the creation of a more 'racially valuable' society. It was intended that the people of Hitler's Germany should be protected from what was considered to be a 'creeping and addictive racial poison.' However it was a policy that the German government found impossible to maintain during World War II and it is ironic that by the end of the war cigarettes had become valued as a substitute currency. Perhaps this story relates more to political history rather than the history of food and drink but that does not detract from its interest.

John Boyd Orr's work was also complicated by politicians and political considerations. This collection of essays provides other examples of the reluctance of British governments to put their immediate political interest at risk in making decisions about the quality and safety of food and drink. John E Burnet and P J Atkins provide clear and detailed accounts of the slow but eventually successful efforts of government in Britain to put an end to milk borne tuberculosis. In the nineteenth and into the twentieth century tuberculosis was the chief cause of death of young adults and a crippling disease of children. It now seems reprehensible that it should have taken governments so many years to control the most readily controllable form of the disease, that disseminated in milk. One detects echoes in government's hesitant and uncertain handling of the recent crises described by Professor Pennington to this symposium.

This book will be a source of sound and useful information for anyone interested in the history of food and drink. It also offers valuable new insights for those making particular study of any one of a number of aspects of the interplay of food, drink and health. For those with a more general interest, it offers a very good read and much food for thought.

Morrice McCrae

LETHAL WORK. A HISTORY OF THE ASBESTOS TRAGEDY IN SCOTLAND
Robert Johnston and Arthur McIvor
East Linton, Tuckwell Press, 2000
xv + 256pp. £12.99. ISBN 18232 178 7

This story of desolate personal tragedy and callous corporate neglect seems startlingly out of place in the twenty-first century. The Industrial Revolution came late and harshly to Scotland but by the end of the nineteenth century an 'economic miracle' had put Scotland at the industrial heart of the Empire. This was achieved at great social cost. Scotland's population was no longer distributed principally north of the Clyde and Forth but had become concentrated – and for the most part badly housed – across the central belt with Glasgow and Clydeside now home to the heaviest concentrations of people in Europe. A vast new industrial proletariat had been created, much of it poorly paid, underfed, unhealthy and stunted in growth and largely dependent for employment and subsistence on a few heavy industries, particularly shipbuilding and heavy engineering.

It might be reasonably assumed that, in the course of the twentieth century, the relief of poverty, decent housing, better nutrition, free medical care and the regulation of working conditions must have secured the working population of Scotland from the worst effects of urbanisation and the industrial environment. Johnston and McIvor now show that such confidence has been sadly misplaced. From a cohort of the working population, not born until the 1940s, as many as 20,000 who found employment in shipbuilding, heavy engineering and the construction industry in Scotland, will die in the twenty first century of a single industrial disease. The old and now defunct industries on which Scotland's economic miracle was based have left a dreadful legacy.

Those whose environment causes them to inhale fibres, or even the smallest particles, of asbestos are at once exposed to the risk of progressive lung damage leading eventually to breathlessness and respiratory failure. Even short-term exposure creates an even graver risk, indeed a probability, that many years later they will develop a particular and incurable form of lung cancer, mesothelioma. While primary contact with asbestos almost invariably occurs in the workplace the worker may then carry asbestos fibres and particles into his home, putting his family at risk.

In *Lethal Work* Johnston and McIvor have set out, by oral interviewing and by archival research, to determine the dimensions of this modern problem in industrial health, to identify its causes and to analyse its impact upon the lives of those who have suffered. The strength of the book is in its presentation of the oral histories of twenty six of those who have suffered the consequences of exposure to asbestos in the workplace or to asbestos carried into the home. The authors have assembled a vivid and moving account of the suffering, the stoicism and the almost incredible fatalism of those whose health has been destroyed by asbestos. We are left in no doubt of the extent and severity of this human tragedy.

In *Lethal Work* the oral evidence is expertly presented. Archival material has been used to set these individual histories in context. The authors first set out the catalogue of occupational health hazards that have afflicted Scottish workers in the nineteenth and twentieth centuries. They then go on to give a commentary on the long period of occupational exposure to asbestos, the protracted process of discovery of the hazards of such exposure and the slow emergence of legislation to offer at least some protection to the workers. Perhaps the most telling chapter describes the gradual – often grudging – change in the attitudes of the employers, managers, trade unions and the workers themselves.

All this is well done but there are a few disappointing deficiencies. The authors make a number of intriguing statements that deserve at least a footnote in explanation. For example, 'the asbestos industry made sure that this research [on animal models] was not published'. (113) How? 'The different legal system north of the border made it more difficult to obtain a *post mortem* and thus to definitively prove asbestos lung tissue damage.'(217) Surely not. The *Glasgow Medical Journal* is offered as the only witness to a lack of proper medical interest in asbestosis in the West of Scotland although, even in Glasgow, that journal had only a very limited distribution and commanded little scientific or medico-political attention.

However, it is the conclusions reached in *Lethal Work* that will provoke questioning and debate. Johnston and McIvor put the blame for this tragedy chiefly on the calculated callousness of the primary producers and primary users of asbestos who put 'profit before workers' health, neglected basic safely precautions and failed to educate and develop a safety conscious workforce.' The authors fully justify an accusation of criminal negligence and managerial malpractice. The trade unions are judged to have contributed to the disaster by their willingness to accept money in recognition of an admitted risk rather than press for safer working conditions. Clearly the unions failed to act as an effective counterpoise to the power of the asbestos companies.

But does the ultimate responsibility not rest with government? Are the authors right to exculpate the regulators and policy makers on the grounds that in the 1930s their energies were still fully occupied by other dangerous work processes even several years after the Department of Labor in the United States had recognised and turned its attention to the problems of asbestos. There were other circumstances in Britain in the 1930s in which government intervention in health was hesitant and uncertain, the eventual legislation a compromise reached to placate powerful interests and the agreed regulations ineffectively implemented. Contemporary experience of government management of Mad Cow Disease and outbreaks of E Coli infection suggests that the efficiency of state intervention in urgent health problems still stands in need of improvement. In this admirable book Ronald Johnston and Arthur McIvor have drawn attention to, and analysed, a continuing tragedy that should not have happened. Perhaps the publication of *Lethal Work* will help to stimulate

measures that will make further tragedies less likely in future.

Morrice McCrae

SATAN'S CONSPIRACY: MAGIC AND WITCHCRAFT IN SIXTEENTH CENTURY SCOTLAND
P. G. Maxwell-Stuart
East Linton: Tuckwell Press, 2001
225pp. £16.99. ISBN 1 86232 136 1

Since the Enlightenment, Western man has dared to know – *sapere audi* – and to examine rationally the circumstances, the influences and the events that shape his every day existence. In this fascinating book Maxwell-Stuart takes us back to a previous age. In sixteenth century Scotland, before the dawn of modern scientific inquiry, the vacancy of reasoned understanding was occupied by faith and imaginings. People of every class saw their physical world suspended between the celestial world of God and His angels and the demonic world of Satan. The course of their lives, leading inevitably either to Heaven or to Hell, was deemed open to the powerful agency of spirits from these Other Worlds and to the influence of emanations from the planets and the stars. Inevitably there were those, at every level of society, who professed an ability to access these sources of preternatural power on behalf of themselves or their clients. Everyone in Scotland had his own awareness of *sithean* (fairies), witches, diviners, astrologers, physiognomists and alchemists. Maxwell-Stuart now brings together, for the first time, much of the scattered archival record of magic and witchcraft and presents an interpretation of the role of the preternatural in the tumultuous Scotland of the sixteenth century.

While consciousness of the power of the preternatural formed a constant 'background noise' to everyday life, a heightened and manipulated consciousness of the preternatural could also be brought to bear in affairs of state. After decades of rebellion and discord, legislation was introduced in 1563 to promote a 'common peace.' It included a Witchcraft Act to suppress 'all sic vane superstition' as 'Witchcraftis, Sorsarie and Necromancie and the credence gevin thairto,' all of which were pronounced to be against the Law of God. Prosecutions could be brought at the instigation of the Kirk but were to be executed by the officers of the state. Those promoting the new Reformed faith condemned the Mass (and other Roman Catholic practices such as resort to healing wells) as vain superstition and found the Roman Catholic Church guilty of heresy and idolatry. The suppression of witchcraft, identified with suppression of the Catholic faith, became an instrument in the struggle to secure the Reformed Church as the established faith in Scotland, and was carried over into contemporary struggles for temporal power. In 1567, Mary Queen of Scots had been deposed and, after a period of imprisonment, had fled to England. The Regent, the Earl of Moray, in his campaign to replace the former Catholic and French oriented government of Scotland with his own Protestant regime, used accusations of heresy, idolatry and witchcraft to undermine the still active Catholic Marian sympathisers.

In a particularly fine chapter – *Magic In League with Treason* – Maxwell-Stuart explores James VI's confrontation with witchcraft in the early 1590s. While highly sceptical of the reality of the powers claimed by those who practised the Black Arts, the King was well aware of their potential as instruments of propaganda directed at the mass of the population. He certainly had reliable intelligence of a large network of professed witches in the Lothians capable of calling a convention of perhaps as many as a hundred members to be harangued by a figure clad in black gown and black hat in keeping with the common perception of the manifestation of the Devil. That figure may have been the Earl of Bothwell or one of his Marian allies; certainly this subversive organisation produced a propaganda pamphlet – *Newes From Scotland* – against the King's interest. The King may not have feared death by direct preternatural intervention but the invocation of witchcraft against him could reasonably be feared as the voice of treason, revealing the aspirations of those who might contrive his assassination by

means that were entirely mundane. We have long known that in his *Basilikon Doron* James VI (by 1598 less afraid of assassination) put witchcraft ahead of murder, sodomy, incest, poisoning and the issue of false coins in his list of crimes against civil order; from Maxwell-Stuart's work we can now more clearly understand why.

Maxwell-Stuart presents his work as a report to scholars on the extent and importance of the material to found in previously unexplored archives and as a preliminary interpretation of the role of witchcraft in sixteenth century Scotland. There can be no doubt that scholars will look to his book as a sure foundation on which to develop their own further assessments of the impact of Satanic conspiracies on the course of history.

For every reader Maxwell-Stuart has produced a lively, enjoyable and informative account of a magic world that, even in the twenty-first century, has not vanished completely from Scotland. On every May Morning people still climb to the fairy *sithean* at the summit of Arthur's Seat to wet their faces in the early dew.

Morrice McCrae

The Rough Wooing:
Mary Queen of Scots 1542–1551
Marcus Merriman
East Linton: Tuckwell Press 2000
448pp. Illus. £25.00. ISBN 86232 090 X

The 'Rough Wooing' has left a visible legacy across the southern counties of Scotland. The shattered aisles and naves of ancient Abbeys from Jedburgh and Melrose to Holyrood and St Andrews and the many ruined fortifications from Dunbar to Blackness, remain as venerable monuments of what lives in folk memory as but one short episode in the long history of Scotland's struggle to retain its existence as a nation. However the historian can find a mass of archival material that bears witness to the full import of the turbulent years from 1542 to 1551. For some forty years Marcus Merrimen has explored almost every repository and examined almost every relevant document, publishing his observations in a series of contributions to learned journals. He now brings his work together in a single elegantly produced volume.

Merriman endorses the essential story of these years as told succinctly by Gordon Donaldson in his history of *The Making of Scotland*[1] but now sets that story in the wider context of the great dynastic rivalries in sixteenth century Europe. In this protracted struggle for dominance, the chief players were the Hapsburgs, the Valois and the Tudors and the Pope, leading the Holy Roman Empire, France and England into conflicts in which Ottoman Turk, Denmark, Sweden, Norway and Scotland all played important but subsidiary roles. In his comprehensive account of the recurring shifts in the balance of power, Merriman supports his text with a series of ingenious diagrams illustrating the changing complex of treaties, alliances and openly declared wars. The place of the Rough Wooing in the shifting balance of power in Europe is explained and demonstrated with commendable clarity.

Of perhaps more immediate relevance to the domestic history of Scotland is the part played by the Rough Wooing in the introduction of Protestantism as the predominant faith in Scotland. Rosalind Mitchison[2] has already discussed the events of 1542-51 in the context of the Reformation and it is well recognised the Henry VIII used ruthless armed force in his attempts to dislodge the Roman Catholic Governor of Scotland (Earl of Arran), Cardinal Beaton and the Dowager Queen Mary of Guise as the rulers of Scotland and to break the alliance with Catholic France. Merriman now draws attention to the extent of Henry's use of propaganda. Henry promoted books, pamphlets (and sermons) to justify his war by asserting the right of the King of England to rule Scotland and to establish his Reformed church in both Kingdoms. Merriman is not persuaded that this propaganda had any effect on the military outcome of the war but suggests that it 'implanted in men's minds' the idea that Union with England had a 'godly purpose' in bringing the Reformed faith to Scotland. From Merriman's evidence it could be argued that, while the siege of St Andrew's was of little lasting military significance, its lasting significance was in providing the opportunity for an obscure priest, John Knox, to emerge as the successor to the executed George Wishart and, building on what had been 'implanted in men's minds,' to become the voice of the Reformation in Scotland.

The Rough Wooing has an important place in a number of related but different stories and Merriman deals extensively with all of them. This does create problems in the structure of the book. It has clearly not been possible to establish an easy chronology. A further problem is the sheer extent and depth of the author's scholarship. Many years of careful research have given Merriman a deep understanding of the period from which he has drawn important conclusions; they have also allowed him to collect a formidable accumulation of detail. The reader is informed that the Duke of Hamilton's French château in the sixteenth century has since become a municipal library; that the nineteenth century Duke of Hamilton grew up in a house that is now a local golf clubhouse; that the cost of Captain Ubadini's lodging in Edinburgh in 1548 was £11; and that the bill for the improvements in the fortification of Edinburgh castle between 1548 and 1550 was £6,387 2s 10d. In this abundance of detail errors are rare (although Hector Boece could not possibly have been Principal of the University of Aberdeen in 1494) and much of it is intriguing. However the excessive wealth of background information tends to impede the flow of the argument.

Merriman tells us that it was his daughter who finally persuaded him to bring the results of his researches together in a book. Perhaps if she had exerted her influence at an earlier stage we might have had two books in which the wealth of information could sit more comfortably. Nevertheless, this is an excellent book and those who bring their full attention to bear will be well rewarded.

Morrice McCrae

1 G. Donaldson, *Scotland: The Making of the Kingdom James V-James VII*, Edinburgh, 1994.
2 R. Mitchison, *A History of Scotland*, London, 1970.

THE AUTOBIOGRAPHY OF SAMUEL LAING OF PAPDALE 1780–1868
R P Fereday ed and suppl
Kirkwall, Bellavista Publications 2000
xviii + 308pp. £14.95. ISBN 0 9525350 5 X

Samuel Laing is amongst the many Orcadians who have made their mark on the wider world. This book will be of interest in Europe generally, for he spent time in various countries – Norway, Sweden, France, Prussia, Italy, Switzerland, etc. – made copious notes, and wrote books about them. He had the gift of tongues and was responsible for the first translation from the Icelandic of the *Heimskringla or Chronicle of the Kings of Norway* in 1844, so unlocking this great reservoir of northern literature to an English-speaking audience.

This 'autobiography' was begun in 1816 and ended in 1856. It is a copy made in 1957 of a manuscript that has subsequently gone missing. It is a kind of diary, notes for his family, and was not kept up systematically, but nevertheless it tells a great deal about the man himself, his energy and strong views, his contemporaries, his family, and much else, including the role of the holder of an estate vis-à-vis other family members in supporting them. Implicitly rather than explicitly, there appears a picture of nineteenth landed society in Britain, and the role of marriage in relation to status and estate economics.

Samuel Laing in his time played many parts. He started life in Orkney as the son of a merchant, but as the youngest son he had no great expectations and the supply of wealthy godfathers had run out. He showed little interest in academic education in Edinburgh, nor in commercial training in Liverpool, though this gave him the opportunity to spend time in Germany and Holland. He became a soldier at the time of the Napoleonic War, and at various times was manager of the Wanlockhead lead mines in Dumfriessshire, and agent at Leith for Orkney kelp.

On the death of his brother Malcolm in 1818 he found himself taking over the Papdale estate, and here he behaved very energetically, carrying out various improvements which included doing away with payments in kind, trying to make kelp making pay better, and in effect developing the herring fishing and curing trade. He sought reform rather than revolution, embracing utilitarian ideas and considering that enterprise and efficiency were the keys to prosperity.

Inevitably, he began to play a part in local authority activities, and was for 12 years from 1822 provost of Kirkwall. This in turn led to involvement in educational and political interests. He stood as a Liberal after the Reform Acts became law in 1832, but failed to get into parliament. But the difficulties of running an estate were immense and once his children were well settled, he gave it up and started a new life, staying and travelling in many countries, and writing about them. If he had at one time felt there was a lack of purpose in his life, he now seems to have found fulfilment as a writer. His books were full of original observations, and the views expressed were much coloured by the 'liberal utopia' he felt he had discovered in Norway, in which liberal capitalistic values might spread, bringing 'free trade, free speech and free political institutions to other parts of Europe'.

The editor of this volume, R P Fereday, has fully supplemented Laing's own account of his activities and thoughts, and has provided annotations where necessary. The book will certainly revive interest in Laing, not only at home, but also very much in Sweden and Norway, where his memory is well respected. It also throws much interesting light, from an insider's pen, on political life in nineteenth century Britain as a whole.

A Fenton

ROTHIEMURCHUS. NATURE AND PEOPLE ON A HIGHLAND ESTATE 1500–2000
T C Smout and R A Lambert eds
Edinburgh, Scottish Cultural Press, 1999
ix+150pp. Illus. £9.99. ISBN 1 84017 033 6

Very different aspects of Rothiemurchus, described as 'the gateway to the Highlands', are touched on in this wide-ranging volume: the medieval background, the Gaelic heritage, the Grant lairds, the architecture of The Doune, the house in which Elizabeth Grant of Rothiemurchus lived and wrote for some of her life, her literary heritage and the Victorian popular press, the birds and mammals, nature and sport and visitors who sought these, the history of the woodlands, and the ecology of the forest and its future management. The chapters, which are the outcome of a two-day conference, have each their own level of interest.

It can be seen how the changing fortunes of the Grant lairds depended heavily on the forest from as early as the late seventeenth century, when an Aberdeen merchant secured a 13 year lease of the fir woods, with permission to build sawmills. He fell into financial trouble, and other agreements were made early in the eighteenth century, but before the mid-century, outsiders had ceased to be invited to exploit the woods. The trees appear to have been of small size, and there were difficulties with other lairds about floating timbers down the Spey, so that profit to the Grants was not as great as had been hoped, though the demand for timber, especially pine, during the Napoleonic Wars somewhat boosted their fortunes. The technique of rotational clearfelling replaced what seems to have been an earlier more random system, or rather lack of it, according to which the best timbers had been cut out wherever they were found.

But by the final quarter of the nineteenth century, Rothiemurchus had become a sporting estate, with the shootings for deer and grouse bringing in revenue. And though the story of the woodlands shows that they have been subject to constant heavy use, nevertheless the pine forests have proved to be resilient, and following the declaration of a National Nature Reserve in the Cairngorms in 1954, and subsequent agreements, the Caledonian pine forest is protected by both European and British legislation as a priority habitat. In terms of conservation, management, biodiversity etc the 33 native pinewoods designated as Sites of Special Scientific Interest under the Wildlife and Countryside Act of 1981, are targeted as important ecosystems for which

a Native Pine Woodland Habitat Action Plan has been prepared. This will take into account the past and present history of the forests to guarantee sustainability not only of the woods but also of the dependent plant and insect species. Insect and other species are listed on pp 92–103.

Rothiemurchus is, therefore, changing very much in its character. It is no longer the economic imperatives of a family estate that drive actions, but a more global concern for the earth and its environment. It is interesting to speculate on whether or not Elizabeth Grant, author of *Memoirs of a Highland Lady*, would have given wholehearted approval.

A Fenton

SCOTLAND'S ENVIRONMENT: THE FUTURE
George Holmes and Roger Crofts, eds
East Linton, Tuckwell Press in association with The Royal Society of Edinburgh and Scottish Natural Heritage, 2000
x + 150pp. £14.99. ISBN 1 86232 162 0

This volume presents the outcome of a Millennium conference on 'The Future for the Environment: Resetting the Agenda?' In addition, it notes the views of the younger generation of students from secondary fourth to sixth years from Scottish schools resulting from a one-day workshop on 'Scotland's Environment: What Future?'

The rural environment is primarily in focus, and the material is structured to take into account the historical background, present trends, the main drivers of change, an assessment of future aims and the likely kinds of policy instruments required to achieve these.

The historical scene-setting takes a long view of the patterns of rural change over 6000 years, from the beginnings of settled agriculture. The picture is somewhat depressing. Clearance of forest and shrubby areas to make cultivated fields is seen as leading to soil degradation and the creation of podzols, and the concept of deterioration is linked with settlement expansion. The Little Ice Age, a period of global cooling that lasted from the thirteenth to the nineteenth centuries, had an effect on the limits of cultivation and on the growth of young trees in old woods, with an accompanying spread of peat and of moorland. The agricultural improvements that took place from about the 1760s, driven on at a considerable speed in Lowland Scotland with new technologies and buildings, liming and manuring and drainage, stock improvements and better marketing opportunities, and more finance coming from nascent industrial developments, can be seen as a co-ordinated attempt to counteract problems that had been accumulating in intensity over centuries. With the growth of industry and the production of new kinds of pollution, there evolved new levels of conflict between economics and environmental issues. Global warming, whether man-induced or a phenomenon of nature, appears to be a reality, and acidification, nitrogen deposition, problems with the ozone layer, etc are factors that greatly affect land use. So too does the increasing demand from urban populations for recreational access to the countryside. Against such factors has to be set the need to achieve sustainability of resources, and that is to a great degree what this book is about.

An over-arching factor is the economy, with its inter-related elements of financial institutions, often global in their extent, Government policies and statutory bodies that implement these, and the impact of the EU which means that no member state or indeed any state within Europe can remain complete unto itself or go its unilateral way. Another increasingly important factor is that of ethics. The old view of man's dominion over nature is no longer viable, but there is an almost religious movement that seeks to protect nature and her creatures, whatever banner it flies – the green movement, anti-genetic modifications, organic foods and the like. The first United Nations Conference on the Human Environment took place in Stockholm in 1972, another in Rio de Janeiro in 1992 (the 'Earth Summit'), and the one in Nice in 2000, have all been concerned with sustainability and have

had a marked ethical foundation. Interestingly, the Schools Discussion Forum reported in the present volume produced few conclusions from young folk about ethical issues, though the need for education in environmental matters and the fostering of environmental awareness loomed large.

Part 3 of the book, on 'the future', pinpoints the key issues in sustainable development. It is clear that no country can now stand alone, for factors such as globalisation, population increase, the better use of natural resources with less environmental impact, patterns of consumption and lifestyle, climate change, etc are matters that concern the earth as a whole. But the application of measures for sustainability have to be at local level, and a case study of the Scottish Uplands lists the diversity of interests and factors that have to be reconciled, whether by accord or by regulation: agriculture, forestry, sporting interests, recreation and tourism, renewable energy, extractive industries, conservation of the natural heritage. And the flooding of the year 2000 gives sharp actuality to the question of urban drainage which collects foul drainage and rainwater through sewers and conveys both to the nearest available watercourse, carrying elements of pollution and denying the hydrological cycle by which rainwater carries essential nutrients to plants and animals and shapes the natural environment through processes of erosion and sedimentation. Much more attention will be paid to this question in the future, no doubt, as for other sectors, through the use of economic instruments such as tax concessions, subsidisation, financial incentives, and the like. These are well established, but not all have had the expected desirable consequences, as in the case of the great expansion of agricultural activity in the 1970s–80s, or the private sector quick-return afforestation of sensitive areas like the Flow Country in the 1980s. Planning and policy-making seem to have to make progress on the basis of past mistakes, though the outcome of actions as 'mistakes' may only appear in retrospect.

Perhaps this is why there is a move to shift from state regulation to community involvement as the framework of decision making, and why the concept of 'stewardship' has gained fairly general acceptance in the land reform debate, with its potential for greater accord between owner, occupiers and users, and in a way looking more strongly at ethical issues. But the world being what it is, the people on the ground, and even the local and central authorities, will still be tinkering on the edge of what have become global concerns to an increasing extent, and their task will be to translate into regional terms the broad-brush rulings from on high. In such a scenario, the Editors' 'Agenda for Action', pp 134–40, deserves particular attention.

A Fenton

ROBERT TOWNSON MAGYARORSZÁGI UTAZÁSAI. ROBERT TOWNSON'S TRAVELS IN HUNGARY
Péter Rózsa, ed
Kossuth Egyetemi Kiadó, Debrecen, 1999
219pp. ISBN 963 472 495 1

This multi-author volume contains the proceedings of the 'Townson Symposium' held in Debrecen, Hungary, on 26 September, 1997. Robert Townson, 1762–1827, was a 'Hungarophile polymath', the son of a London merchant, who abandoned a mercantile apprenticeship in favour of becoming a naturalist. He studied medicine, chemistry and later botany at Edinburgh University, at a time when Edinburgh was at the height of the Enlightenment period, and was influenced by a number of brilliant teachers: James Hutton, geology; Alexander Munro, anatomy and surgery; Daniel Rutherford, natural history and botany; Joseph Black, chemistry; John Walker, natural history.

His second book, *Travels in Hungary with a short account of Vienna in the year 1793* was published in 1797 and there quickly followed Dutch and French editions. It was the result of a tour, largely on foot. It included a map which was one of the earliest attempts at mapping 'petrography' by any English scientist, and

speleological investigations, with accounts of pioneering ascents in the Tatra Mountains. For this he was awarded an LL D degree by Edinburgh University in 1796. His geological practice and ideas were much influenced by Abraham Gottlob Werner, professor at the mining school in Freiberg, one of whose major contributions to the development of the science of geology was to add the concept of time – relating to successive deposition of rocks from a primeval ocean – to thinking about the earth.

In all his wide-ranging work, whether geological, meteorological, botanical or entomological, he was one of the group who helped to shape, in the eighteenth century, the foundation of the modern world. But he also observed and tasted Hungarian wines, describing the wines and wine-growing of the Tokay region. In Debrecen he described the making of a special type of large, high, white bread, and of a white, hard kind of soap. Forms of dress, fairs, girls' games and dances were also of interest to him. Like a true enlightenment figure, he had a rounded view of life, and this present volume does much to restore to memory one whose ideas were shaped and stimulated in the hotbed of the Scottish Enlightenment.

All papers in the book are given in Hungarian, with full English translations.

A Fenton

LOOKING BACK. AN AUTOBIOGRAPHICAL JOURNEY THROUGH SOUTH EDINBURGH AND BEYOND
Charles J Smith
Edinburgh: Malcolm Cant Publications 2000
xi, 116pp. Illus. £12.00. ISBN 0 9526099 4 0

Charles Smith has written 10 previous books on Edinburgh and now at the age of 80 he presents some of the highlights of his life. These can be divided into three sections: his young days, his work in the Department of Medical Microbiology in the University of Edinburgh which went in parallel with his years of community service, and his very productive activities as a writer and lecturer on the local history of Edinburgh. Since he left school early, he was largely self-trained, but there is no doubt that the training in a methodological approach in a microbiological laboratory guided him in a systematic approach to local history, as he describes on pp 96–7.

He started to earn pocket money by early morning milk delivery at the age of 12. Other boys delivered morning rolls and newspapers, and here light is thrown on the infrastructure of the street economy as part of city life. Street games, those both of boys and girls, are described, as well as details of home life and domestic circumstances – including the coming of gas lighting. Holidays in the 1940s were to the west of Scotland, to Rothesay, by train and steamer, in boarding house accommodation.

Religion and social welfare played a large part in Charles Smith's life, at first through membership of the Boys' Brigade and in the late 1940s through the Young Christian Workers' Youth Movement. He became leader of one of the Edinburgh Sections and as a result came to play a role in the Kilbrandon Council, the Standing Consultative Council on Youth and Community Service in Scotland. He was much involved in the setting up of a youth club at Hyvot's Bank farmhouse at Gilmerton in 1964. It had great initial success but closed in the following year. The chapter that tells of this activity is an important one, as it points to what may or may not be possible to accomplish for young folk in an area, in a way that will provide lasting benefit.

In his work place, he was also involved in matters of national importance, for he was one of a small team that was producing penicillin, after its importance was realised, for clinical trials in Edinburgh Royal Infirmary.

Chapter 8 deals with his writing and lecturing, revealing a man who is methodical in assembling data and assiduous in presenting it for the public weal, and in this way continuing a life of dedicated public service. The book tells as much about the man as about his times.

A Fenton

RUIN AND RESTORATION: ST MARY'S CHURCH, HADDINGTON
Rosalind K Marshall

East Lothian Council Library Service, 2001
76pp. Illus. ISBN 1 897857 23 3

Ever since I came to Edinburgh in the 1950s, I have paid periodical visits to St Mary's Church in Haddington. It has a magnetic quality, that draws visitors back to it time and again. In its ruined state, it had this effect and its restoration has done nothing to change this. This new, lavishly illustrated booklet by Dr Marshall provides a welcome and convenient means of understanding its attraction. It is much more than a guide book, for it recounts the mixed fortunes of the church against over 800 years of the history of Scotland.

When the parish church of St Mary the Virgin was founded is unknown, but it existed in the first half of the twelfth century, lying outside the town of Haddington, by the River Tyne, and surrounded by its graveyard, as it still is. In 1400, the new church of St Mary, designed in the Gothic style, was consecrated. At 206 feet long by 62 feet wide, it was the largest parish church in Scotland. Details of the conduct of the Mass are given, as well as of the endowment of Masses by wealthy individuals, and of the role of the Trades Incorporations.

In 1548, the English laid siege to Haddington and the church received a battering. The east end deteriorated and was being used as a quarry by townspeople who wanted stone to repair their own houses. A barrier wall was erected, leaving the choir and transepts in a ruined state and allowing the rest to be used for Protestant worship. Repair work continued through the sixteenth century, as well as burials of the élite, in spite of the fact that the General Assembly of the Church of Scotland had forbidden burial within churches in 1581. Lofts were built in the seventeenth century for the Haddington magistrates and for the Trades Incorporations, and space within the usable part of the church was at a premium. Meantime, the tower was becoming dangerous and various remedial measures were tried in the nineteenth and twentieth centuries.

John McVie, former Town Clerk of Haddington, deserves full credit for his long battle to achieve a total reconstruction of the church, and provides a sound example of the important role that an individual can sometimes play within the life of a community. Power was added through the establishment of the 'Lamp of Lothian Trust', chaired by the Duchess of Hamilton. Yehudi Menuhin agreed to initiate a fundraising initiative by playing in the church in 1968, and Queen Elizabeth the Queen Mother became Royal Patron of the Friends of the church. High level activity led to substantial support for the project, and restoration work began in 1971. In 1973, the first service for over 400 years was held in the choir. A fine new organ was built in, and renewal was completed by the acquisition of a set of bells, dedicated in June 1999.

The story of the restoration of the church of St Mary is a fine example of what can be done through private initiatives, and through voluntary organisation. Dr Marshall has documented the story in fascinating detail. The only thing I find missing is a discussion of the graveyard around the church, for this also commemorates much of the history of the people of Haddington. When I go there, I never fail to pay due homage to a table tombstone, probably of the eighteenth century, on which there is a graphic representation of an oval and a round loaf, lying on a pair of crossed peels, ready to be popped into a baking oven.

A Fenton

GLENESK: THE HISTORY AND CULTURE OF AN ANGUS COMMUNITY BY MARGARET FAIRWEATHER MICHIE Compiled and edited by Alexander Fenton and John Beech with a chapter by Christina Mackenzie
East Linton, Tuckwell Press, 2000
301pp. £20.00. ISBN 1 86232 181 7

Glenesk is the longest, the most complicated historically and still the most populous and interesting of all the Angus glens. Although a good deal has been written about it, no detailed work has hitherto been attempted. The idea of the present work belongs to Greta Michie, the charismatic native of Glenesk whose zeal as a born educator impressed and enlightened everyone with whom she had contact. Her collections of life in the Glen, past and present, were preserved in a pioneering series of guard books in the Glenesk Museum which were available for public access and consulted by scholars and other visitors from far and wide. She had always intended that these should be the sources for a book on the Glen, as a kind of microcosm of a disappearing way of life, but her drafts were far from completed by the end of her life. She fixed on her friend Alexander Fenton to bring her work to publication – an unsought task which he has brought to a satisfactory conclusion with the help of John Beech, taking account of everything which has been published about Glenesk since Miss Michie's death. The book covers a wide range of subjects from the underlying geology and the archaeology through the lords of the Glen and the histories of the churches and schools to the television programme preferences of the inhabitants in the 1960s and 1970s. There are some unexpected nuggets like the letter of William Scot in 1587 with an appreciation of nature in the Glen every bit as lyrical as the writings of the Romantic poets of a couple of centuries later or the detailed dimensions of the vanished 'castle' of Auchmull built in 1607. A thorough analysis of seventeenth century testaments reveals a surprising amount about lifestyle and agricultural success curiously at odds with continual complaints in the same period about depredations by highland caterans and others. This agricultural analysis is continued for the eighteenth and nineteenth centuries using additional sources like rentals accounts and diaries.

The story of a changing and declining culture and the radical solutions introduced by the estate in the name of progress are echoed in many other parts of Scotland where the spiralling process of agricultural decline and consequent emigration is at work aided by the selfish interests of an absentee or distant landlord. The process is traced from the multiple tenancy holdings of the seventeenth century to the single farms of the eighteenth and their rapidly declining numbers through amalgamations and the creation of deer forest and grouse moors in the nineteenth century. The population of the Glen declined steadily from about 700 in 1755 to 120 in 1992, but there are signs that the rate of decrease has slowed slightly in the last forty years. These changes are closely tied to the lives of particular individuals and families, and there is extensive information about some of them, where they came from and where they went. Some of the emigrants are even followed to their new homes overseas in some detail and notice taken of their descendants return visits to the Glen.

Individuals are one of the notable features of this book: James Stewart and Robert Middleton, nineteenth century day labourers, who kept meticulous accounts of their lives, Jess Cattanach, whose life at Whigginton is so well documented in memories and artifacts and many others whose houses, tools, animals and lives are discussed in illuminating detail. Chapters on summer grazings and illicit stills, sport and game, and hearth and home flesh out the story of life in the Glen and recount the anecdotes which bring it alive.

The final chapter by Christina Mackenzie deals with the recent past and records the life of the Glen people as a community and the changes which outside pressures have brought.

The book begins with and autobiographical foreword by Greta Michie and an elegant memoir by the late Dr Ronald Cant. There is an excellent series of over eighty illustrations to accompany the text and there is a good index. This comprehensive book is a work of general importance as it preserves much of the information about people and places which perishes with depopulation.

Robert Smart

SPORTS CULTURE: AN A-Z GUIDE
Ellis Cashmore
London: Routledge, 2000
xvi, 482pp. £18.99. pbk ISBN 0 415 22335 0

This is a guide to current sociological work on the culture of contemporary sport. As an analysis of sport, it may not be balanced, but this is a characteristic of the academic world, which is far more interested in race, gender, sexuality, film and television, than in historical origins, regional variation, or sports writing. In *Sport Culture*, sport is implicitly defined as something that can be seen on television. The ordinary player, who is seeking pleasure rather than a wage, is not present. Neither is the meaningful local contest that can hardly be understood by outsiders, as when Lugar Boswell Thistle engage in mortal combat with Irvine Vics on the football park. Instead, we have something that approaches the soap opera: 'the incidence of illegitimate births and subsequent legal actions involving sportsmen is full of possibilities to the student of culture.' (329) Cashmore is largely concerned with golf, athletics, basketball, baseball, American football, and association football. Not yachting or badminton, not sports like bowls which are largely played in the former British Empire, not the sports which over the span of history have most affected the history of sport in general, archery and horse racing. In this perspective, the shapers of modern sport are men like Roone Arledge, the television executive who forced the camera close enough to see players' facial expressions, Mark McCormack, who made himself rich as Arnold Palmer's agent, and now represents David Coulthard and the Pope, and Rupert Murdoch.

Sport Culture is a clear and incisive guide. It plays down the theoretical side of sociology, emphasising real people trying to live real lives. Each entry ends with a short bibliography, and there is a helpfully full index. And the book is readable. 'Motor racing and horse racing are the only two sports in which the participants are routinely followed by ambulances.' (81)

John Burnett

SPORT, SCOTLAND AND THE SCOTS
Ed Grant Jarvie and John Burnett
East Linton: Tuckwell Press, 2000
x + 277pp. Illus. £16.99. ISBN 1 86232 130 2

Sport, Scotland and the Scots is an immensely informative and readable volume which succeeds admirably in capturing the country's enduring passion for its traditional and contemporary games. This lucidly written publication by an array of acclaimed authors, assesses the growth and development of Scottish sport from medieval times to the turn of the twenty-first century. It is a comprehensive, thoroughly researched and thought-provoking work deserving to be widely read by sports academics and general enthusiasts alike.

Rather than discussing sports in a vacuum, contributors address their evolution within a dynamic and changing society. Thus, among other issues, the impact of industrialisation, globalisation and devolution, are considered, with the effects of the former particularly prominent in revolutionising sport. The formation of governing bodies during the Victorian period, in line with the new order and regimentation imposed on society at large, transformed uncodified folk games into structured activities, which were initially promoted across Britain by educational institutions before becoming widespread. With the odd exception, the historical and modern eras are treated equally: perhaps the chapter on hockey, for example, could have dwelt a little longer on early twentieth-century events rather than concentrating primarily on the last thirty years. The hockey piece, however, is the only one in which both sexes receive similar attention. While the rise of women's participation is frequently commented on, that sport remains a predominantly male arena is emphasised by the small space devoted to female involvement, evidently indicating that their contribution is yet to be fully realised.

Sports' national significance is demonstrated by the opening chapter's claim that eighty-six per cent of the Scottish population regard it as important to have winning teams. Eminent native athletes are, therefore, held in high esteem, and indigenous sports, as well as those that the country has successfully adopted, are broadly promoted. Despite a lasting debt to other European countries for inspiring this adoption, Scotland takes pride in its own distinctive sporting heritage, with curling, shinty, golf and bowls all being enjoyed long before the widespread formalisation of sports during the late nineteenth century. Having begun as an annual event around 1820, the Scottish Highland Games continue to delight by presenting to a global audience a festival combining athletic competition with music, dance, and geniality. Even association football, a game created by the English, has become a national obsession, which the Scots embrace unreservedly.

Although the volume largely celebrates Scottish sport, it does not shirk from discussing thornier topics such as lack of facilities, financial shortages, and the threat posed to indigenous games by those that are played internationally. The contributors stress that in order to survive in the twenty-first century and avoid being obliterated by more prominent spectator sports like football and rugby, the organisation of 'Scottish' games requires fundamental revision. In the case of shinty, Hugh Dan Maclennan warns that without 'a radical approach to the game's administration and development' its ability to 'progress and remain competitive and attractive' is nigh impossible. Indeed, a distinct pessimism is expressed concerning the future of shinty and quoits, both presently suffering from falling attendances through public apathy. It would be tragic if the only communities eventually left to fly their flag were Scottish societies abroad, which utilise their national sports to demonstrate their loyalty to their country.

The contributors' obvious enthusiasm toward their subjects is marked by the fluent and engrossing text, enlivened by colourful quotations and humorous touches. Alan Bairner's opening remarks in his football paper gently mock the national team's consistently woeful World Cup performances, while Joyce Kay and Wray Vamplew vividly portray the horse-racing world, in which gentry balls and parties contrast starkly with working class crime and hooliganism. With such an abundance of contributors, one might expect the book to be incohesive. This is never the case, however, for while the chapters stand as valid discussions in their own right, they are neatly drawn together by the editors' introduction, which provides an overview of the main themes and periods under consideration. A generous use of black and white photographic illustrations accompanies the text, and the book concludes with a useful chronology of Scottish sport over the centuries, along with list of recommended publications for further reading.

By raising, as yet, unanswerable questions concerning the future fortunes of Scottish sport, the volume not only charts its progress to date, but also invites further comment and debate. It constitutes a stimulating read for those seeking to obtain a solid grounding in Scotland's most popular sports and become acquainted with the surrounding social issues which have influenced the directions in which the games have travelled. With British sports literature currently England-dominated, accessible publications such as this go some way toward redressing the balance. The sporting tradition of Celtic countries needs to be clearly defined, in order to underline their own significant place in history. That sport is integral to Scottish culture is undeniable – a fact that *Sport, Scotland and the Scots* proclaims with confidence, vitality and panache.

Emma Lile

THE OXFORD COMPANION TO FOOD
Alan Davidson
Oxford: OUP, 1999
xx, 892pp. £40.00. ISBN 0-19-211579-0

This is a beautiful book, laid out as formally as an Oxford reference book should be, but also with elegance and wit. The drawings by Soun Vannithone are beautiful as well as informative. The text is endlessly interesting, and staggeringly wide ranging. And the book may also be quite useful.

The *Oxford Companion to Food* is largely about ingredients, and what we might call simple food – say bread or sausages – which may themselves become the ingredients of more complex dishes. It says less about cooking and dishes, and more or less nothing about the various structures of the meal. It feels as though it has been written from a kitchen near late twentieth-century Oxford, with an emphasis on the things one puts on the table in order to impress. The ethnologist will be saddened that the author's energy and scholarship have not been directed towards the nature of meals, or their timing, or tableware, or the role of Sunday food in extending the diet, or the diet itself, or cooking utensils, or the professions which prepare and sell food, or famine, or fasting. There is good material on food and calendar customs. But food eaten on festivals is usually richer than normal food, pointing us to the author's enthusiasm for the special rather than the quotidian or hebdomadal. The food which most people ate (or eat) on most days of the year is not a central theme of the *Oxford Companion*. The entry on vegetarianism treats it as a matter of choice from Pythagoras to the present, but a meat-free diet was inevitable for much of the population of Europe before the late nineteenth century. The bibliography focuses on specialist food writers rather than ethnologists; there is a mild flavour of the *Sunday Times* colour supplement.

Alan Davidson was a diplomat. This is reflected in his interest in language and etymology, the naming of different kinds of dal, the problematical *Sally Lunn* (a Bath bakeress? Alsatian *soleil et lune*?) and the Sanskrit origin of the Spanish word *paella*. One of the few words he does not unpick is the Scots dye *cudbear*, extracted from lichen, and once used to improve the colour of red wine (the name comes from that of Cuthbert Gordon, the inventor). The global span of diplomacy also leads to the global vision of the book, though the breadth of vision is accompanied by an enthusiasm for detail. In Asia 'dragonflies are widely eaten, but are not an important foodstuff anywhere; catching them is a sort of a "sport", and this aspect is as important as anything to do with nutrition or flavour.' (255)

'The standard Albanian loaf is dark beige in colour, on the heavy side, with a slightly sour flavour.' (9) Perhaps the most useful entries in the book are those on national and regional cuisines.

That said, one of the least satisfactory essays is the one on Scotland. One sixth of it is taken up with a description of the Auld Alliance. Unhappily, it accepts F. Marian McNeill's mutton-headed discussion of the debt of Scots cooking terminology to the French, in which she deployed unsatisfactory etymologies, and also implied that a number of words were Scots when they were also used in England. The *Oxford Companion* says nothing of the Scots tradition of soup making, or of our liking for sweet things, or of the very limited tradition of making leavened bread.

Taken in its own terms, this is a most enjoyable book, but perhaps as well placed in the kitchen, for intellectual entertainment while the spuds are boiling, than in the ethnologist's study.

John Burnett

THE EDINBURGH EDITION OF THE WAVERLEY NOVELS
Editor-in-chief Professor David Hewitt

GUY MANNERING (1815)
Walter Scott
P D Garside, ed
University Press, Edinburgh, 1999
xvi + 599pp. £30.00. Hb. ISBN 0 7486 0568 1

THE ABBOT (1820)
Walter Scott
Christopher Johnson, ed
University Press, Edinburgh, 2000
xvi + 555pp. £30.00. Hb. ISBN 0 7486 0575 4

THE FAIR MAID OF PERTH (1828)
Walter Scott
A D Hook and Donald Mackenzie, eds
University Press, Edinburgh: 1999
xvi + 532pp. £30.00. Hb. ISBN 0 7486 0585 1

ANNE OF GEIERSTEIN (1829)
Walter Scott
J H Alexander, ed
University Press, Edinburgh, 2000
xvi + 581pp. £30.00. Hb. ISBN 0 7486 0586 x

The Edinburgh Edition of the Waverley Novels was launched in 1993, and publication continues. The volumes have been carefully and critically edited from the original manuscripts and now the texts, which in each case capture large numbers of readings never before printed and clear away elements of corruption in existing editions, are as close to what Scott originally wrote as the skills of the editorial team can make them. Full emendation lists are given in each case, and though the majority are minor, there are also changes of substance, as for example the inclusion of the pen-portraits of Edinburgh literati in *Guy Mannering* – even if this is an example of Scott letting his pen run away with him in the first instance.

The publication of *Waverley* in 1814 was an event in terms of the history of the novel, of European significance. It marked the emergence of the historical novel, and as the series grew, it was increasingly seen as a mirror of Scotland's identity, Lowland as well as Highland. The speech of Scott's actors varies from a high chivalric mode to that of good dialect, and throughout he uses a wide ranging vocabulary (as, for instance, the hawking terms used in *The Abbot*), in which many of the Scots terms have left an enduring mark on the English language as such.

Whether at home, or on foreign soil as in *Anne of Geierstein*, Scott's approach is to set the old against the new. Traditional feudal loyalties and patterns of behaviour come up against economic and social imperatives. The Laird of Ellengowan in *Guy Mannering*, trying to restore family fortunes, took to farming and attending markets, 'but what he gained in purse he lost in honour'. In *The Abbot*, it is the interface between the old pre-Reformation loyalties and those of the new religion that highlight the drama. In *The Fair Maid of Perth*, Lowland ways spell the doom of Highland traditions of life and thought. As David Daiches says in his Foreword (repeated in each volume), such contrasts were used by Scott to make a pattern that he saw as 'the living fabric of history'. And in each case he sets his dramatic conflicts against the background of scenery that harmonises with the emotions of the characters and is described in terms that can well inspire awe in the reader.

Equally deserving of comment is Scott's close degree of observation of the minutiae of everyday life, which gives his work a sound ethnological flavour. In *Guy Mannering*, he lists the handicrafts of 'gypsies, jockies, or cairds'. In *The Fair Maid*, there is a lively description of Fastern's E'en revels in Perth, and Simon Glover was fed by his Highland host on 'graddan, or bread made of scorched barley'. Here and in innumerable other instances, he has absorbed what he saw – or read – and contextualises it, giving the details life in the broad setting of his novels.

It is not intended to review this sample of four of Scott's novels in any detailed way, for they are well known. My intention is simply to indicate some of the highlights, and to emphasise how much valuable ethnological detail is to be found in them, even though that has to be checked against other sources for Scott, with his omnivorous imagination, was not above setting items out of their true chronologies. But he gave them life, and Scotland owes him a great debt.

A Fenton

MAYALES Y TRILLOS EN LA PROVINCIA DE LEÓN [FLAILS AND TRIBULA IN THE PROVINCE OF LEON]
José Luis Mingote Calderón in collaboration with Asunción Limpo
Diputación Provincial de León, Spain, 1990 116pp. Line drawings, maps, tables, 28 colour photographs. ISBN 84 87081 31 2.

A slim but informative volume, *Mayales y Trillos en la Provincia de León* arose from a Spain-wide study of the topic of threshing, much of which

has now been published in the *Anales del Museo del Pueblo Español* [*Annals of the Spanish People's Museum*]. The initial broad investigation helped focus a year's local government-funded research in Leon, an inland province in north-western Spain, and enabled the authors to undertake a remarkably comprehensive investigation of the topic. The project was led by José Luis Mingote Calderón, a member of the International Committee for Research on the History of Agricultural Implements and Field Structures, Copenhagen, whose other publications have included the *Catálogo de Aperos Agrícolas del Museo del Pueblo Español* [*Catalogue of Agricultural Tools in the Collections of the Spanish People's Museum*].

Work began by sending a questionnaire with covering letter to all the local councils in the province (some 220), asking about the presence or absence of both flails and threshing boards or tribula (see fig). It was largely from the 15 per cent that replied that the authors chose specific places of study – one village for each grid box drawn on the map – and in these a total of 20 days were spent in the field in 1985, gathering information through questionnaires corroborated by occasional questions on specific points. Field results are augmented in the book by a close examination of visual and documentary evidence (a list of references to flails and tribula in medieval Leonese texts is appended), including a number of English-speaking travellers' accounts from the eighteenth and nineteenth centuries.

Direct Percussion

Before examining flails and tribula a range of other methods of separating grain from the stalk, used largely in the mountainous north-east of in Leon, is outlined. These include rubbing or beating sheaves with straight rods, and hitting sheaves against a bench, cart or threshing stool or the lower part of a tribulum. Direct percussion against a tribulum is in fact fairly common in a number of parts of Spain and is usually conducted as a preliminary measure by a solo worker. It is stressed that there has been no straightforward evolution of technology from these methods to the flail. Indeed, in a few places the flail has been ousted by forms of direct percussion.

Flails

Nomenclature

Words used to denote the entire flail vary greatly across the province and reflect contacts with neighbouring regions, especially Galicia and Cantabria, the standard Castilian term *mayal* being scarcely used. Separate geographical distribution maps can also be generated for the nomenclature related to each of the flail's component parts. None of these bears relation to the distribution of the Leon dialect.

Distribution of the Flail v the Tribulum

The flail is found only in the western half of Leon. The boundary between its use and that of the tribulum constitutes a line of retreat which cuts through, rather than follows, the north-south highland-lowland divide in the province. The flail/tribulum distribution in no way accords with the distribution of racial, linguistic, topographical, administrative and most other agricultural phenomena, though there is some slight correlation with plough type, size of holding and cereal dealt with (generally speaking the flail can be used with all cereals but the tribulum is preferred for wheat). Mingote favours the view that the explanation lies primarily in a form of preference, based on perceptions of status (one of a number of points in the book which indicate the capacity of emotion and feeling to override economic and other more 'practical' concerns). His fieldwork throughout Spain has shown a sense of inferiority among people who use the flail, a tool which makes use of human power rather than the animal power associated with the tribulum. However, he points out that in Central Europe, where agriculture is generally more advanced than in Spain, the tribulum is unknown and threshing is carried out with the flail.

Characteristics of the Flails

Five types of flail are identified in Leon, the boundaries marking the types' geographical distributions, like that of the flail/tribulum line, graduating. All of these varieties can be decorated, with turning or carving ranging from the rudimentary to the fairly intricate.

Smaller flails exist for children to work with and women generally use lighter implements. One small zone in Leon makes use of flails in which the handstaff is bigger than the souple, but elsewhere the opposite is the case (this is in contrast to Galician and Portugese flails where the souple is half the size of the handstaff). New flails are made using the measurements of an existing tool or might occasionally be constructed using measurements taken from the human body.

The woods of handstaffs are light and flexible – hazel, chestnut, willow, blackwood, alder or poplar – while the souples are created from heavy and resistant oak or elm.

Form of Use

The laying out of sheaves in preparation for threshing takes two forms. The sheaves can be placed in two rows with the ears opposite each other. Though limited to one particular zone in Leon this technique is known in both Navarra and Catalonia. The other method consists of laying the sheaves in a north-south line with the ears pointing in the same direction. More sheaves are placed on top but leaving the ears of the first layer visible, and this continues until a surface of ears is obtained.

The Threshers

Throughout Leon both men and women thresh with the flail (unlike Galicia and Portugal where it is an exclusively male activity). Each thresher needs a clear space to his or her side to allow the long souple to be swung, and works with a partner, one person swinging to the right and the other to the left. This is mirrored by the couple opposite. The basic group is therefore of four workers, often two men and two women, and other units are added on to this. Blows are normally given at the same time though sometimes the four workers give their blows in succession which gives rise to a more lively rhythm.

Usually the group of threshers goes up and down the line of sheaves in an east-west direction. Once the sheaves have been threshed they are be turned over and threshed again more lightly. Finally the straw is shaken out (formerly it was gathered up and then threshed again in the evening). The number of sheaves threshed in a day varies considerably, depending on the dryness of the ears and of course the strength of the threshers.

Organising the Work

Formerly, the work of threshing with the flail could be organised in one of three ways: it could be contracted (never important in mountainous parts of the province where holdings are small); reciprocal (common in all parts of Leon, the order of work being chosen by pulling numbers out of a hat); or voluntary (in the case of a sick neighbour, for example). It is the latter which has largely fallen out of favour.

Folklore

The folklore associated with flail threshing was once considerable in extent and variety, largely owing to the sense of festivity surrounding the work, itself a product of several households coming together. Although the practice of flail threshing continues, its festive ambience is remembered only by the oldest members of communities. They recall numerous sayings associated with threshing such as 'eat wheat and thresh barley' (wheat being a more highly regarded grain but barley easier to thresh), competitions between threshers to see who was the fastest, loudest or otherwise most able, betting on who would finish first or on who could jump furthest over the heap of threshed corn (recreations accompanied by particularly generous quantities of wine), the hiding of objects such as stones or clothes under spread sheaves, intended primarily as a joke but with fertility ritual overtones, or leaving one tied sheaf amongst the spread ones on the threshing floor (this being called the 'vixen'). Fun could also

be had chasing the rats out of the last sheaves to be threshed.

Song was very important, in co-ordinating the rhythm of the work and also in buoying the workers' spirits. Likewise shouting. Certain sexual liberties might be taken during a threshing. These included tying girls up to a sheaf or stuffing a handful of straw under their skirts. Slapping women on the bottom with a handful of corn while they bent to turn sheaves also provided diversion, though the women could respond by attempting to push straw down the lads' trousers. Such antics were augmented by the generosity of the *dueño de la maja* or 'lord of the threshing' (the person responsible for paying or feeding the threshers) in supplying an alcoholic punch for the workers, usually made with honey, egg and sugar. At the end of the threshing, and accompanied by much song, the *dueño* would be carried back to his home by the young men.

Food and Drink

As a threshing day constituted something of a festival, food and drink would be of a special quality or quantity. In addition to punches and enriched wine, a sheep or goat would often be consumed and in one particular village the tail of this animal was given to the best prankster. Extra generous plates of everyday dishes such as chickpea stew, *chorizo* (salami-like sausage), consommé, potatoes with rice, salt cod, sardines, meat with peppers, rabbit in vinegar, potato omelette or salad, followed by rice pudding or *leche frita* (fried custard squares), would be offered for lunch or dinner, while the *merienda*, or late afternoon snack, could consist of delicacies such as *torrijas* (sweetened fried bread slices). There was certainly a measure of competition in providing such fare for one's workers and when people from beyond the area were present the need to impress could increase still further.

Tribula

In contrast with the flail, the tribulum has only one, standard Castilian name, *trillo*, and little

Tribulum: upper surface

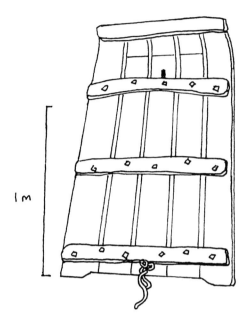

1 m

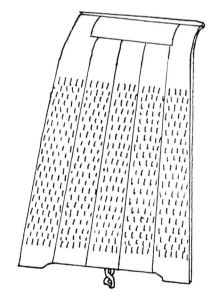

Tribulum: lower surface

variety in the nomenclature of its component parts. Its construction is fairly uniform also, with the only notable differences – neither of which have any geographical distribution – being in shape (rectangular or trapezoidal) and the materials used for cutting parts. Some tribula have stone or ceramic cutters set into the underside of the board whilst others use metal knives (usually these are locally made implements), or a combination of both stone and metal.

Use

Grain is removed from the stalk without any particular order when a tribulum is used, the sheaves simply being untied and forked until sufficiently mashed. A ring is made and one or two tribula go round this. When finished, the straw is collected up. Unlike the straw produced by a flail, this is not suitable as a thatching material. Threshing with the tribulum is usually less productive than with the flail (for this reason, say the authors, flails have survived), but it requires the involvement of far fewer workers, with a higher output per person.

In areas where the flail continues to dominate, other objects and methods can be used as a substitute for the tribulum. These include a small Mediterranean oak or a substantial branch of blackwood weighted down with stones or with people, wickerwork structures and variations on the iron in a wooden frame theme, draught animals (sometimes the tribulum is used after animals have trod the sheaves), and carts. The latter have the advantage of also chopping the straw up sufficiently for it to serve as bedding.

Manufacture and Sale

Tribula can be homemade but more often they are bought from salesmen who travel round the villages. They can also be purchased at weekly, monthly or annual fairs (the latter held at threshing time) in county towns.

Organising the Work

Reciprocal work rarely occurs with the tribulum as most households can provide the necessary labour themselves. However some coming together of people is seen at the collection of both straw and threshed grain, and tools and animals may be borrowed and lent. In addition, help can be offered if an individual household is experiencing difficulty, though normally it is family members in other households who are involved in all of these acts rather than the general community.

Folklore and Food

Owing to the family context of the work, there was relatively little folklore associated with the use of the tribulum. There was however, some competition when carts were being loaded with straw or threshed grain (the last cart to be filled sometimes had a cockerel or rabbit suspended from it) and pranks could include hiding the essential tools of the task from the workers and frightening the beasts.

Food eaten at threshing time is that of the every day. However, when the threshed grain is being stored a small festive meal consisting of meats or omelette can be served.

The Future

By way of conclusion the authors state that much information relating to the non-material aspects of threshing in Leon has disappeared. Festive and community connotations disappeared as the twentieth century progressed (the Civil War having a large role to play in this). It will not be long until the material culture associated with traditional threshing practices goes also – Mingote estimates some 30 years. As new means of dealing with grain gain favour both flails and tribula are being made redundant, and the latter are increasingly to be found serving as doors, gates or firewood, or simply ending their days as junk.

Note: Comparative Scottish material on the topic of threshing can be found in Fenton, A. Hand threshing. In Fenton, A, *The Shape of the Past 1: Essays in Scottish Ethnology*, Edinburgh, 1985, 132–175.

Susan Storrier

AS GOOD AS A HOLIDAY: POTATO HARVESTING IN THE LOTHIANS FROM 1870 TO THE PRESENT
Heather Holmes
East Linton, Tuckwell Press 2000
334pp, 16 plates, 41 tables, 11 figures. £20.00.
ISBN 1 86232 061 6

Don't be fooled by the cheery cover of golden spuds and happy harvesters – this is a serious piece of scholarship, the product of innumerable hours in the archive, the library and, yes, the field. Most of the material was gathered for the author's doctoral thesis (for which she was awarded the prestigious Michaelis-Jena Prize in 1996), but the book also draws on a pre-existing interest and personal involvement in agricultural work. As a Lothian farmer's daughter and a graduate of the School of Scottish Studies, no-one can be better qualified than Heather Holmes to tackle this important topic in Scottish agricultural and labour history, a story intermeshed with aspects of technology, educational policy and migration.

The study is the first ever to examine the full range of individuals employed in the potato harvest. The complex relationship between various types of harvester, harvest technology, harvesting techniques and employment conditions is made explicit by using archive and published material (including parliamentary papers and newspapers), farm records, oral testimony from potato merchants and farmers and their wives, questionnaires, photographic records and personal experience. The result is nearly three hundred pages of text truly packed with information (one has the sensation that reducing the bulk to even that generous size involved making some painful decisions), and if collecting together such a wealth of material is an achievement how much more so is organising it into a readable and useful text.

There are six sections to the book. In the first, both the labour requirements and sources of labour for the Lothian potato harvest are explored (comparative material from other areas is included throughout the book). The task of harvesting the potato crop remained extremely labour intensive until far into the twentieth century and well beyond the capacities of the regular farm workforce. Squads of between 8 and 60 casual labourers were thus employed by farmers, potato merchants or labour contractors for weeks at a time between late June and November. Workers, both adult and children, could come from nearby villages and urban areas, or might be migrant labourers from Ireland. In times of national crises, such as the World Wars, harvesting could also be undertaken by emergency workforces, the best known of which came from the ranks of the Women's Land Army. Usually, however, the choice of type of labourer depended on availability and also on the quality and length of the work to be done.

The uneven transition from hand tool to full mechanisation is charted in the section on harvesting tools and techniques where the processes involved in harvesting the crop, from opening up the land to transporting the harvested potatoes from the field, are meticulously described. A single chapter, and probably the most fascinating of the book, on local women and their employment conditions, deals with types of women who worked at the tatties, how they were recruited and organised childcare among themselves, and why they often chose to be employed at an undoubtedly uncomfortable job year after year. The author has candidly recorded the women's complaints about their work, grievances which in the second half of the twentieth century were to appear more significant as the economic circumstances of working-class homes improved and the roles of women in society changed. The last local squads were composed of a higher percentage of men, often the unemployed or those of ethnic backgrounds, a trend frequently deplored by farmers.

Children's employment forms a substantial part of the book (and this importance is reflected in the inclusion of an appendix dealing with School Boards and Schools in the Lothians in 1901). The tradition of employing minors at the potato harvest began in the second half of the nineteenth century and continued until the

1970s, but from the 1880s was almost always accompanied by polemic over the rights and wrongs of taking children out of school. Children could be released by being granted a number of exemptions from school attendance or by being given a 'tattie holiday'. Either way a good amount of legislation was required and regulations had to be continually created and reinforced to control children's working conditions. The children themselves seem to have been very much aware of what their rights were, and what perks they could expect:

> So important was the giving of a drink, especially tea, that children rated farms according to how good the tea was at them and preferred to work at those where they knew they could get a good cup. (171)

Irish migratory harvesters, consisting of two distinct groups – Achill and Donegal workers – were in many ways considered the élite of potato labourers. However, despite the high levels of skill and discipline displayed, wages and conditions could be far from ideal. Dr Holmes looks at Irish workers' recruitment, gaffers, wages, food, and especially their accommodation. We read of repeated attempts by authorities and the workers themselves to improve conditions, and ironically how, in the latter part of the twentieth century, the long-sought advances coincided with an upturn in the Irish economy and a reduced need for involvement in foreign agricultural work.

The ample supply of Irish and other seasonal labour until the 1960s and '70s had much to do with the delay of mechanisation in potato production, the subject of the final section of the book. As labour shortages developed and the remaining workers became less reliable, so the adoption of various means of mechanisation increased. The earliest attempts at mechanical harvesting had been expensive and only partially successful. Later refinements proved however to be cheaper, faster and more reliable than the squads. It is clear that some present-day farmers miss the harvesters despite the practical advantages of mechanisation but others seem only too happy to have replaced intractable human difficulties with simpler mechanical ones.

This book is a fine resource for the scholar, or for the general reader wishing to know something of the statistical and legislative background to the lowland Scottish agricultural environment. What you will not find here, despite the tantalising glimpses of oral testimony, is a very profound sense of what it felt like to be digging tatties. For this one must turn to a book such as Ian MacDougall's *Hoggie's Angels* (Flashbacks No 3). Indeed these two Tuckwell Press publications complement each other so superbly that one can scarcely be recommended without the other.

Susan Storrier

THE BEDESMAN AND THE HODBEARER. THE EPISTOLARY FRIENDSHIP OF FRANCIS JAMES CHILD AND WILLIAM WALKER
Ed and Intro Mary Ellen Brown
Aberdeen University Press for the
Elphinstone Institute, 2001
117pp. ISBN 1 85752 299 0

William Walker first came to my attention when, as a student at Aberdeen, I acquired a copy of his *Bards of Bon-Accord, 1375–1860* (Aberdeen, 1887). Later, I picked up his *Extracts from the Commonplace Book of Andrew Melville, Doctor and Master in the Song School of Aberdeen, 1621–1640* (Aberdeen, 1899). But I never came across his *Letters on Scottish Ballads from Professor Francis J Child* (Aberdeen, 1930). Now Mary Ellen Brown, in editing and presenting both Child's letters and also Walker's answers (which he modestly did not reproduce in his own publication), has given us both sides of the coin.

Walker first wrote to Child in 1890, and Child died 6 years later. Though they never met, they eventually exchanged photographs, and through their correspondence, became friends. Child was the generalist, working on his *The English and Scottish Ballads* (1882–98), and Walker was the regional specialist, on whom Child came to depend for local information on Scottish ballads, in particular the glossing of Scottish terms and the interpretation of obscure terms and phrases, the background topography, and the personal names and interrelationships of the characters mentioned.

Walker also helped Child by seeking out books and other material that would help to make the approach as comprehensive as possible. There is a kind of sub-theme in the letters, regarding the publications and papers of Peter Buchan on ballads and songs. Walker evidently had a strong bias against Buchan and had no high opinion of Buchan's nephew, David Scott, who had acquired the Buchan manuscripts. He was forced to revise his opinion, and admitted that there was more in the material than he had at first thought. Child died in 1896, and was not able to take into account (in his efforts to 'get behind' printed versions), of the Buchan material sent by Walker in August of that year.

This volume does two things, beyond the simple presentation of information. It throws light on the methods Child used in preparing his texts on the one hand, though it was unfortunate that the letter exchange took place in the last few years of his life, when he was becoming frail. On the other, it gives William Walker the credit that is his due. Walker had little formal education, though he became managing director of the Equitable Loan Company, and he fitted his literary and antiquarian interests into a busy life. Though self-taught to a great extent, he is rightly to be regarded as a scholar of the North-East, even though he himself was too modest ever to have claimed such a distinction.

A Fenton

A GUIDE TO CONTRIBUTORS

Submission of Articles

Contributions for possible publication in ROSC should be sent to Professor Alexander Fenton at:

EERC, c/o National Museums of Scotland, Chambers Street, Edinburgh EH1 1JF.

Submissions are required by the end of June in any year if they are to be included in the volume of that year. Hard copy should be provided, double-spaced, along with a computer disk, which should be Microsoft Word compatible.

Length

Up to 10,000 words, but an average of up to 6000 is preferred. Shorter Notes should not exceed 2500 words. Items for the Noticeboard, and Reviews, should be of around 500-600 words.

Style

A paragraph should be included at the beginning to summarise the contents of the article. This may or may not be published. Authors are encouraged to incorporate sub-headings to clarify the argument for readers.

References

References should be given running numbers in the text and included as Endnotes. Samples of the form of reference are:

1 Book. Handley, James. *The Navvy in Scotland*, Cork, 1970, 61.

2 Article in a book. Heron, R. Memoirs of the life of the late Robert Burns. In Lindsay, M., *The Burns Encyclopaedia*, London, 1980, 166–82.

3 Article in a journal. Gemmill, Elisabeth. Signs and symbols in medieval Scottish trade. *Review of Scottish Culture*, 13 (2000–2001), 7–17.

4 A repeated reference takes the form Handley, 1970, 63.